In 2006 **Catherine Mulbrandon** launched VisualizingEconomics.com, a website dedicated to publishing infographics about economic data. She received a bachelor's degree in economics from the University of Chicago and a master's degree in design from Carnegie Mellon University and has worked in the finance industry for 10 years. A native of Washington, DC, she currently lives in Jersey City, NJ.

The data graphics in this book, along with supplementary materials, data, and updates can be found at VisualizingEconomics.com.

This book was published through the direct support of my backers on Kickstarter.com and a grant from the J-Lab at American University funded by the McCormick Foundation.

Contents

Distribution 8

To draw the income distribution of the United States, US Census Bureau data is used to illustrate the bottom 99% of income earners because it has the best statistics for households earning less than $250,000. For the top 1%, I relied on IRS data and the top incomes reported in the media to estimate how long to make the "long tail."

Top Incomes 22

There has been a huge increase in incomes at the very top of the income distribution. But who are the top earners, and what are their incomes? Although the IRS knows who the high-income taxpayers are, they can't tell us because of privacy laws, so the available public information is used here.

Income Sources 45

Sources of income vary dramatically for each income group. The higher the income, the more important nonsalary sources become. Taxes on these different sources vary as well, affecting not only the amount of money that people have to spend but also the rate at which they can accumulate wealth.

Demographics 57

Even if the share of income going to the top 1% were unchanged, inequality would still have increased for the bottom 99% of income earners because of changes in household structure. For example, since the 1970s, there are more two-income families than one-income families. Two incomes are common in households earning more than $80,000 a year.

Geography 79

Cities and their surrounding urban areas tend to have higher incomes, especially coastal cities in the Northeast and in California. Some states have greater income inequality, such as New York, while others have less inequality, such as Utah. Although New York State has a higher GDP per person, Utah's median income of $57,000 is higher than New York's at $50,000.

Wages 91

Median wages have stagnated since the mid-1970s, and in some occupations, wages have fallen. At the same time, the number of people of working age and their participation rate in the labor force has increased.

Industries 113

One reason income inequality has increased is because of fewer jobs in goods-producing industries such as manufacturing and more jobs in both low-paid service industries such as accommodation and food services and high-paid ones such as finance and insurance. Although labor productivity has grown since the 1970s, wages have not kept pace with that growth.

Occupations by Industries 123

This section provides an overview of nearly 800 occupations. These "maps" take a bird's-eye view of the labor market by looking at patterns of income and job growth by industry and by education.

Standard of Living 149

As incomes have grown dramatically over the last 100 years, patterns of family spending have changed. Food and clothing are relatively less expensive, while more money is spent on bigger and better housing. Although the poverty rate dropped to 12.6% by 1970, it has not changed significantly in the last 40 years.

Introduction

Who is this for?

Economic data is plentiful, and yet it is does not receive the attention of designers skilled in creating data graphics. Everywhere you look, the charts are shallow or poorly designed. I believe this data should be presented in a clear and beautiful manner, to help people understand what the numbers mean. If you love looking at data graphics about economics, or, as a teacher, a blogger, or a reporter, you explain economics to others but don't have the time or skills to create illustrations yourself, then this book is for you.

Where is this data coming from?

The core set of data is from the US Census Bureau, Bureau of Labor Statistics (BLS), Internal Revenue Service (IRS), and Bureau of Economic Analysis (BEA), supplemented by data from the Central Intelligence Agency (CIA), Congressional Budget Office (CBO), and Congressional Research Service and income estimates in the media for individuals. I also include analysis performed by academics such as Emmanuel Saez and Thomas Piketty and firms such as EMSI, which specializes in labor market data.

The data has been adjusted for inflation using the Consumer Price Index for All Urban Consumers (CPI-U), a measurement calculated by the BLS to reflect the change in prices. In most cases the data is adjusted to 2010 US dollars (exceptions are noted). For long-term historical series, I used the work of Lawrence H. Officer and Samuel H. Williamson, which extends the CPI-U back to 1774 (see MeasuringWorth.com).

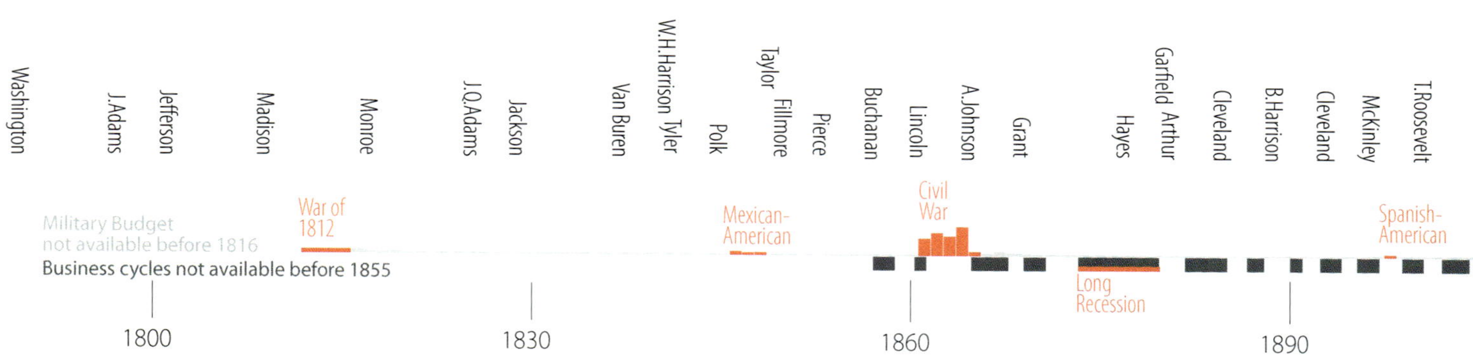

Timeline This 200-year timeline places the data series covered in this guide in historical context. It includes the election of US presidents, major US military conflicts mapped onto military spending as a share of GDP (red and gray bars), and US recessions and depressions (black bars).

Where does income come from?

The labor market is where people compete for paid work, employers compete for willing workers, and wages and salaries are determined. Income from labor comes from a job for which you are paid by the hour (wages) or by the piece (harvesting oranges, $1 a box) or paid every 2 weeks based on an annual salary. Self-employment can be considered labor income when you sell a product you make or charge for a service you provide. Compensation includes everything an employee receives in exchange for a service performed for an employer, which can include not only money but also stock options, use of a private car or plane, or subsidized health insurance, retirement plans, paid sick leave, and vacations. The BLS collects employer costs for employee compensation. Over 8 years of data on civilian workers, the benefits represent about 30% of compensation, while 70% is made up of salaries and wages.

However, there is another source of income—capital income—that includes investments,* dividends, as well as rent for an asset that you own, such as land or equipment, or patents that can be used by others engaged in an economic activity. Celebrity income may be supplemented by endorsement deals that allow their name to be used to sell a product or service. While they may be required to perform some additional work—participate in a photo shoot for a magazine ad, for example—their name is treated as asset that is loaned out in exchange for a payment. Of course, there are markets for capital, as there is for labor, to set the prices for these income sources.

* In the classical economic sense, investing occurs when you are loaning money in exchange for interest payments or financing a new company in exchange for a share of its profits. The income is compensation for the risk that you might not be paid back. The other income commonly referred to as "investing" comes from buying and selling assets, such as art or stocks, which provides liquidity in the market but doesn't contribute to the growth of gross domestic product (GDP) because there is only an exchange of assets (such as money, stocks, art, or gold).

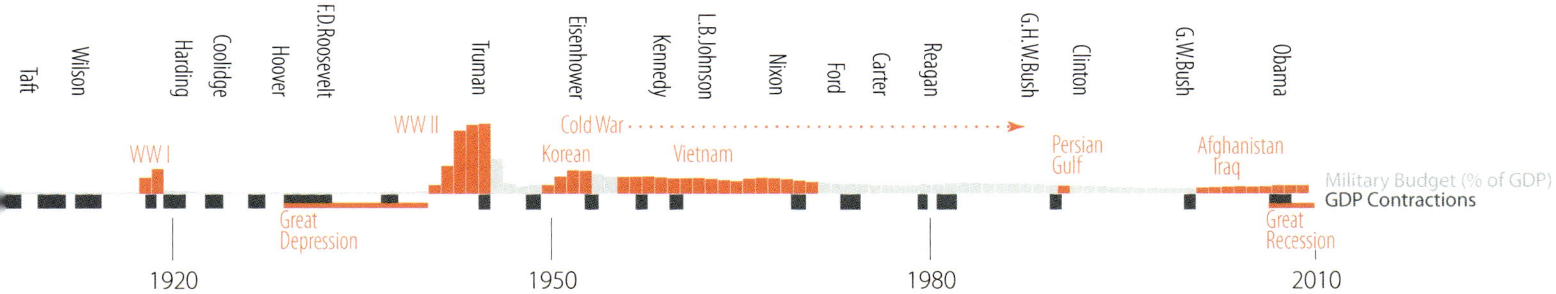

What is included in measurements of income?

Many income data sets originate from government agencies and are collected for the purpose of planing and implementing public policy for federal, state and local governments and not necessarily intended to measure people's standard of living.

Census Bureau reports use **Money Income** (which excludes capital gains and a household's income before taxes), which includes earnings, unemployment compensation, workers' compensation, Social Security, Supplemental Security Income, public assistance, veterans' payments, survivor benefits, pension or retirement income, interest, dividends, rents, royalties, income from estates, trusts, educational assistance, alimony, child support, assistance from outside the household, and other miscellaneous sources. It does not include noncash benefits (such as food stamps and housing subsidies).

IRS data is based on income that is taxable and must be reported. Although there is a lot of overlap between the Census Bureau and IRS data, there are important exceptions. If Social Security is your only income, you would not be taxed and may not even file a tax return. Instead of households, this data set is measured in tax returns or tax units.

The Congressional Budget Office uses data collected by the Census Bureau and the IRS to calculate the **Market Income** for households, which includes cash wages and salaries (including those allocated by employees to 401(k) plans), employer-paid health insurance premiums, and the employer's share of Social Security, Medicare, and federal unemployment insurance payroll taxes, as well as net income from businesses and farms operated solely by their owners, partnership income, and income from S corporations, capital gains, taxable and tax-exempt interest, dividends paid by corporations, positive rental income, corporate income taxes, income received in retirement for past services, and any other sources of income.

A **tax unit** is defined as a married couple living together (with or without dependents) or a single adult (with or without dependents), regardless of whether a tax return is filed.

Household income includes all of the income earned by people living together, regardless of whether they are related. Often, household income is used to understand changes in standards of living, as one's income goes further by sharing living expenses.

Family household income (or family income) includes all income earned by people related by birth, marriage, or adoption and living together. Not all households are families, however, income from unrelated people (lodgers, foster children, wards, or employees) who share a housing unit with a family is not included.

Prisons, dormitories, nursing homes, homeless shelters, and military barracks are not counted as households. Those living in group quarters can be considered income earners or tax units.

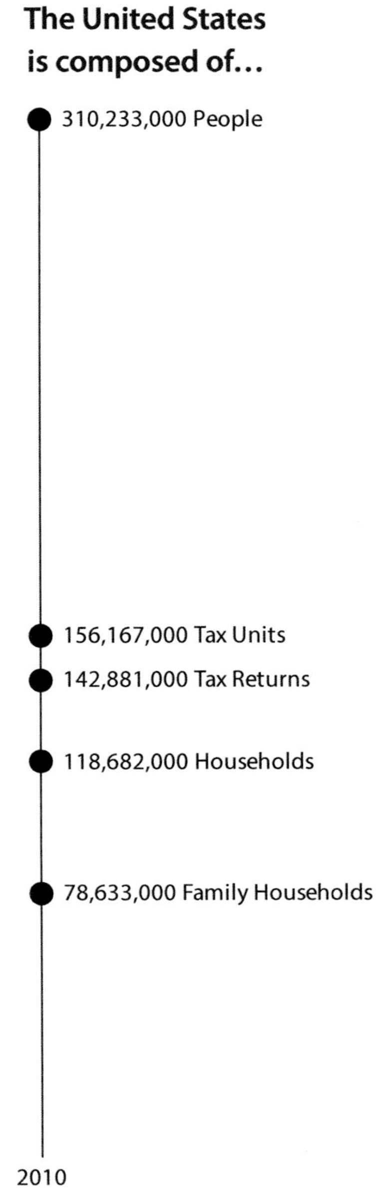

DISTRIBUTION

To draw the income distribution of the United States, US Census Bureau data is used to illustrate the bottom 99% of income earners because it has the best statistics for households earning less than $250,000. For the top 1%, I relied on IRS data and the top incomes reported in the media to estimate how long to make the "long tail."

2010 Household Income of Bottom 99%

Census

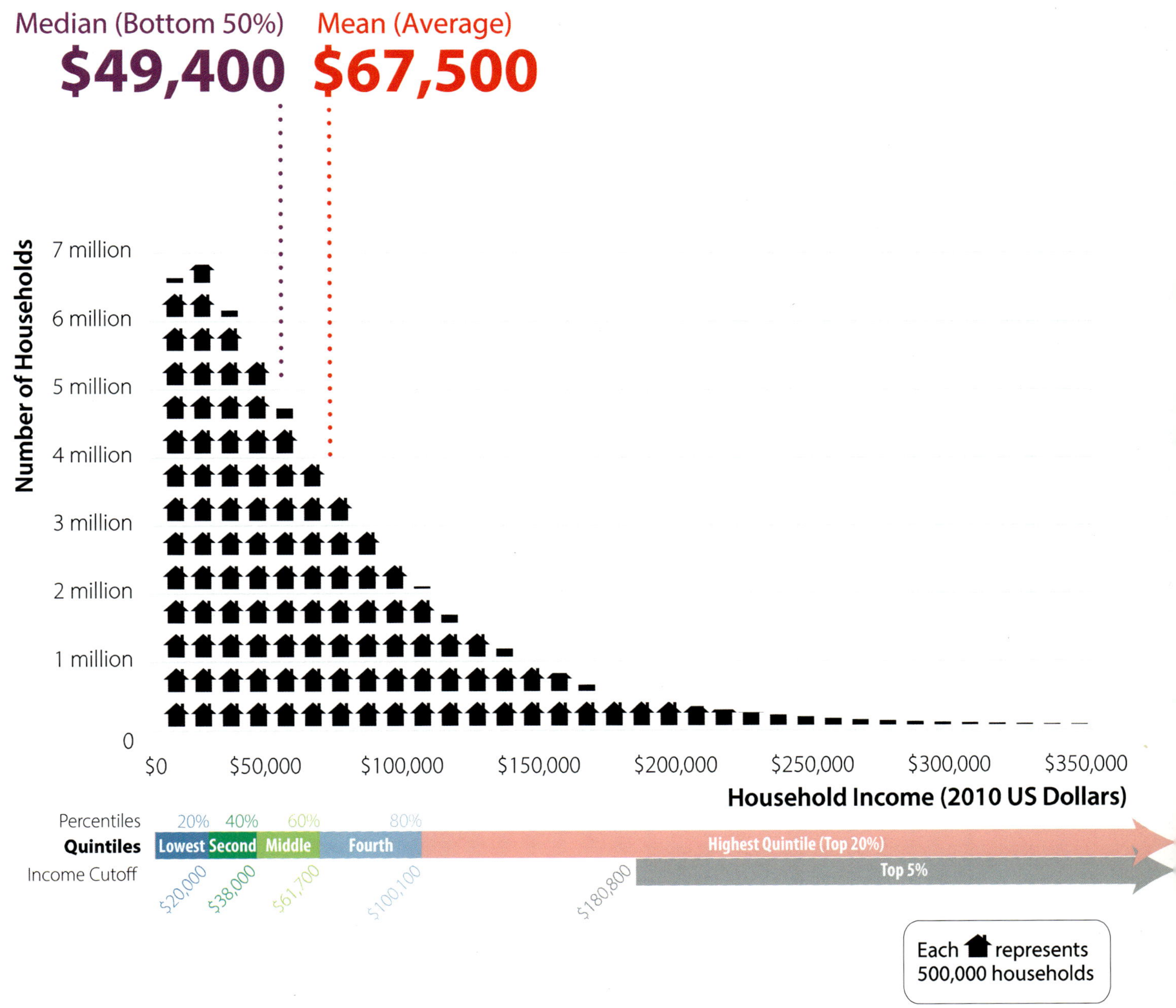

2010 Income Under $1.5 Million

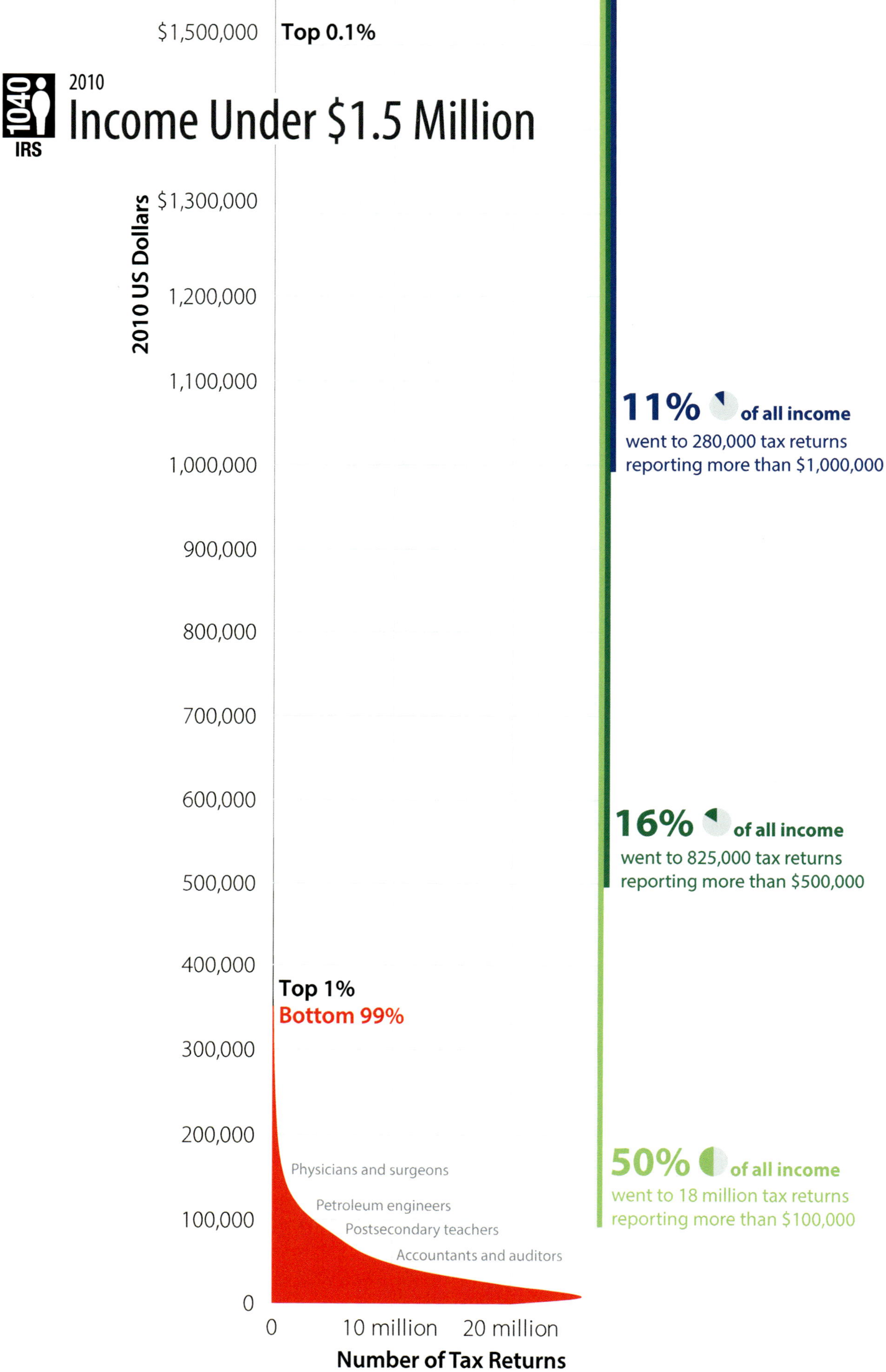

 Sources: IRS, Statistics of Income Division • Worlds Top Incomes Database, March 2012 (Compiled from data collected by IRS)

Various 2010

US Income Distribution

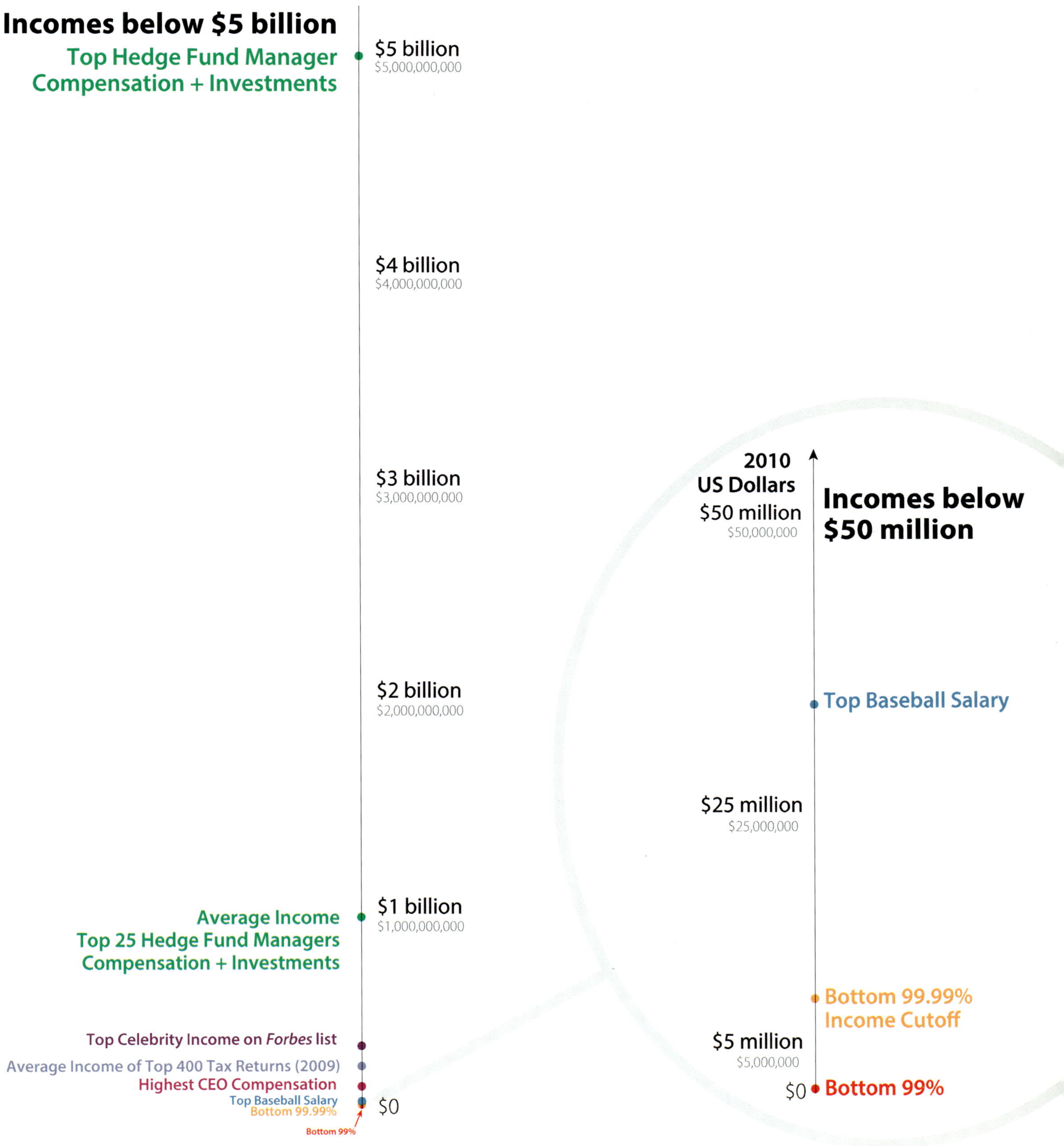

Sources: *Absolute Return + Alpha* • IRS, Statistics of Income Division • *USA Today*, "USATODAY Salaries Databases" • Worlds Top Incomes Database, March 2012 (Compiled from data collected by IRS)

2010
Average Income of Top 10% in 2010

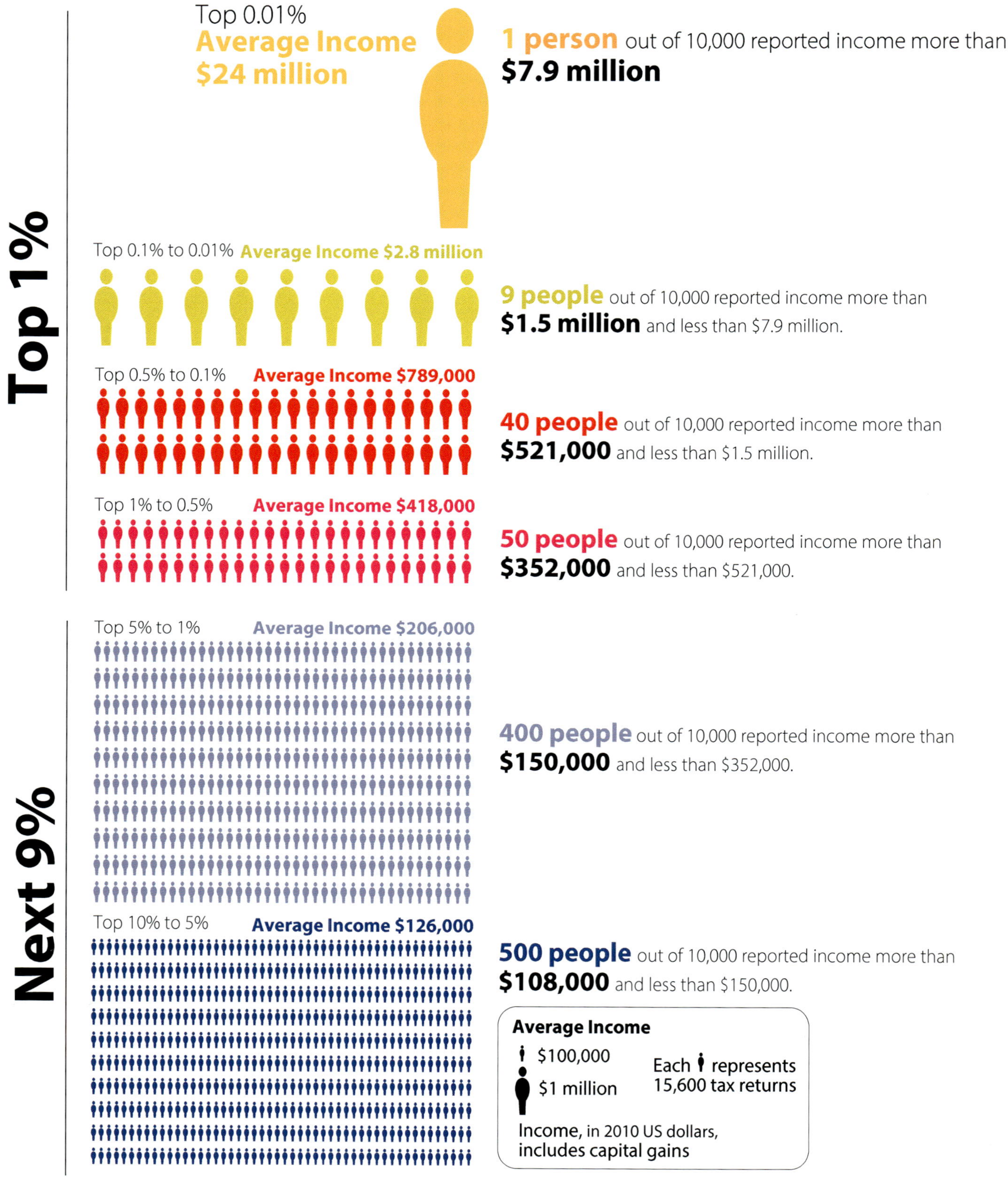

 Source: World Top Incomes Database, March 2012 (Compiled from data collected by IRS)

2010
Income Share of Top 10% in 2010

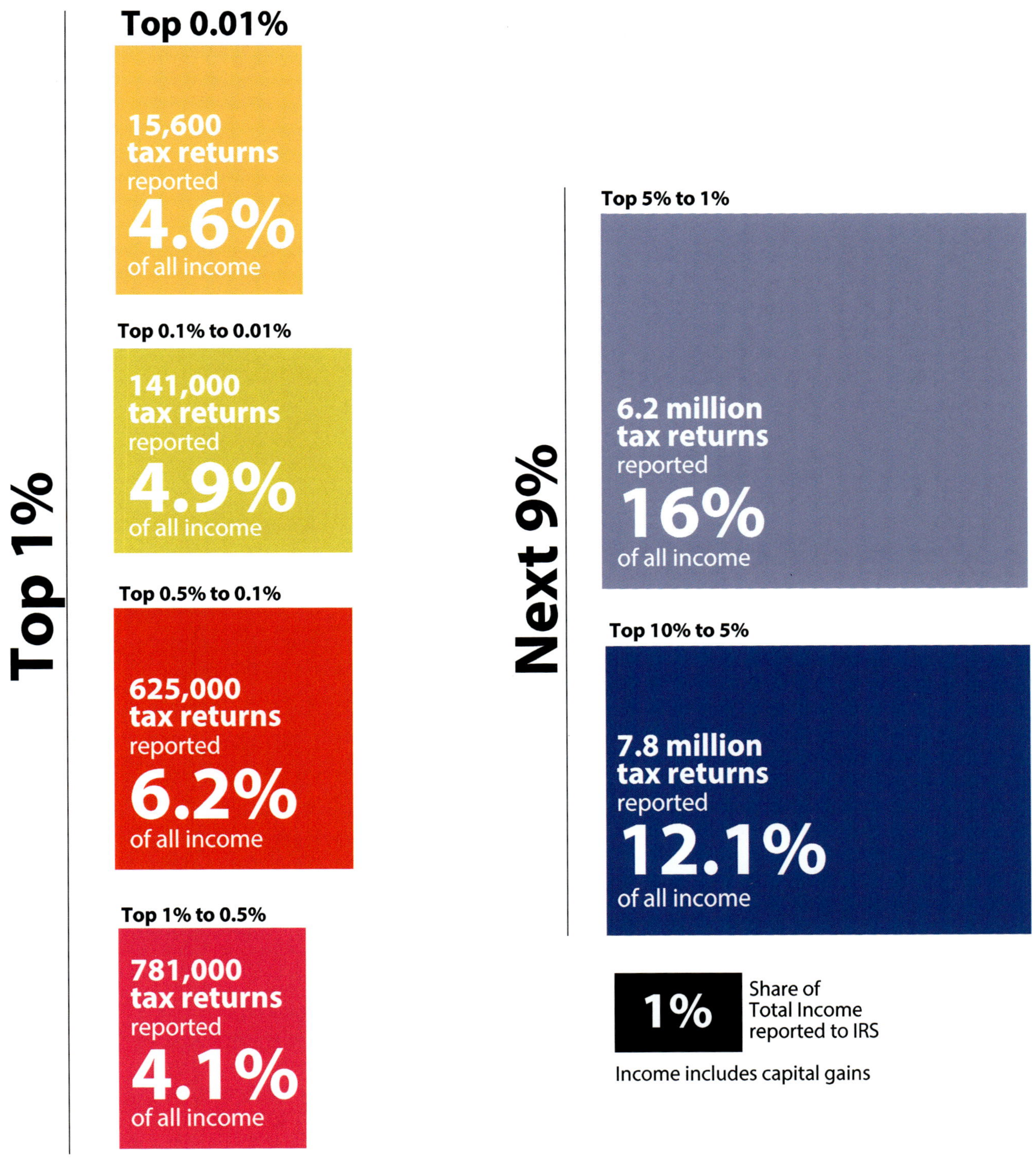

Source: World Top Incomes Database, March 2012 (Compiled from data collected by IRS)

1975
Income Distribution in 1975

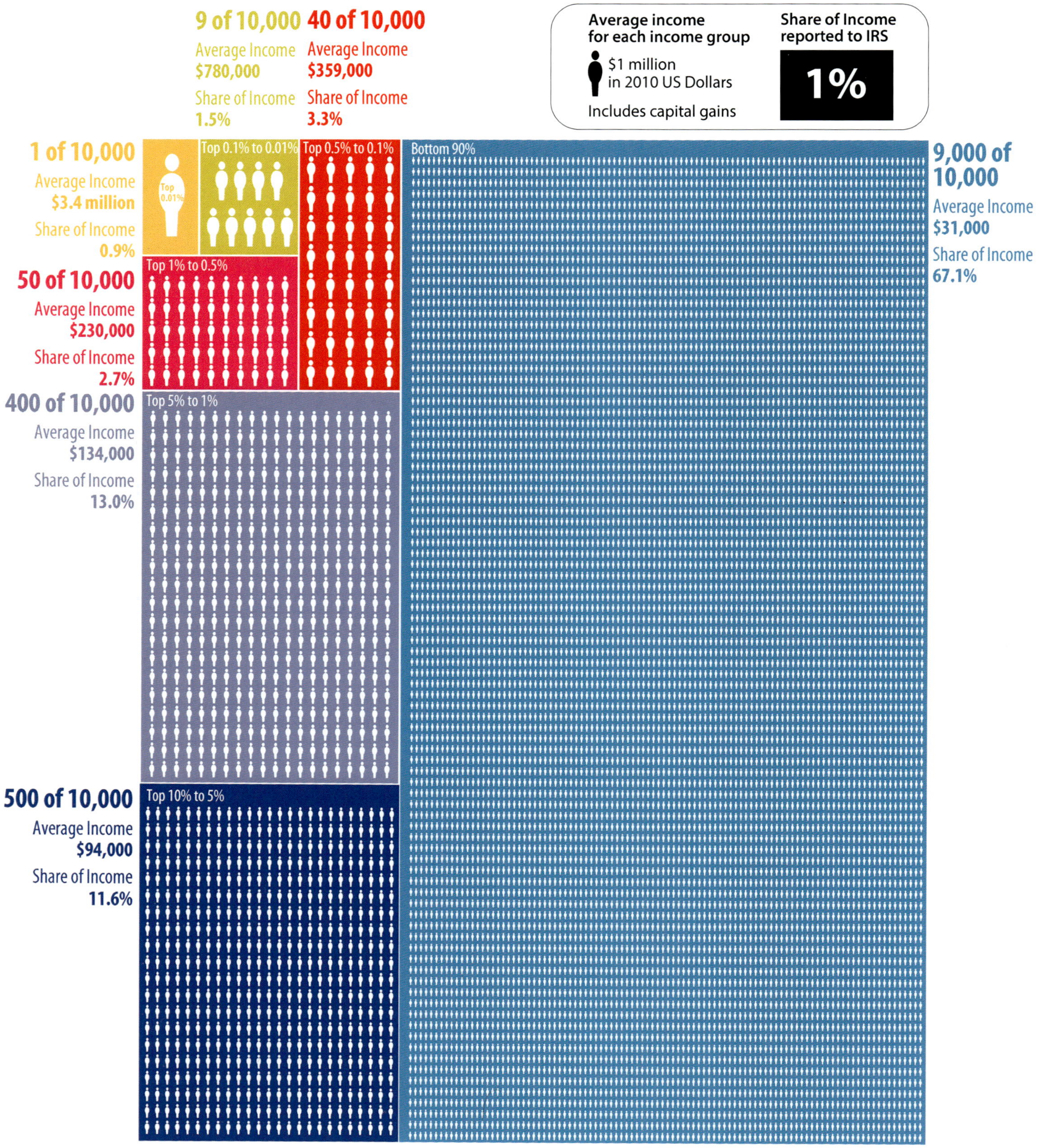

 Source: World Top Incomes Database, March 2012 (Compiled from data collected by IRS)

2010

Income Distribution in 2010

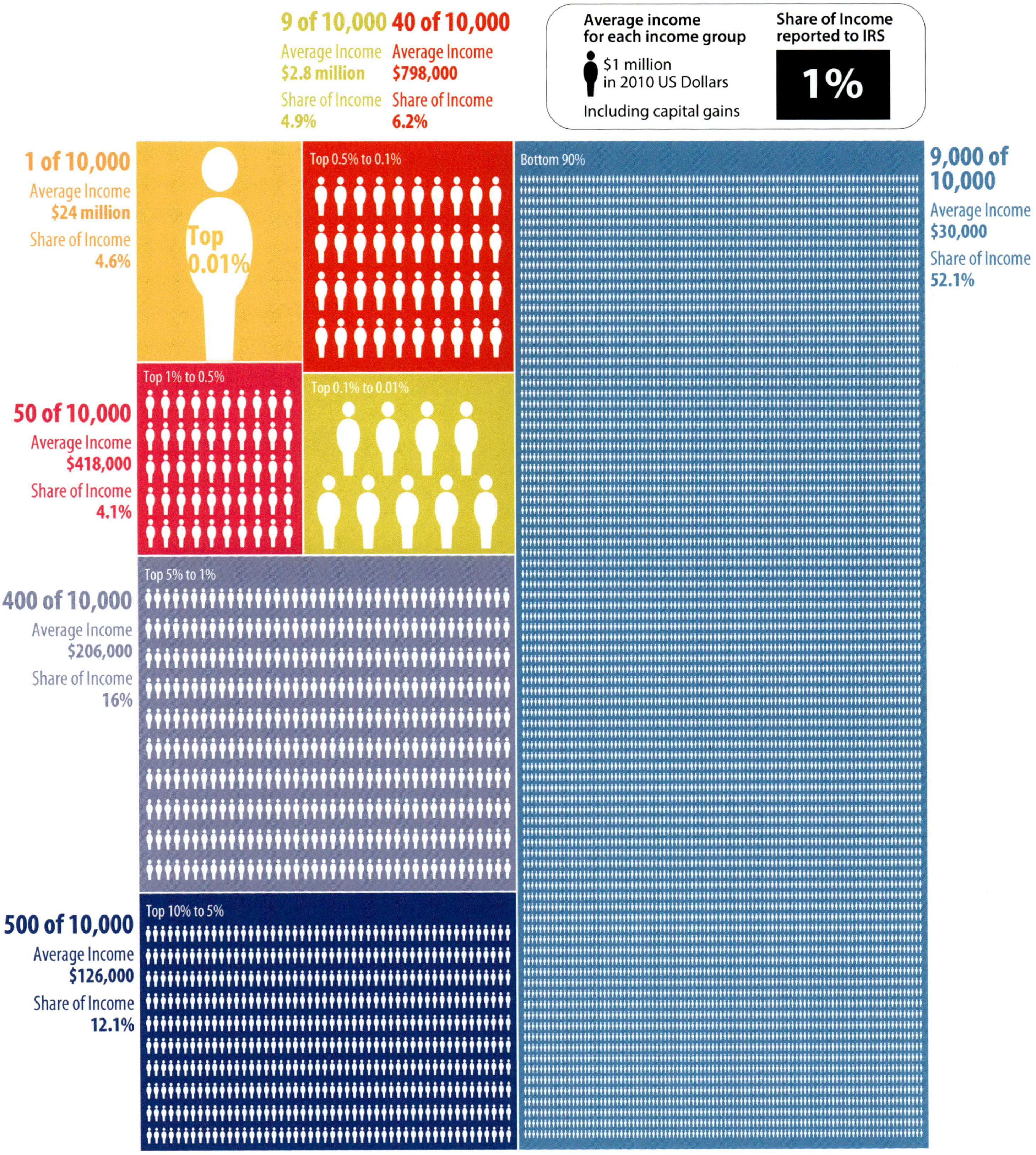

Source: World Top Incomes Database, March 2012 (Compiled from data collected by IRS)

US Census Bureau reports once included categories for just family and individuals. However, as a result of changes in demographics and living arrangements, the Census Bureau now reports income statistics for all households along with family households.

To highlight middle-class families, the following graphs focus on the $30,000–$80,000 income range, which is often used in the media to represent middle-income households.

Share of Middle-Income Family Households

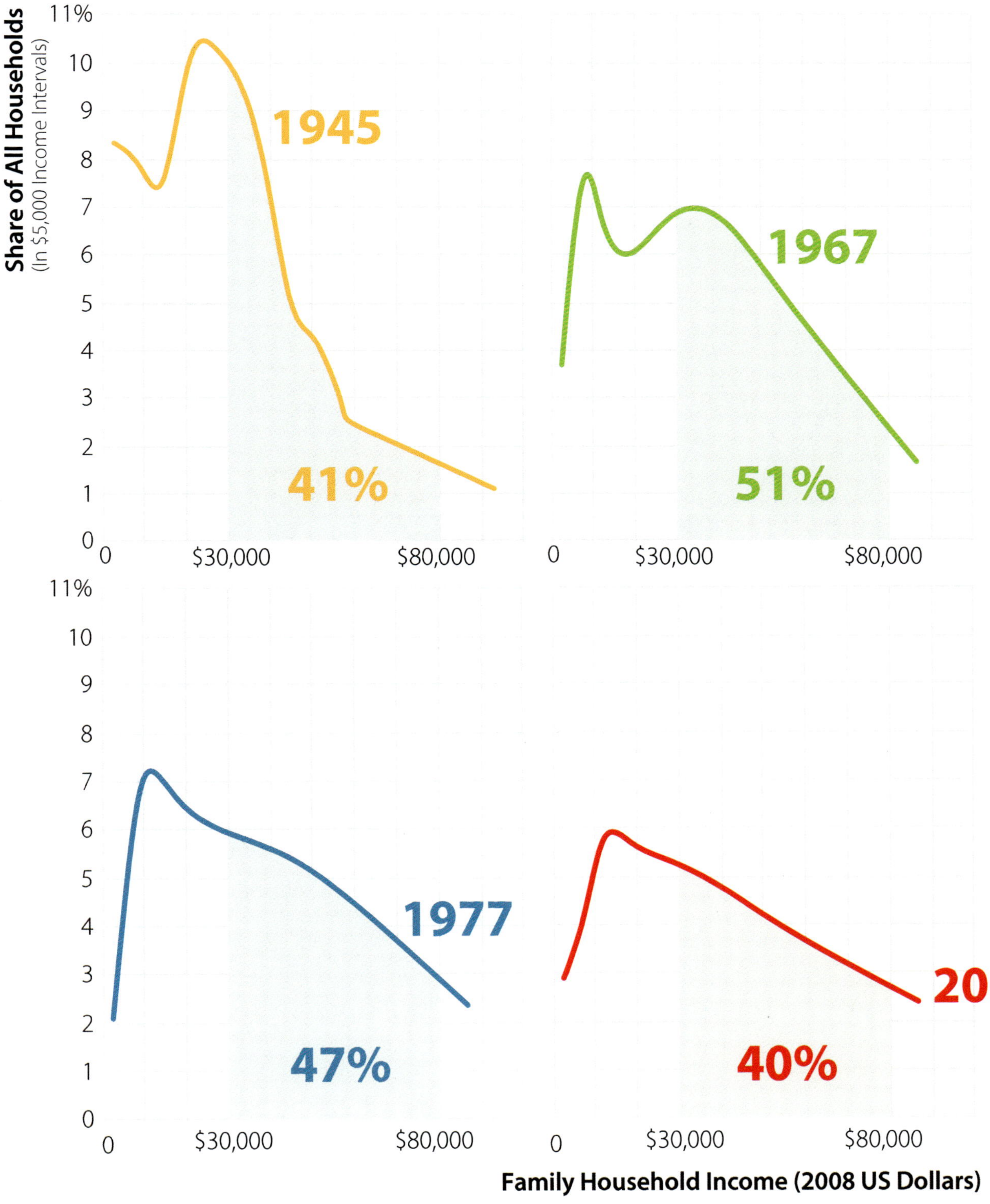

Source: US Census Bureau

1945–2008

Distribution of Income less than $100,000

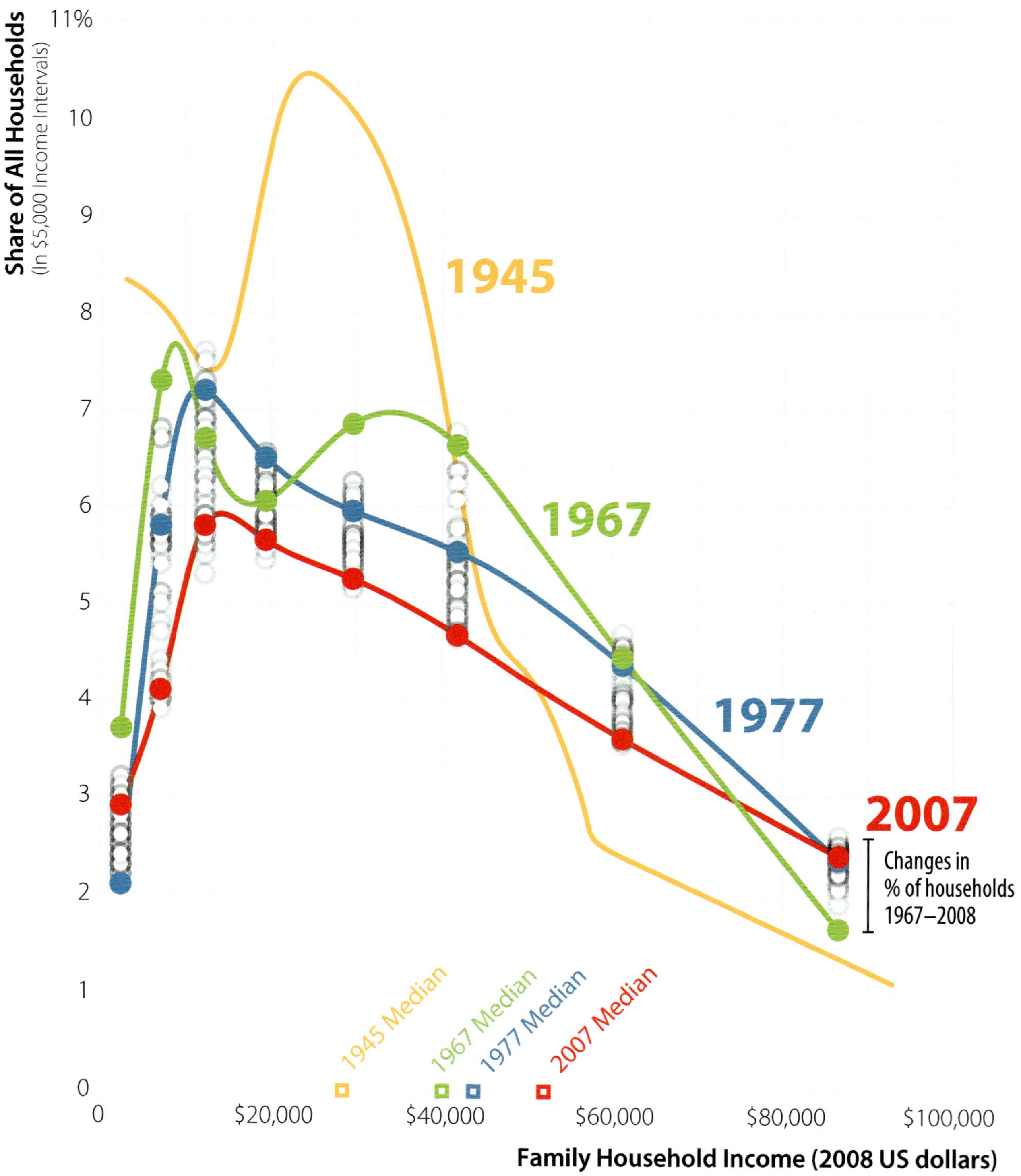

 Source: US Census Bureau

1945 | 1967 | 1977 | 2007

Cumulative Share of Income under $100,000

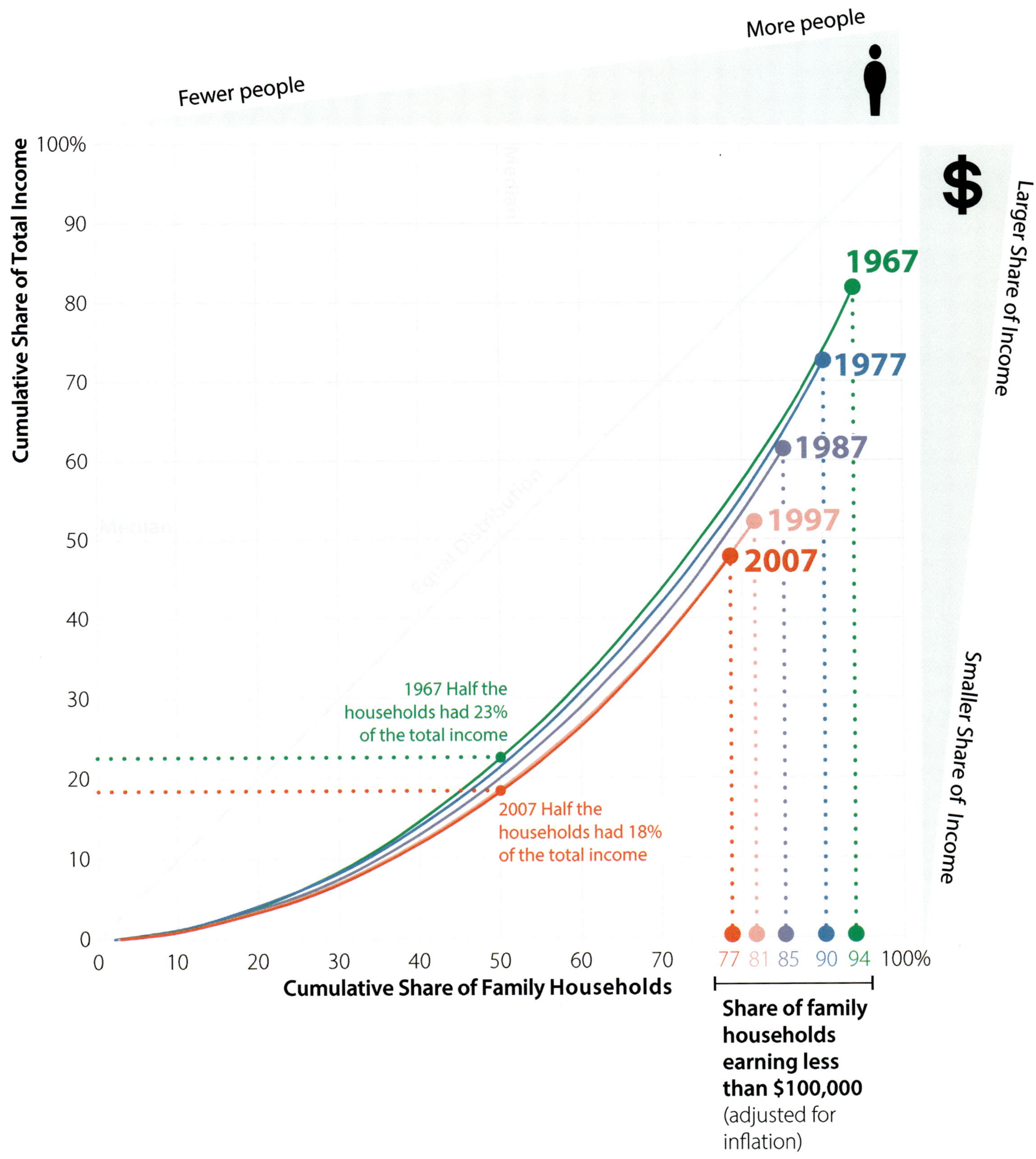

Source: US Census Bureau

2009

US Population Represented by 100 Households

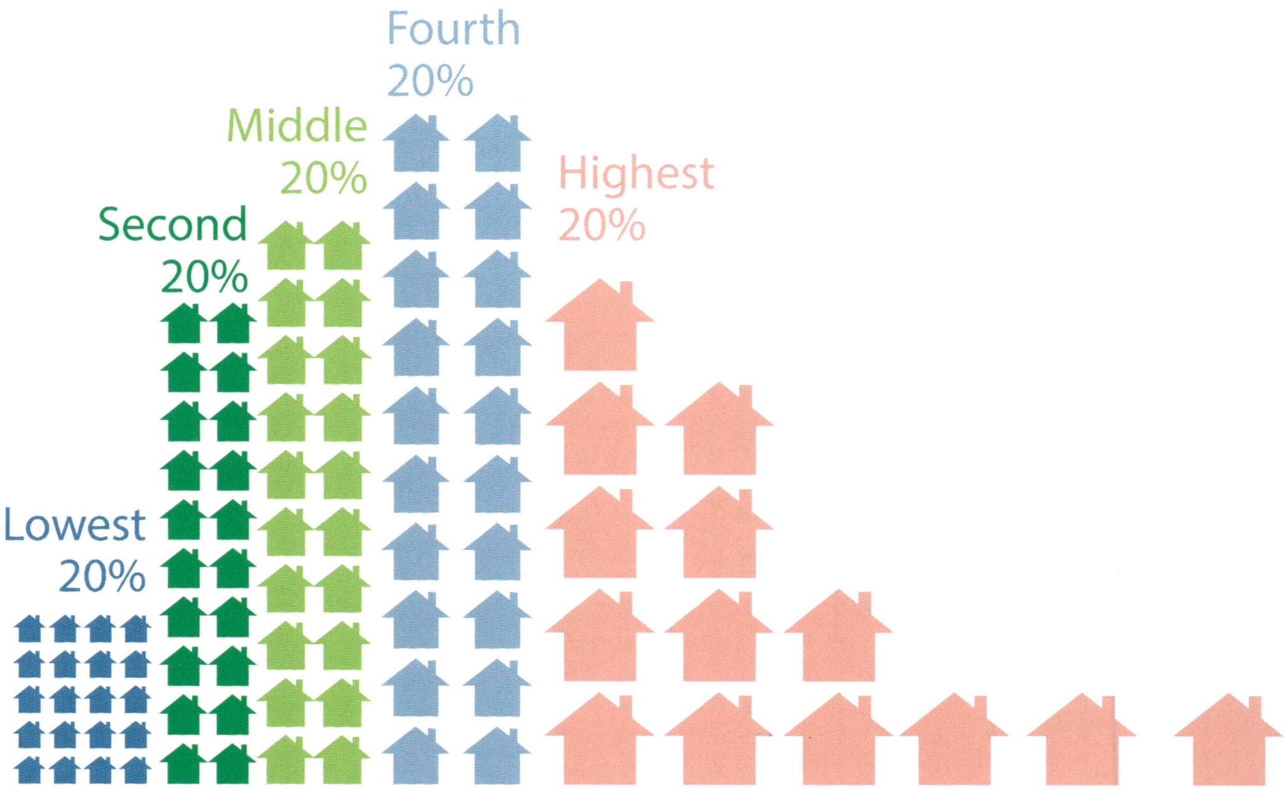

Quintile	Lowest	Second	Middle	Fourth	Highest Quintile (Top 20%)	
Percentile*	**20%**	**40%**	**60%**	**80%**	**90%**	**95%**
Household Size: 4 people	$ 45,200	$ 69,800	$100,200	$148,100	$200,800	$267,800
3 people	39,100	60,400	70,700	128,200	173,900	231,900
2 people	32,000	49,400	70,900	104,700	142,000	189,400
1 person	22,600	34,900	50,100	74,000	100,400	133,900

Income Cutoff (2009 US Dollars)

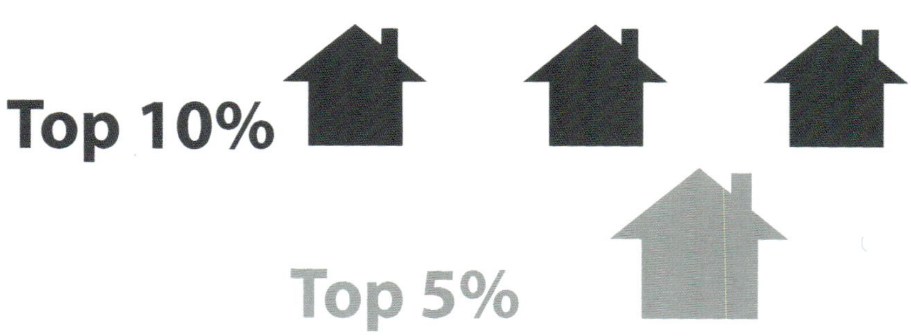

 Source: Congressional Budget Office, Average Federal Taxes by Income Group

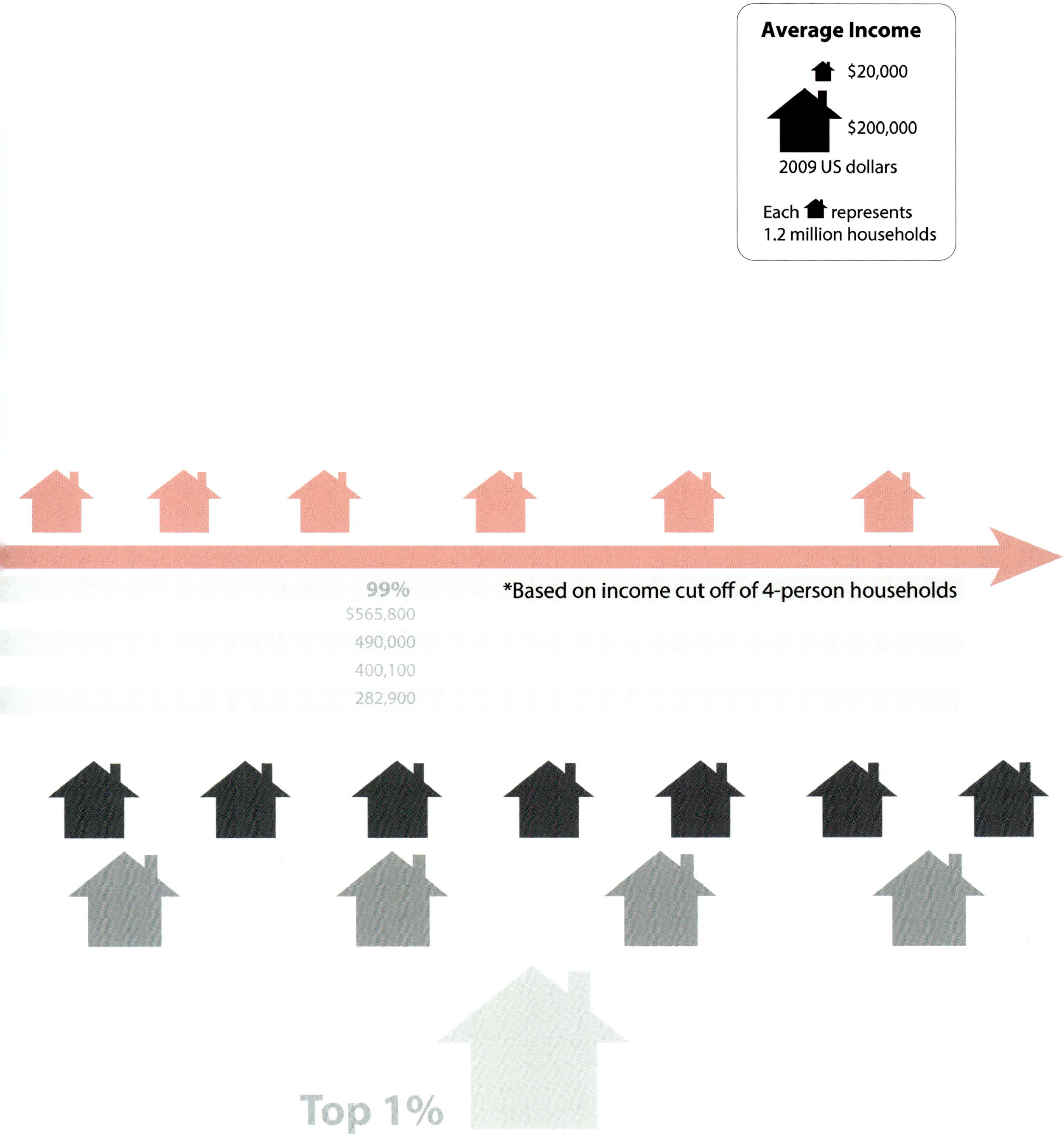

Average Income
$20,000
$200,000
2009 US dollars
Each represents 1.2 million households
99%
$565,800
490,000
400,100
282,900
*Based on income cut off of 4-person households
Top 1%

TOP INCOMES

There has been a huge increase in incomes at the very top of the income distribution. But who are the top earners, and what are their incomes? Although the IRS knows who the high-income taxpayers are, they can't tell us because of privacy laws, so the available public information is used here.

2010 | 2011 Top Incomes in Professional Sports

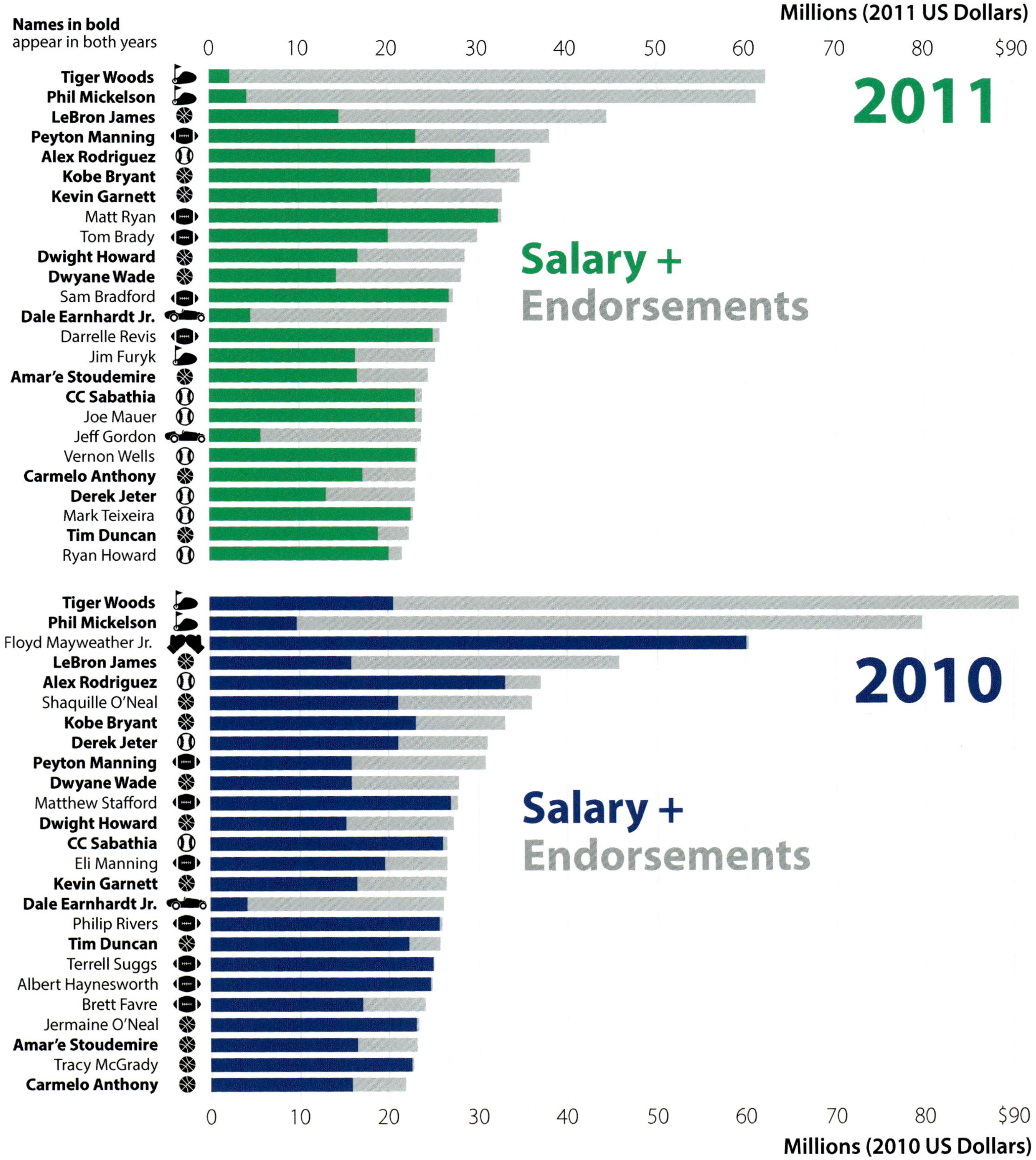

Source: *Sports Illustrated,* "The 50 Highest-Earning American Athletes"

Semi-log graphs In a few cases, when growth in salary or wages is exponential, I have added a second chart graphing the exact same data on a vertical axis with equally spaced increments that are labeled 1, 10, 100, 1000, instead of 1, 2, 3, 4. This log scale helps illustrate the percent change of the small values versus the large values, comparing the slope of the line at different places on the graph.

***Sports Illustrated* income for US athletes** includes salaries, winnings, and bonuses from players' associations, tour records, agents and news reports, along with endorsement estimates from sports-marketing executives and analysts. Auto racing estimates are from FormulaMoney.com.

 Source: *Sports Illustrated,* "The 50 Highest-Earning American Athletes"

1890–2010

Major League Baseball Players

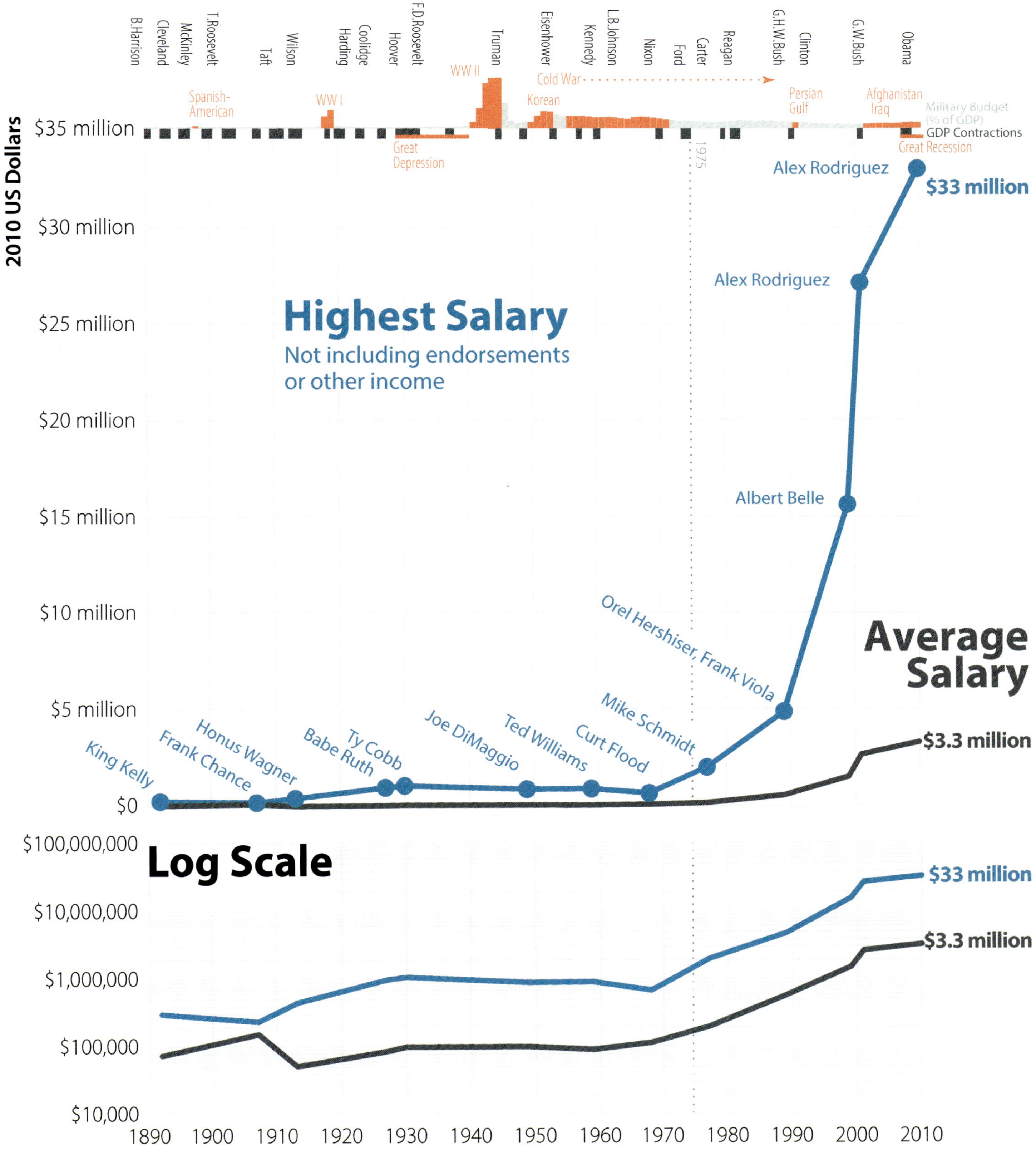

Sources: Michael Haupert, "The Economic History of Major League Baseball" • About.com Baseball

Various 2010

Top Major League Baseball Salaries

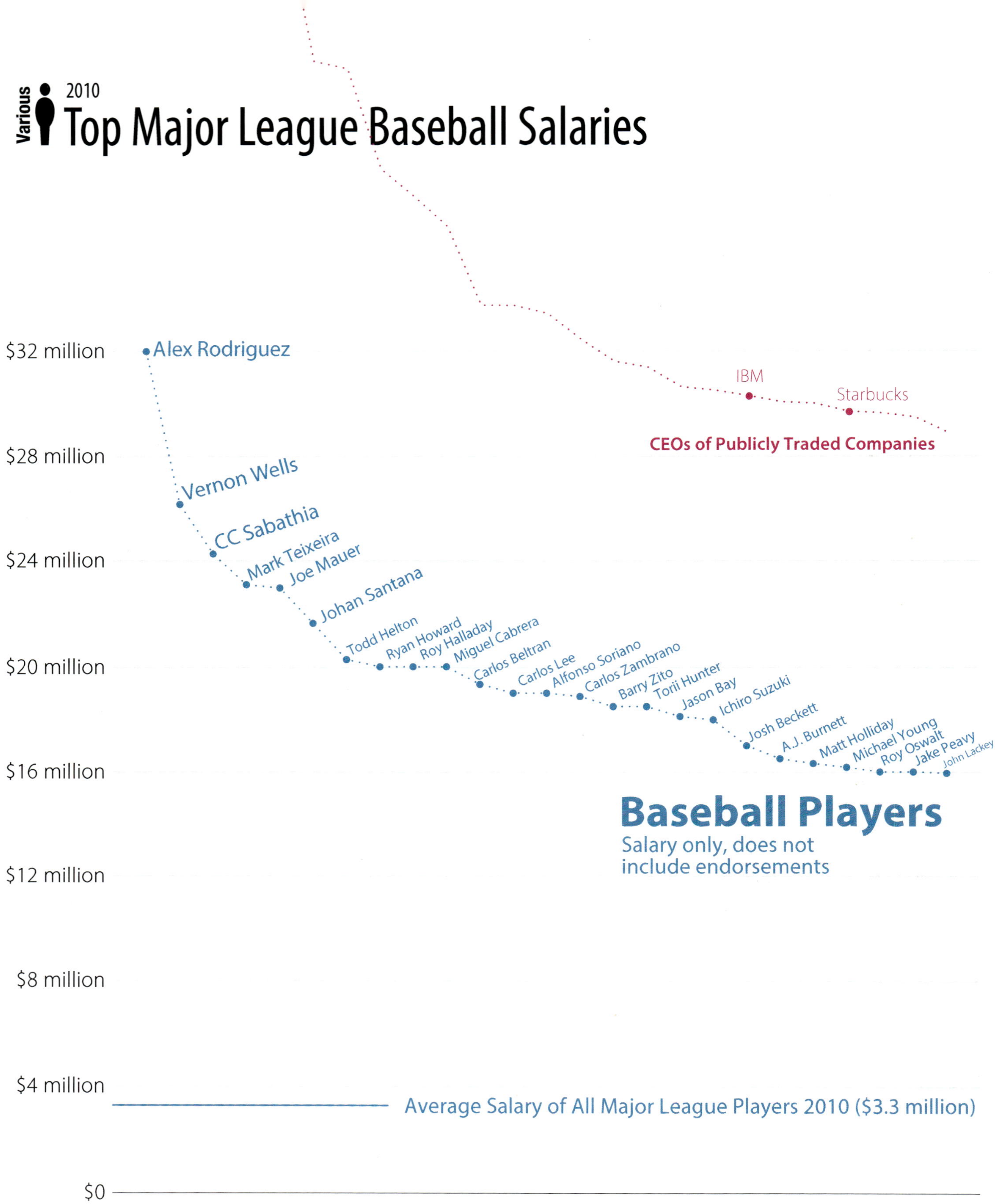

 Sources: *AR: Absolute Return + Alpha*, "The Rich List," April 2011 • *Forbes*, "Celebrity 100, 2011" • *Forbes*, "CEO Compensation, 2011." • *USA Today*, "USATODAY Salaries Databases"

Various 2010

Top CEO Compensation

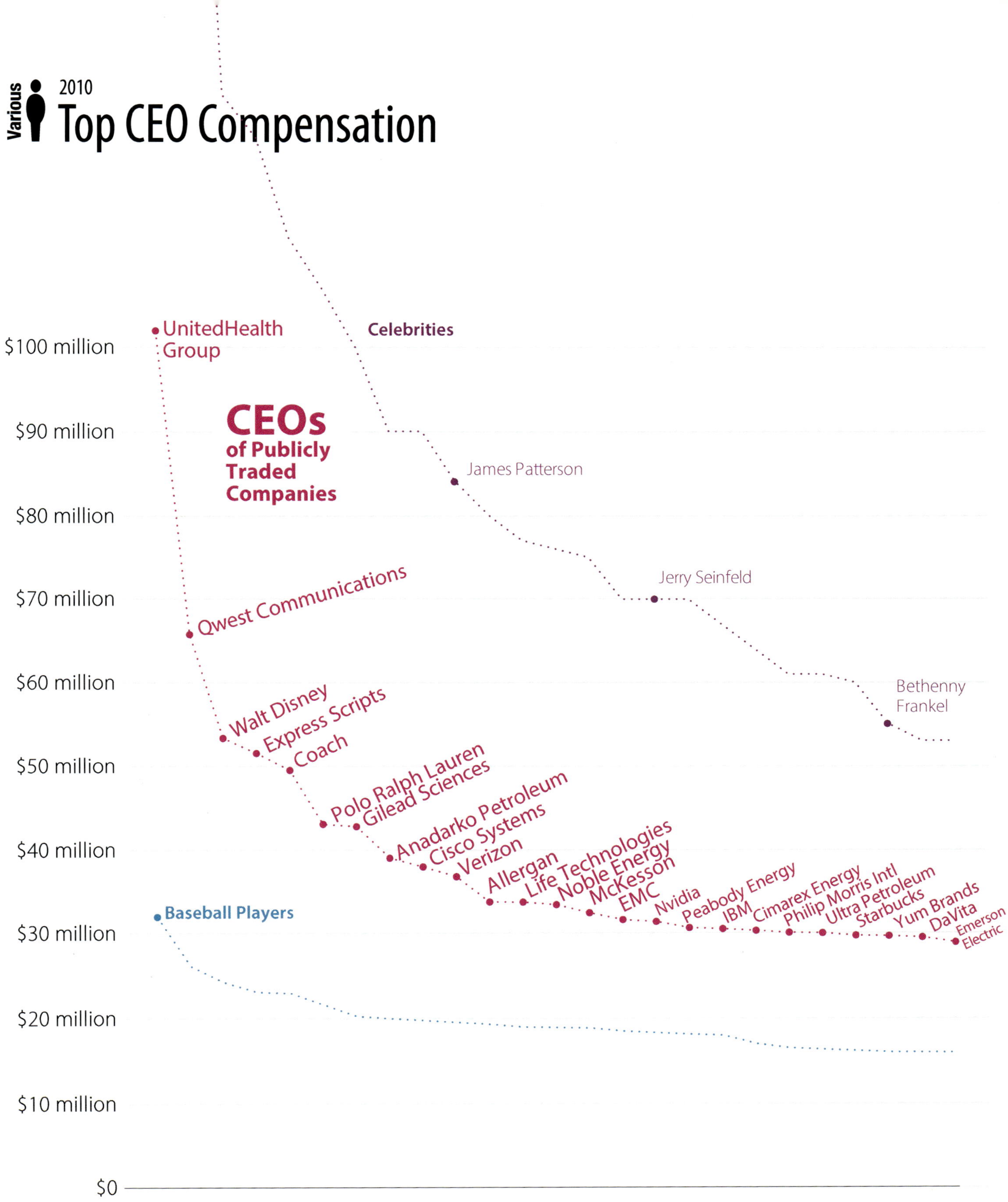

Sources: *AR: Absolute Return + Alpha*, "The Rich List," April 2011 • *Forbes*, "Celebrity 100, 2011" • *Forbes*, "CEO Compensation, 2011." • *USA Today*, "USATODAY Salaries Databases"

Various 2010 Top Celebrity Income

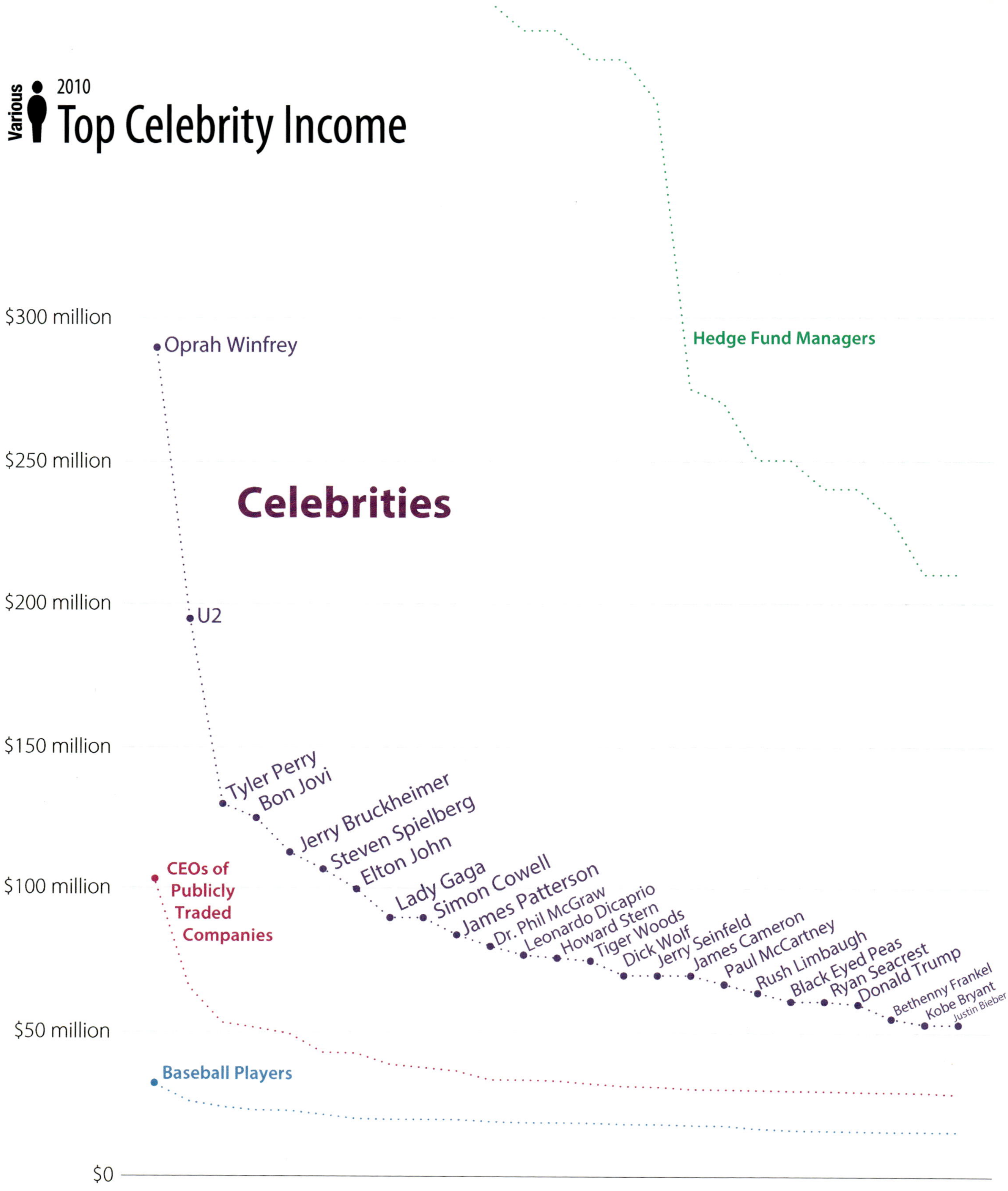

 Sources: *AR: Absolute Return + Alpha*, "The Rich List," April 2011 • *Forbes*, "Celebrity 100, 2011" • *Forbes*, "CEO Compensation, 2011." • *USA Today*, "USATODAY Salaries Databases"

Various 2010 Top Hedge Fund Manager Income

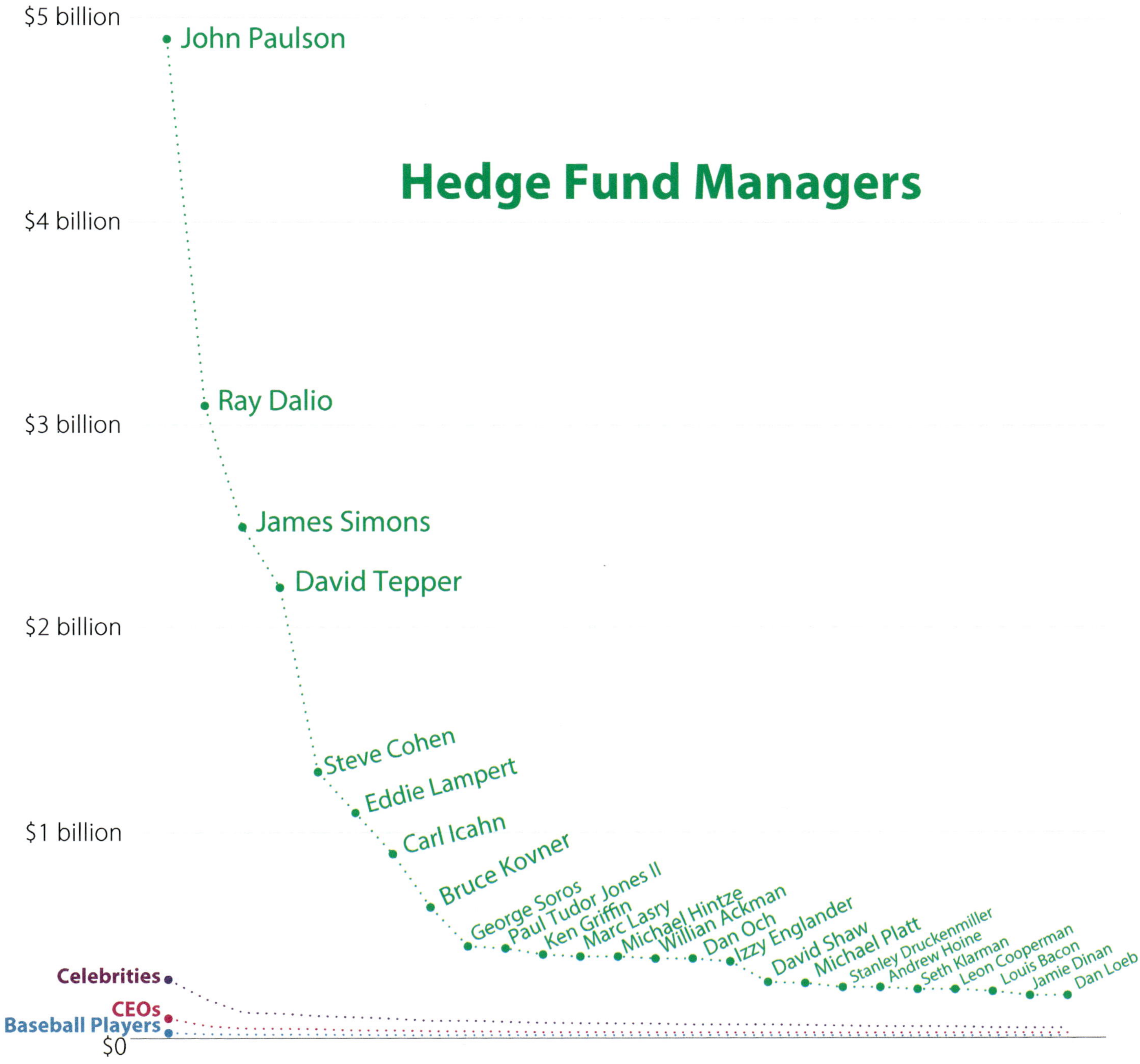

Sources: *AR: Absolute Return + Alpha,* "The Rich List," April 2011 • *Forbes,* "Celebrity 100, 2011" • *Forbes,* "CEO Compensation, 2011." • *USA Today,* "USATODAY Salaries Databases"

Over the years, John Paulson, the number-one-ranked hedge fund manager in 2010, has reinvested his gains back into his funds. In 2010, he had nearly 90% of his personal money (around $10 billion) in either his gold fund or gold-denominated shares of his other funds, accounting for almost $4 billion of his estimated $5 billion income in 2010.

AR's **Hedge Fund Manager** income is calculated from an individual's share of the firm's fees, which include a management fee (between 2% and 5%) and a performance fee, in addition to the gains on the individual's capital (investment) in their funds and the gross gains on personal capital for the year.

Forbes' **Celebrity income** is calculated from entertainment-related pretax gross income of film and television actors, TV personalities, models, athletes, authors, musicians, and comedians. Management, agent, and attorney fees are not deducted.

Forbes' **CEO compensation** for publicly traded companies is based on company proxy statements filed with the US Securities and Exchange Commission. Total compensation includes salary and bonuses; other compensation, such as vested restricted stock grants, LTIP payouts, and perks; and stock gains, the value realized by exercising stock options.

 Sources: *AR: Absolute Return + Alpha* • *Forbes*

1992–2008

Average Income of the Top 400 Tax Returns

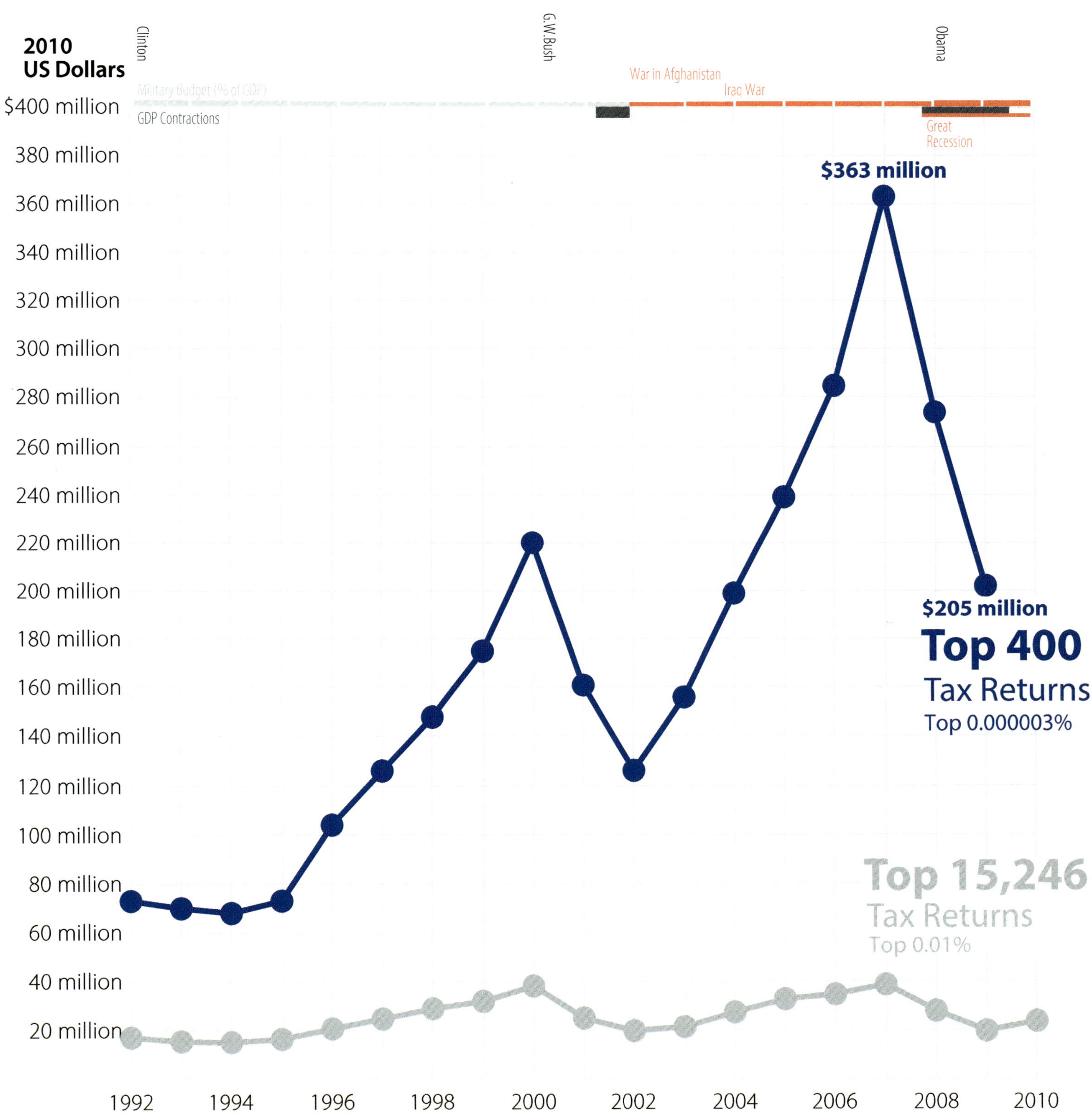

Sources: IRS, Statistics of Income Division • World Top Incomes Database, March 2012 (Compiled from data collected by IRS)

Various 2001–2010

Average Income of the Top 25 Hedge Fund Managers

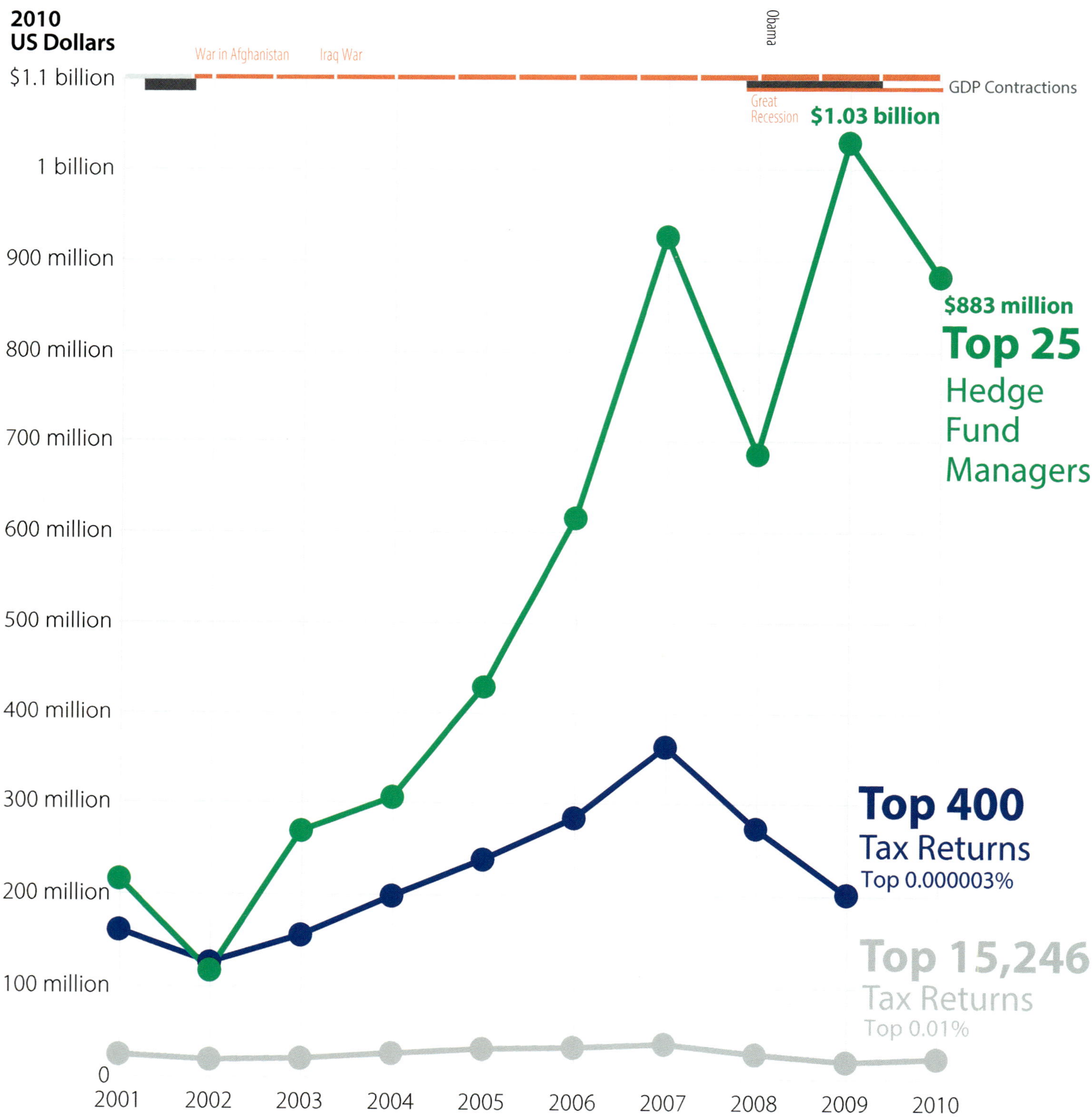

 Sources: *Absolute Return + Alpha* • IRS, Statistics of Income Division • Worlds Top Incomes Database, March 2012 (Compiled from data collected by IRS)

Various

2006–2010

Change in Rank of Top Hedge Fund Managers

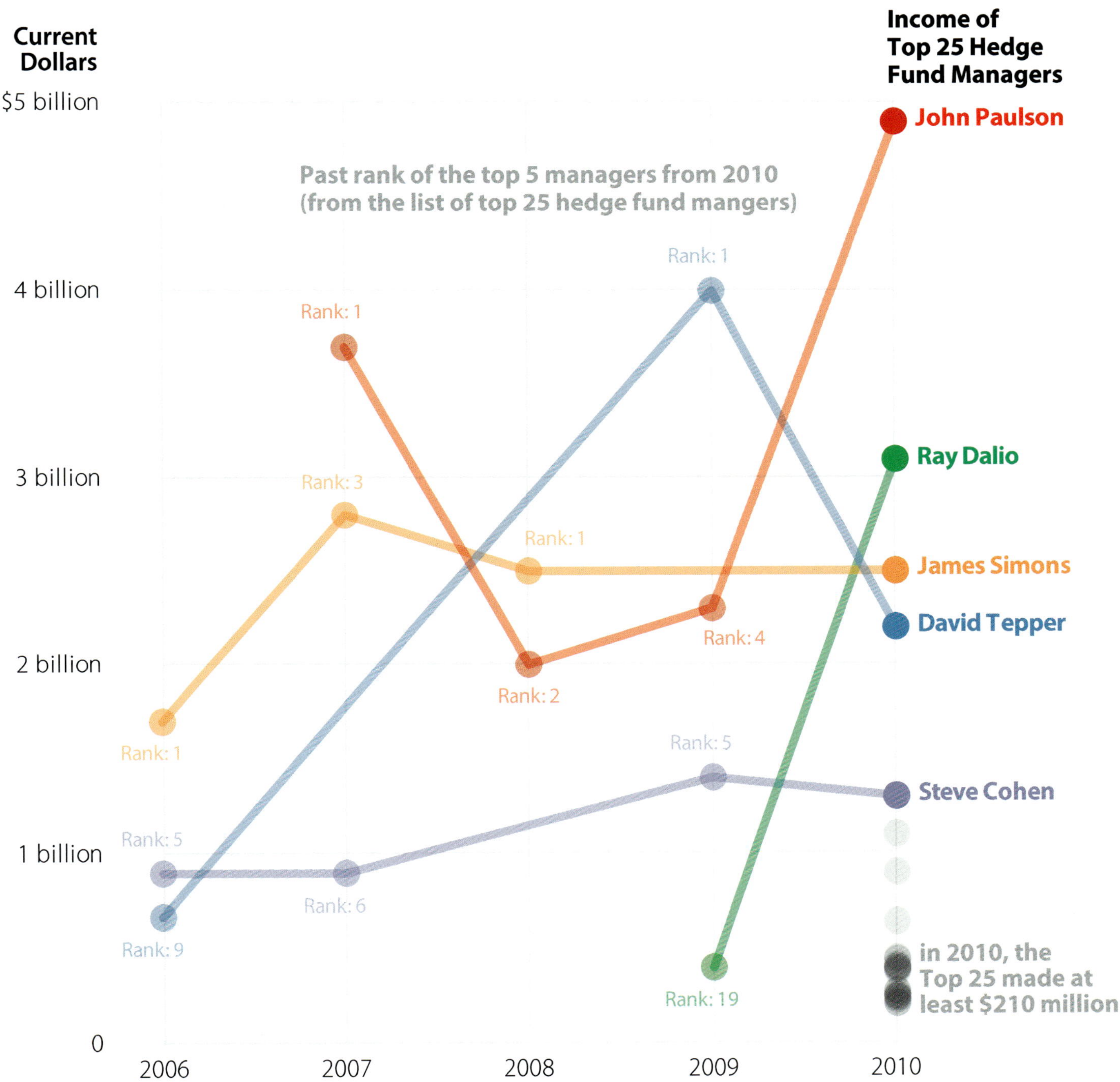

Sources: *Absolute Return + Alpha*, "The Rich List," 2010–2011 • *Institutional Investor's Alpha* 2006–2009

Top 0.01% Income Share and Average Income

1913–2010

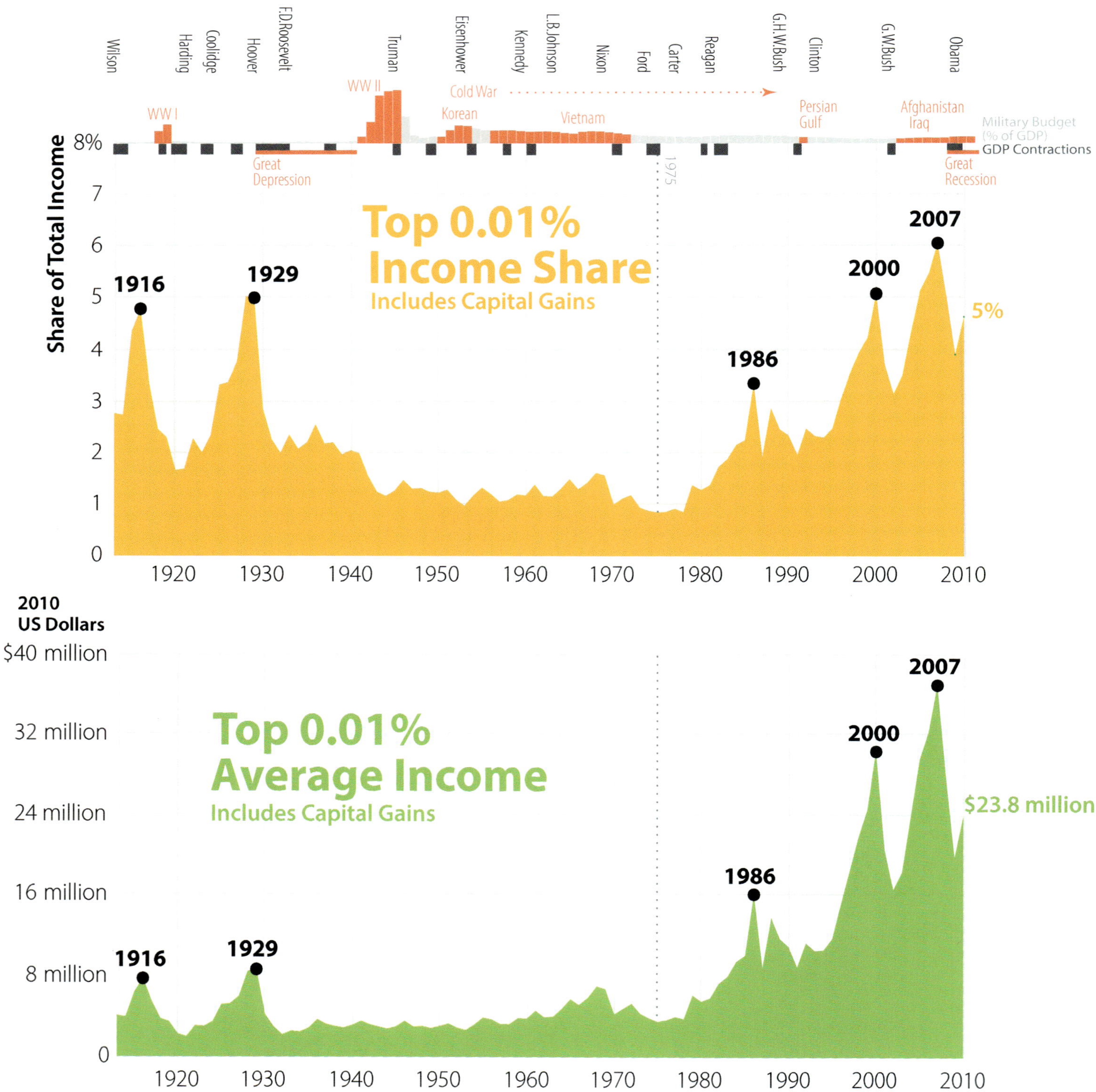

 Source: World Top Incomes Database, March 2012 (Compiled from data collected by IRS)

1913–2010

Top Income Groups since 1913

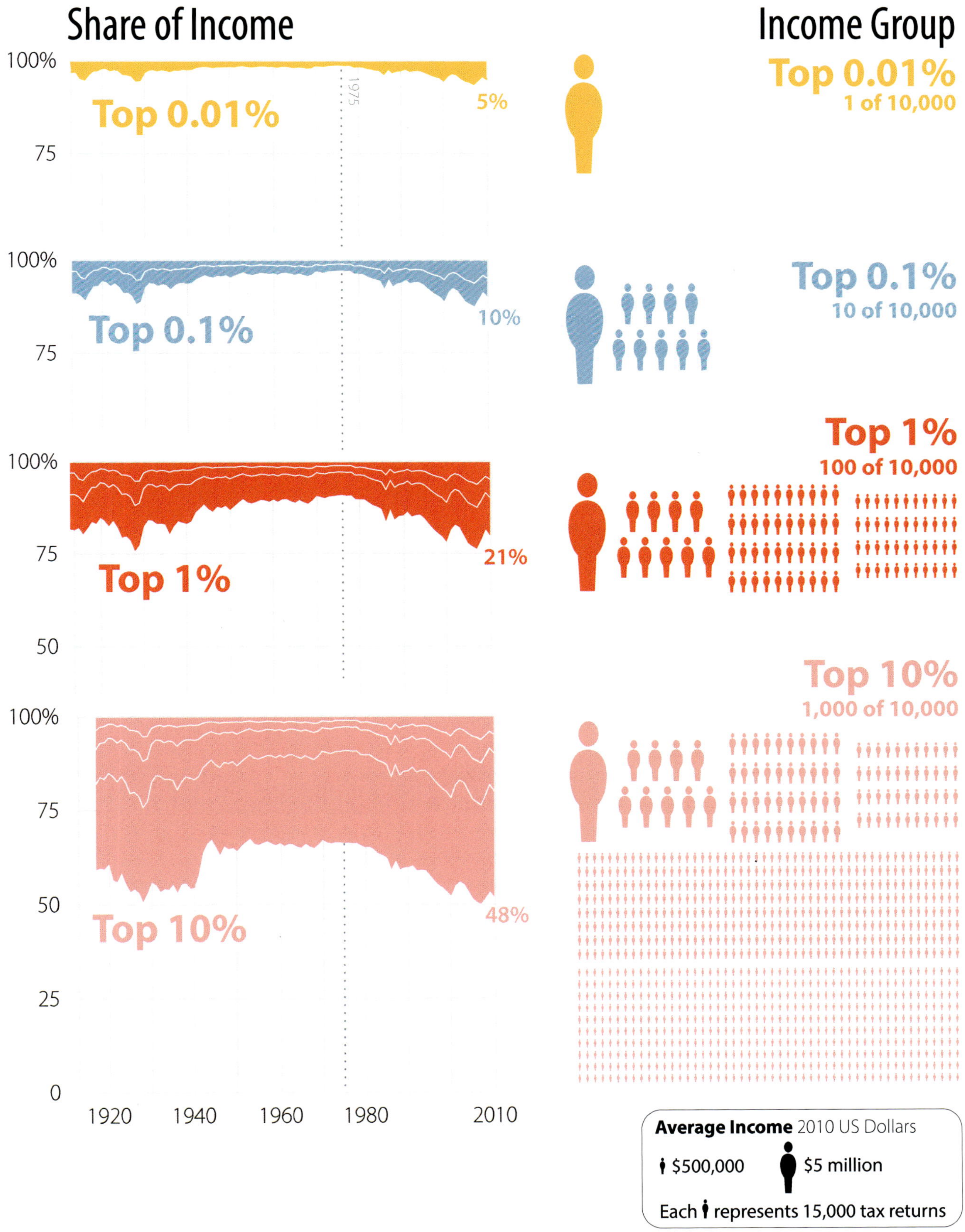

Source: World Top Incomes Database, March 2012 (Compiled from data collected by IRS)

1890–2008

Share of Top 1% by Country (High Income)

Norway

GDP per person (PPP) $54,600

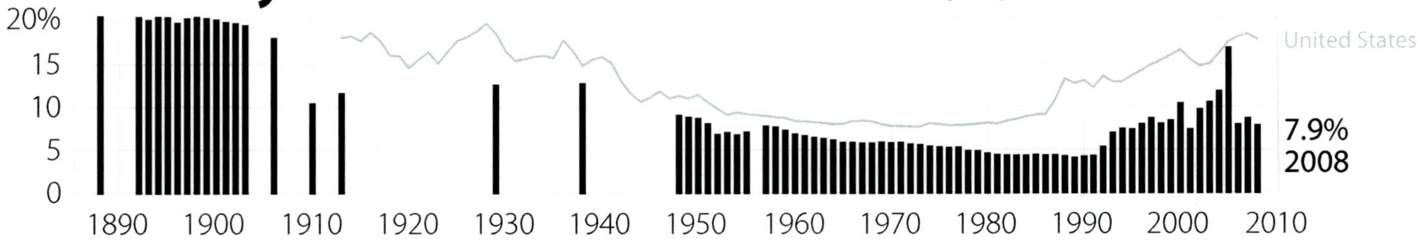

United States

GDP per person (PPP) $47,200

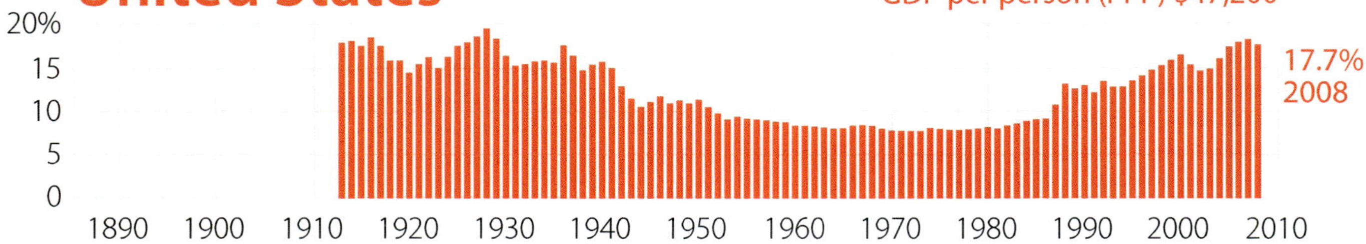

Australia

GDP per person (PPP) $41,000

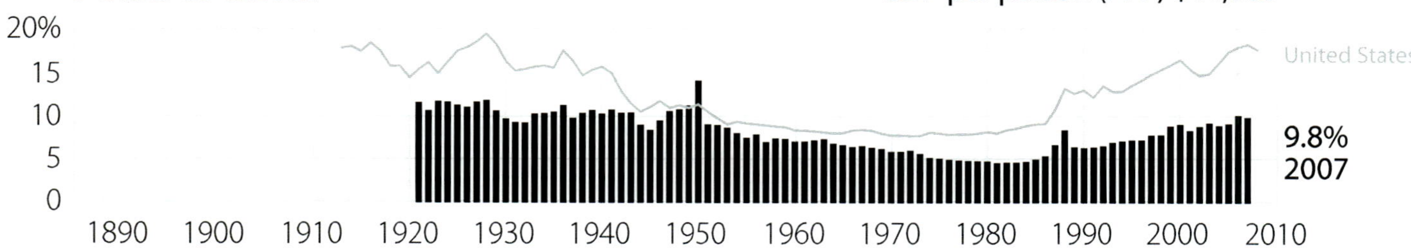

Canada

GDP per person (PPP) $39,400

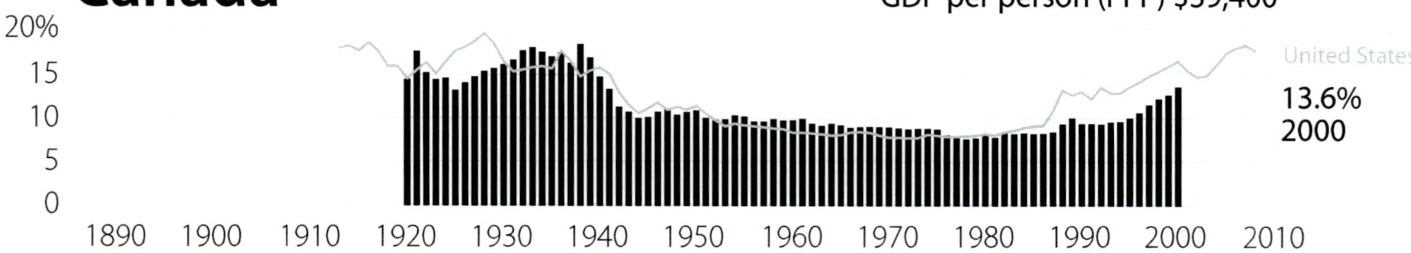

 Source: World Top Incomes Database, March 2012 (Compiled from data collected by IRS)

Sweden

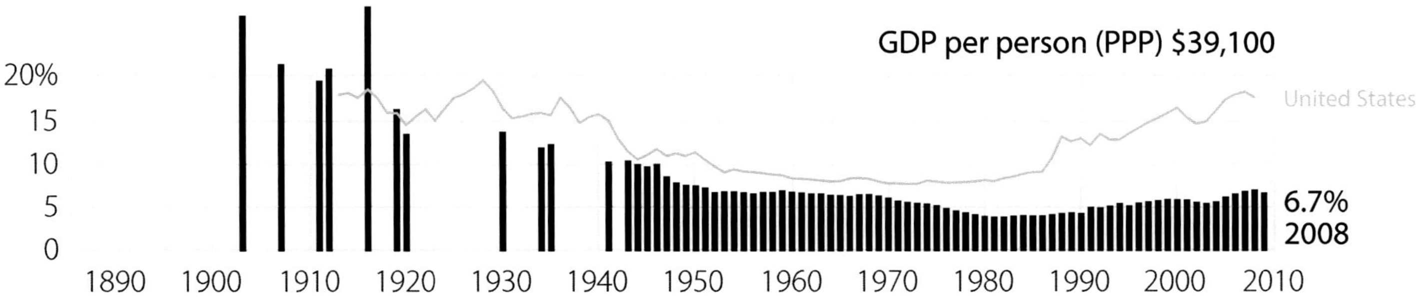

Germany

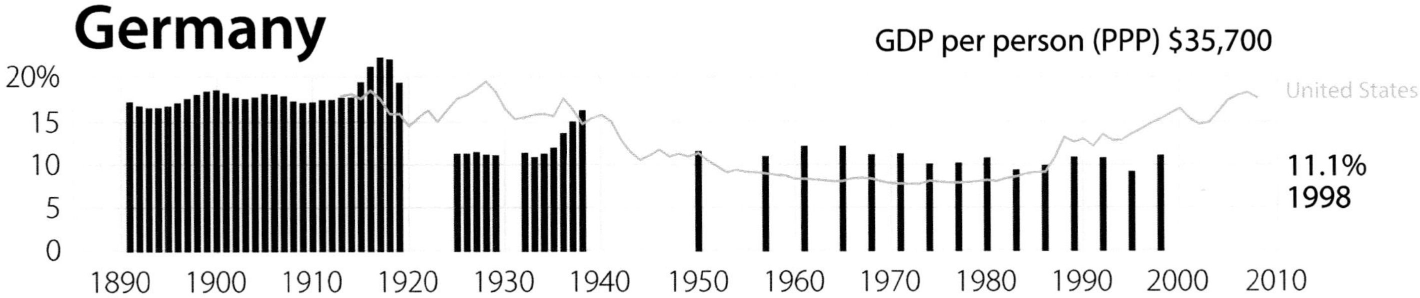

United Kingdom

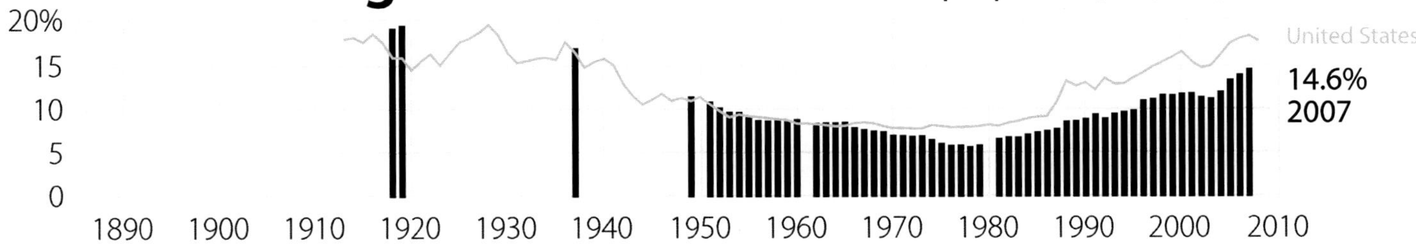

1890–2008

Share of Top 1% by Country (Middle Income)

Japan

GDP per person (PPP) $34,000

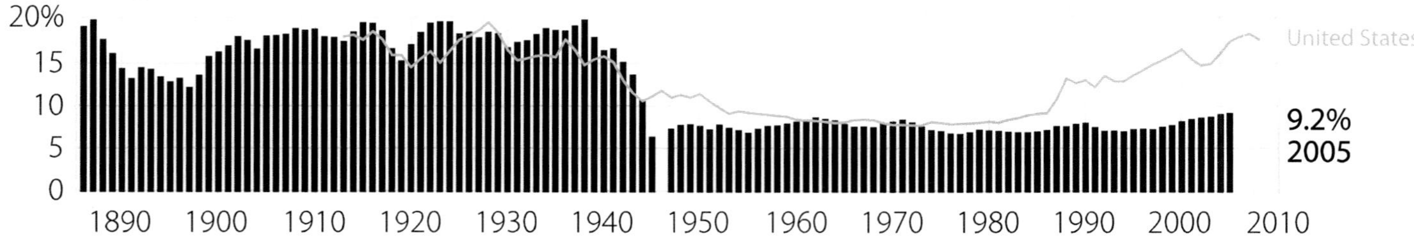

France

GDP per person (PPP) $33,100

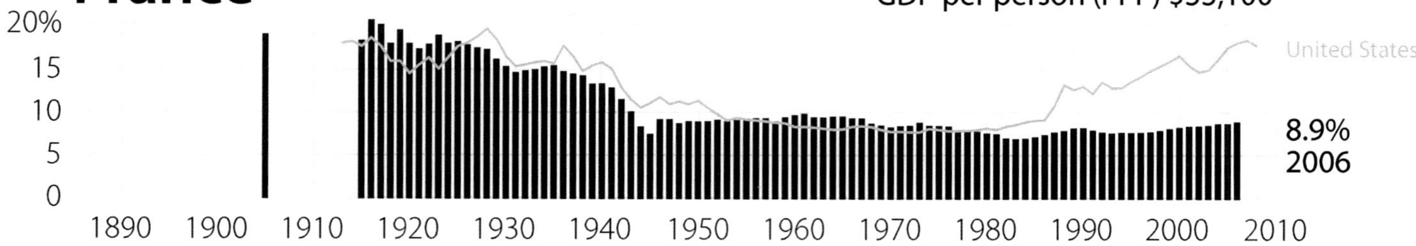

Italy

GDP per person (PPP) $30,500

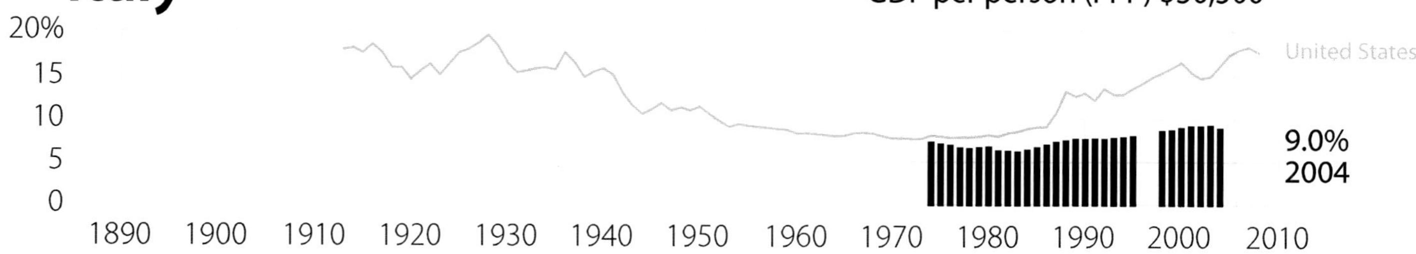

Argentina

GDP per person (PPP) $14,700

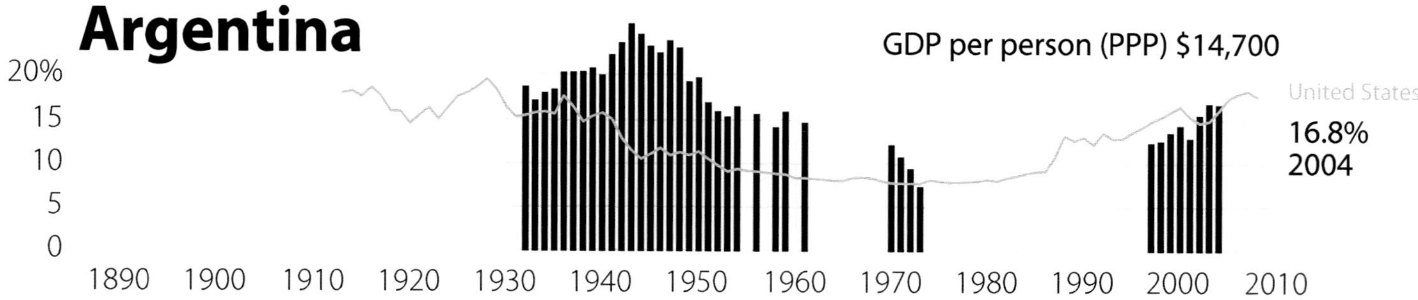

 Source: World Top Incomes Database, March 2012 (Compiled from data collected by IRS)

South Africa

GDP per person (PPP) $10,700

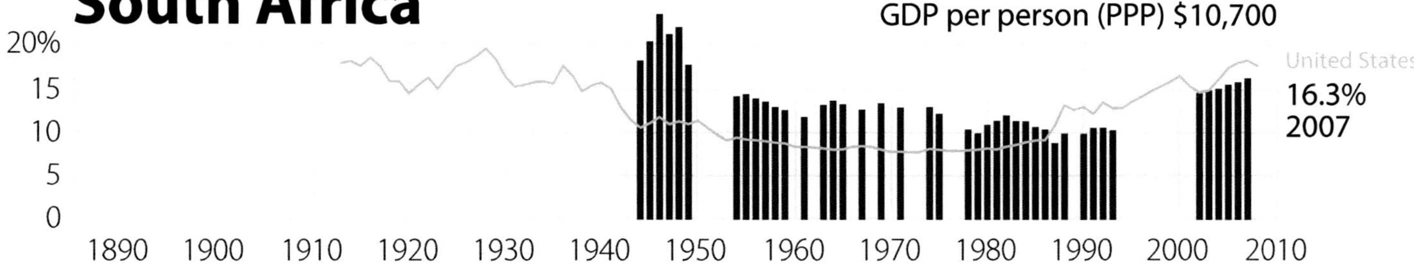

China

GDP per person (PPP) $7,600

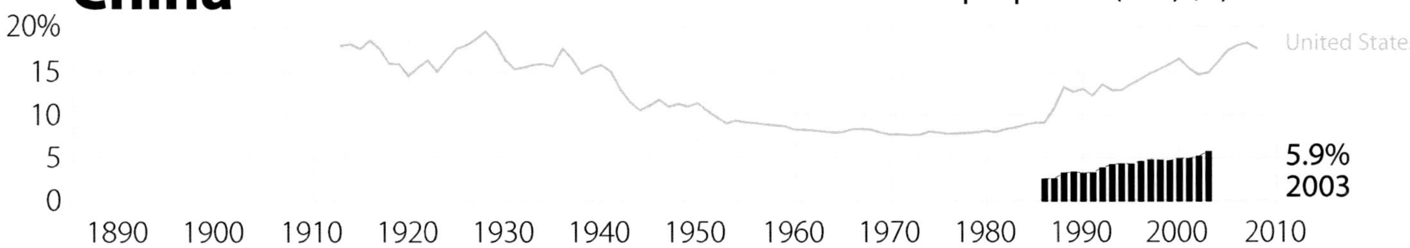

Indonesia

GDP per person (PPP) $4,200

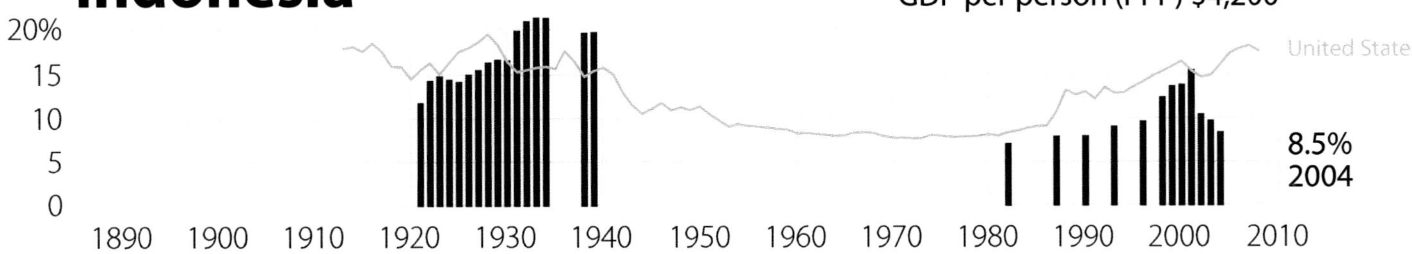

India

GDP per person (PPP) $3,500

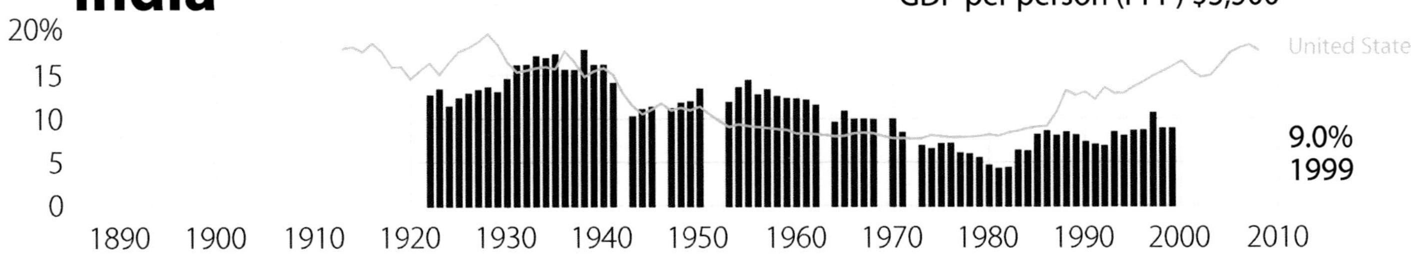

Although articles listing the highest-paid CEOs and celebrities are common, data identifying the occupations of all of the highest income earners is not. The one source I found was from a single research paper by Bakija, Cole, and Heim relying on detailed analysis of US tax returns.

Each year, taxpayers are asked to identify their occupation on their federal income tax form. Since 1979, the Statistics of Income Division of the IRS has coded the occupations of tax filers by converting these text entries into standard occupation codes. The industry of the taxpayer's employer is identified using the employer identification number from the taxpayer's W-2 form; the industry codes come from the Social Security Administration's Employer Information File.

 Source: Jon Bakija, Adam Cole, and Bradley Heim, "Jobs and Income Growth of Top Earners and the Causes of Changing Income Inequality: Evidence from US Tax Return Data," 2008

2005

Occupations of the Top 1% and Top 0.1%

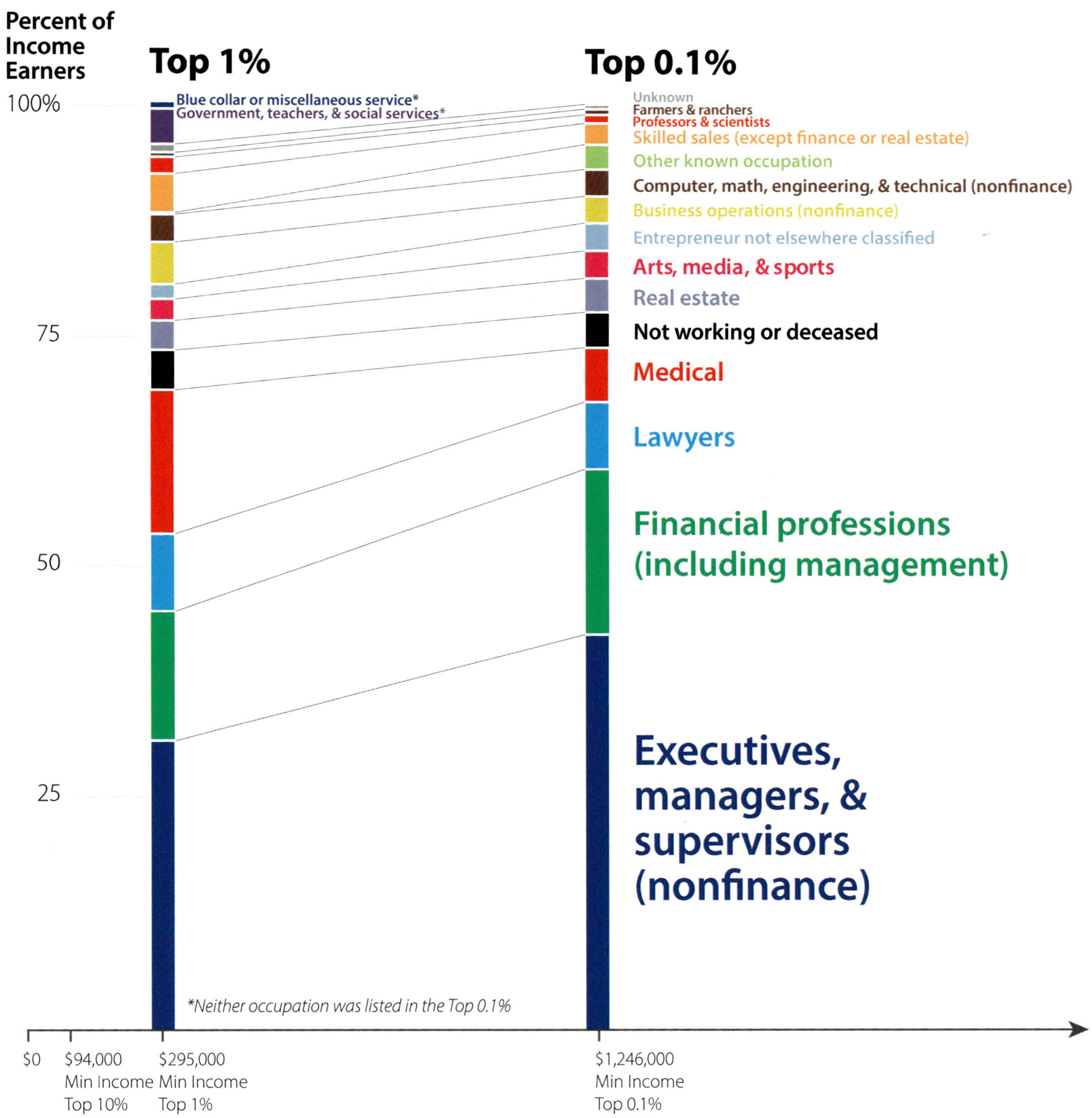

Source: Jon Bakija, Adam Cole, and Bradley Heim, "Jobs and Income Growth of Top Earners and the Causes of Changing Income Inequality: Evidence from US Tax Return Data," 2008

2005

Income Share of Top 1% by Occupation

18% share of total income in 2005

$338,000 Cutoff for the Top 1% in 2005 (income of tax units excluding capital gains)

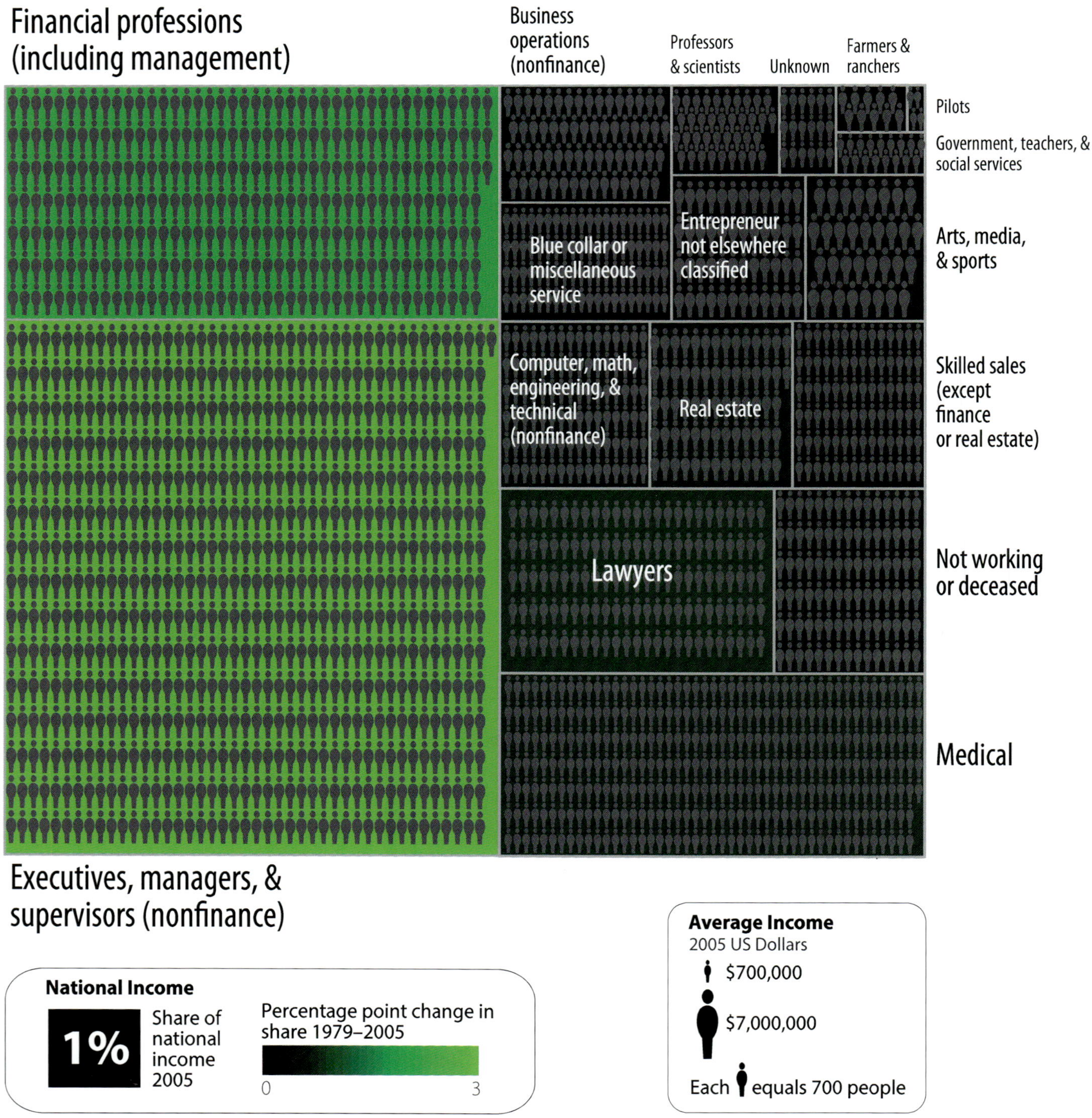

Source: Jon Bakija, Adam Cole, and Bradley Heim, "Jobs and Income Growth of Top Earners and the Causes of Changing Income Inequality: Evidence from US Tax Return Data," 2008

2005

Income Share of Top 0.1% by Occupation

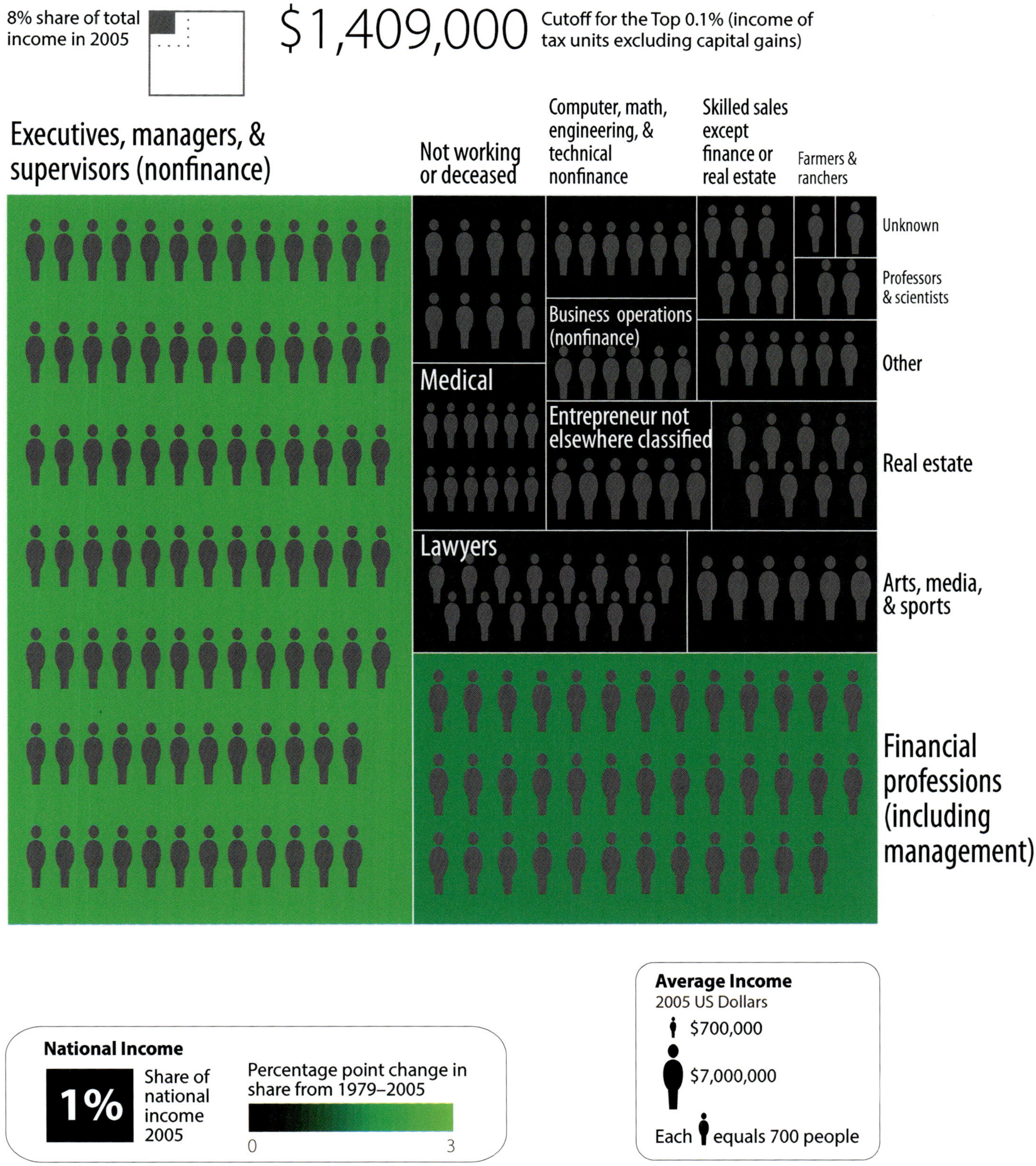

Source: Jon Bakija, Adam Cole, and Bradley Heim, "Jobs and Income Growth of Top Earners and the Causes of Changing Income Inequality: Evidence from US Tax Return Data," 2008

1979–2005

Top Occupations' Share of Taxpayers and Income

 Source: Jon Bakija, Adam Cole, and Bradley Heim, "Jobs and Income Growth of Top Earners and the Causes of Changing Income Inequality: Evidence from US Tax Return Data," 2008

INCOME SOURCES

Sources of income vary dramatically for each income group. The higher the income, the more important nonsalary sources become. Taxes on these different sources vary as well, affecting not only the amount of money that people have to spend but also the rate at which they can accumulate wealth.

1989–2011

CEO Compensation of the Largest US Public Companies

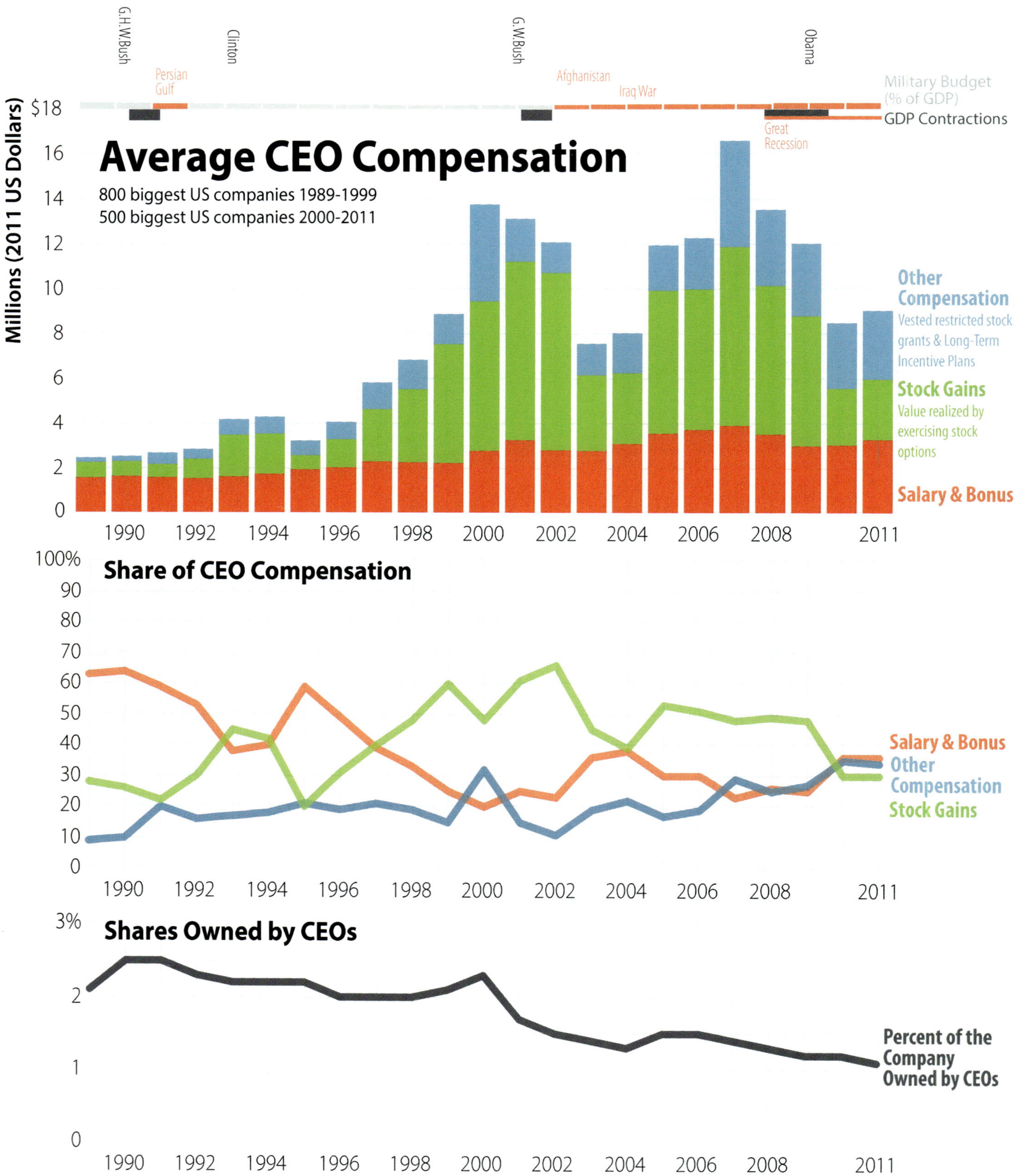

 Source: *Forbes*, "Historical Chart: Two Decades of CEO Pay"

1913–2010

Three Major Income Sources of Top 0.01%

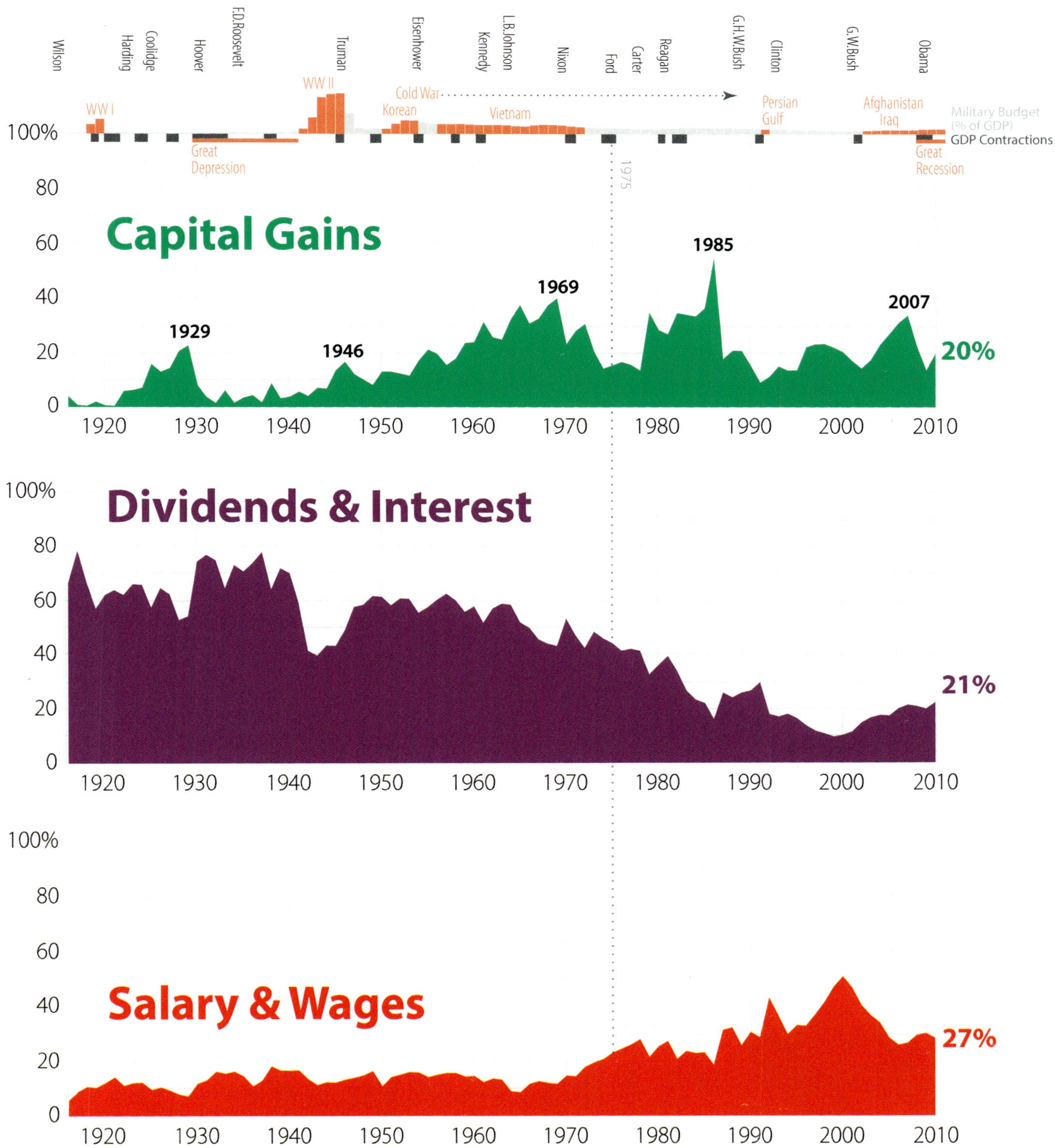

Top 0.01% – 15,600 families in 2010 had incomes greater than $6 million **excluding** capital gains. High-income people whose income comes from captial gains do not appear in these three charts.

Sources: IRS, Statistics of Income Division • World Top Incomes Database, March 2012 (Compiled from data collected by IRS)

Measuring Income Inequality using the Gini Index

It is very difficult to show the income of the poorest, middle, and richest people all on one graph. One approach is to use the Lorenz curve, which plots the cumulative percentage (or share) of income against the cumulative percentage of the population.

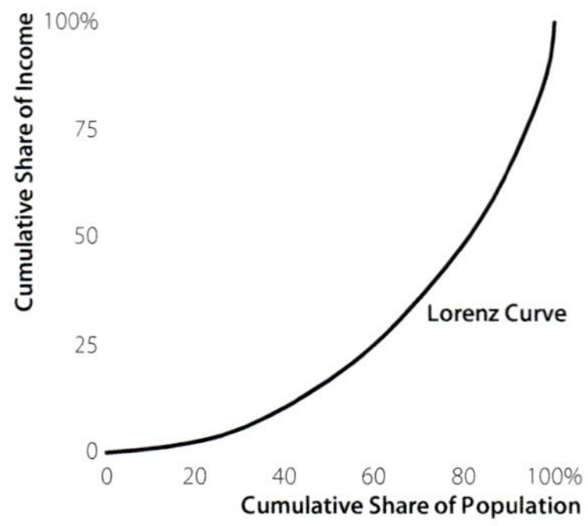

If each income group has the same income, then the cumulative income share would equal the cumulative population share, and the Lorenz curve would follow the "Equal Distribution" 45-degree line.

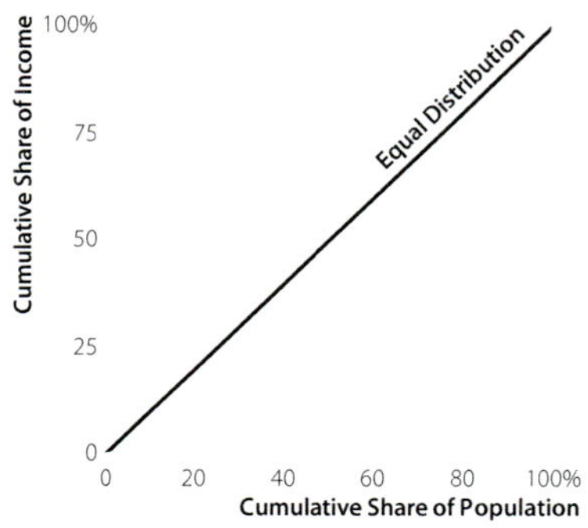

The difference between these two lines is the amount of income inequality. The Gini index is equal to twice the area (in blue) between the 45-degree line and the Lorenz curve.

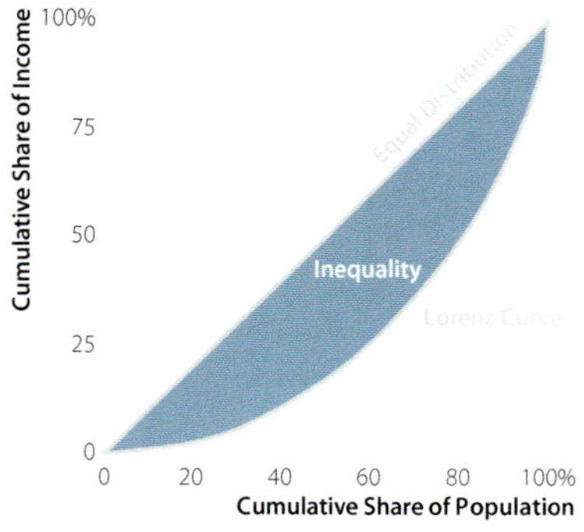

The Congressional Budget Office's measurement of market income includes the following:

Labor income, which includes cash wages and salaries (including those allocated by employees to 401(k) plans), employer-paid health insurance premiums, and the employer's share of Social Security, Medicare, and federal unemployment insurance payroll taxes.

Business income, which includes net income from businesses and farms operated solely by their owners, partnership income, and income from S corporations.

Capital gains, which are profits realized from the sale of assets. Increases in the value of assets that have not been realized through sales are not included in market income.

Capital income (excluding capital gains) which comprises taxable and tax-exempt interest, dividends paid by corporations (but not dividends from S corporations, which are considered part of business income), positive rental income, and corporate income taxes. Capital gains are considered separately and not included in this measure of capital income. The Congressional Budget Office assumes in this analysis that corporate income taxes are borne by owners of capital in proportion to their income from capital; therefore, the amount of the corporate tax is included in household income measured before taxes.

Other income, which includes income received in retirement for past services and any other sources of income.

Source: Congressional Budget Office, "Trends in the Distribution of Household Income Between 1979 and 2007," October 2011

CBO

2007

Distribution of Income by Source

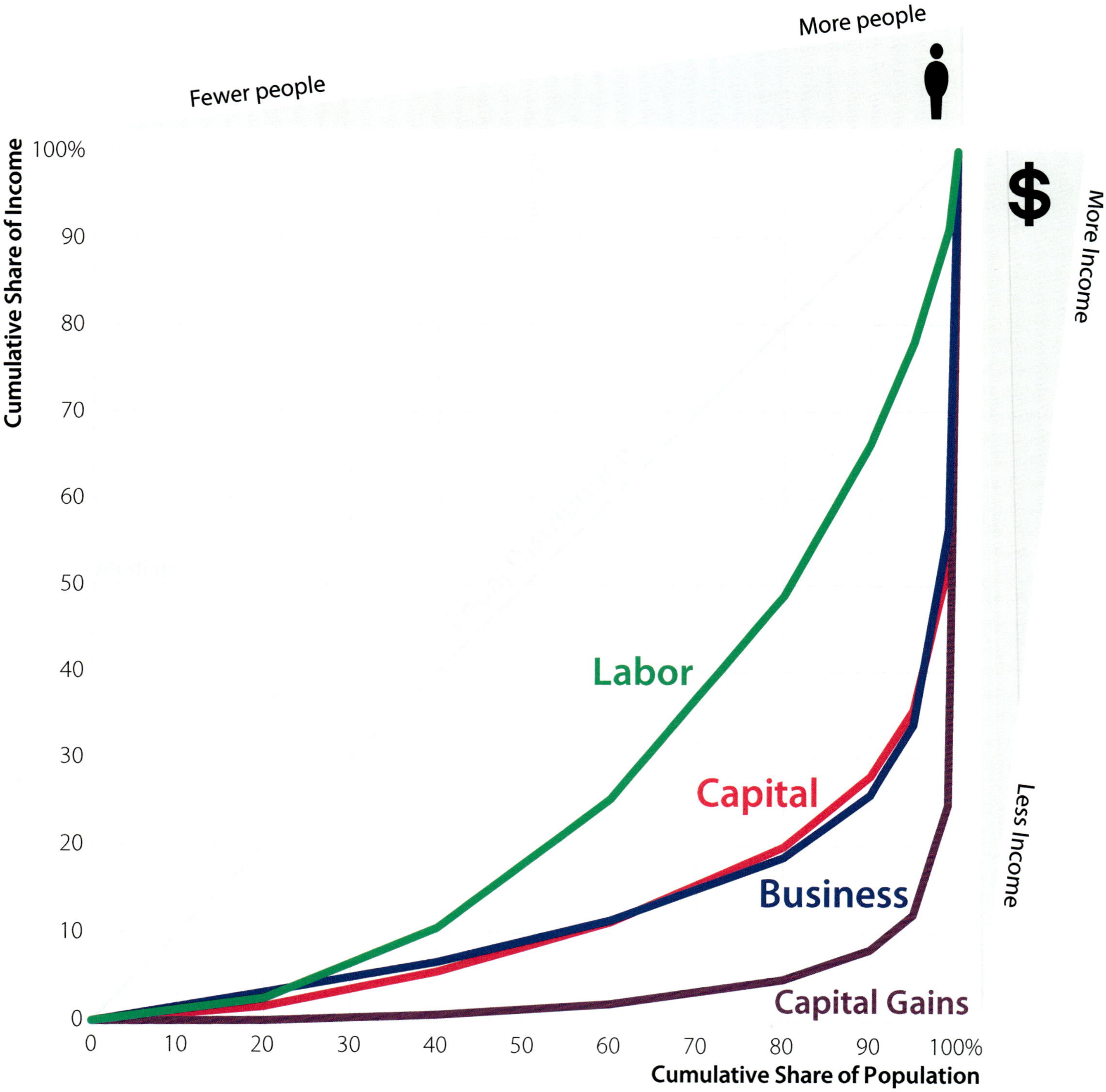

 Source: Congressional Budget Office, "Trends in the Distribution of Household Income Between 1979 and 2007," October 2011

1979–2007

Change in Cumulative Share of Income

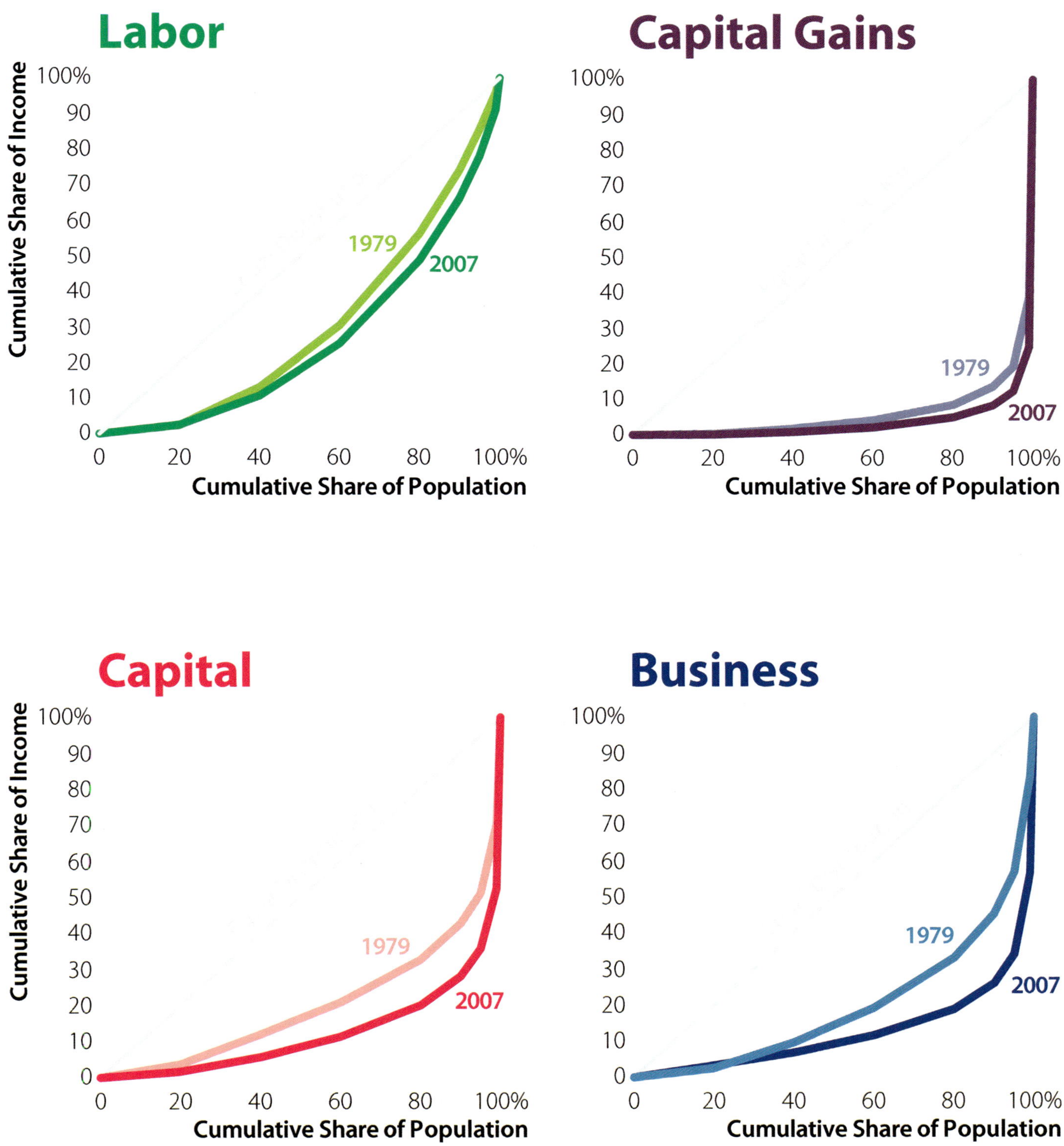

Source: Congressional Budget Office, "Trends in the Distribution of Household Income Between 1979 and 2007," October 2011

When the CBO looks at the effect of federal taxes on income, it includes:

- **Individual income taxes**
- **Social insurance (payroll) taxes**
- **Taxes on corporations**
- **Excise tax on products, such as the gasoline tax**

All of which account for over 95 percent of total federal revenues.

The Congressional Budget Office defines **income groups** by ranking all households by their size-adjusted income (i.e., adjusting for differences in household size by dividing income by the square root of the number of people living together). It assigns equal numbers of people to each percentile (1/100) and quintile (1/5). Households with negative income are excluded from the lowest income group.

The **top tax rate or marginal tax rate** is the rate you pay on the "last dollar" you earn; but when you view the taxes you paid as a percentage of your income, your effective tax rate is less than your marginal rate, especially after you take into account the deductions and exemptions (i.e., income that is not subject to any tax).

 Source: Congressional Budget Office, "Trends in the Distribution of Household Income Between 1979 and 2007," October 2011

2007

Cumulative Share Before and After Federal Taxes

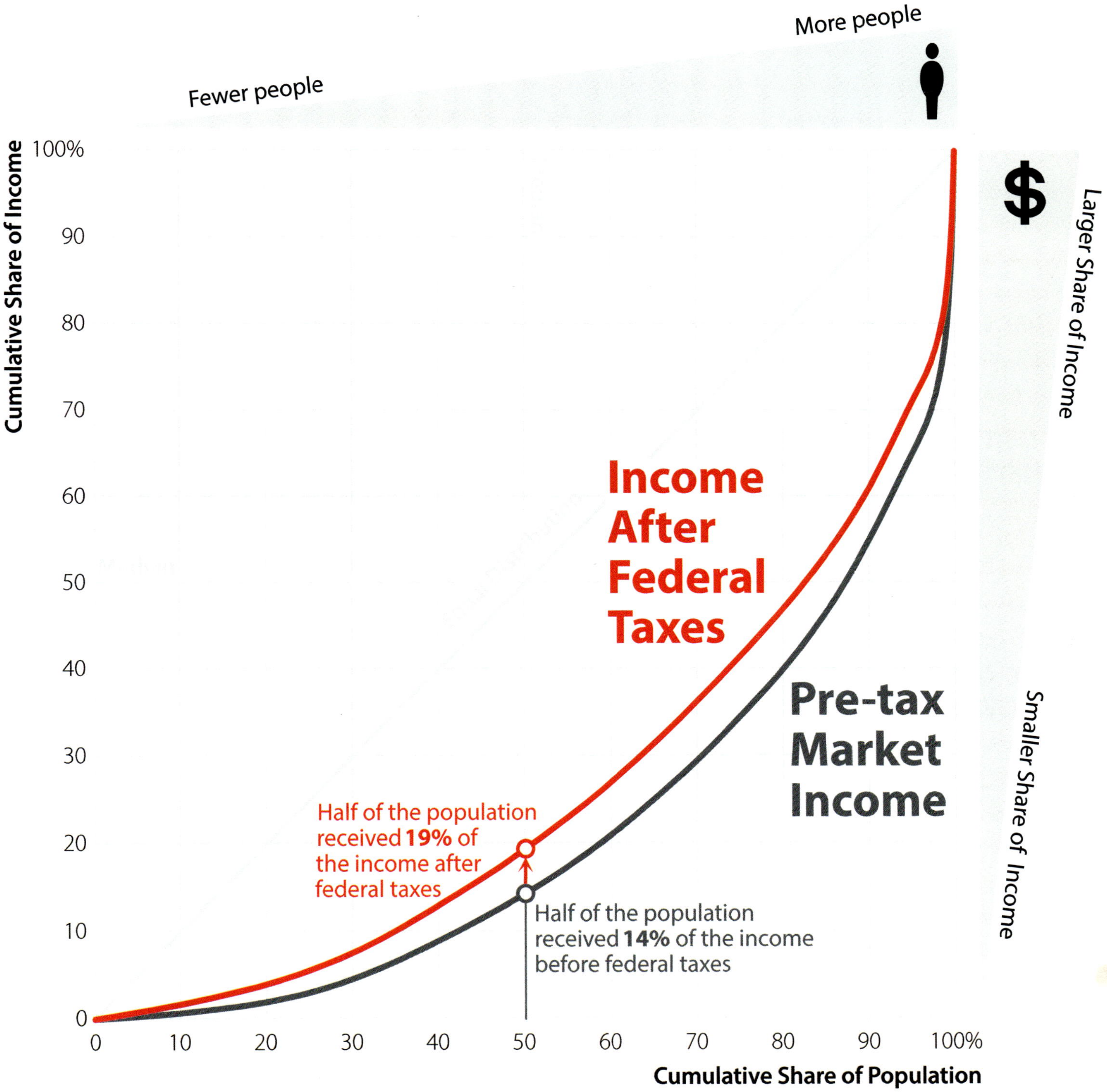

Source: Congressional Budget Office, "Trends in the Distribution of Household Income Between 1979 and 2007," October 2011

1979-2009

Share of Total Income: Before and After Federal Taxes

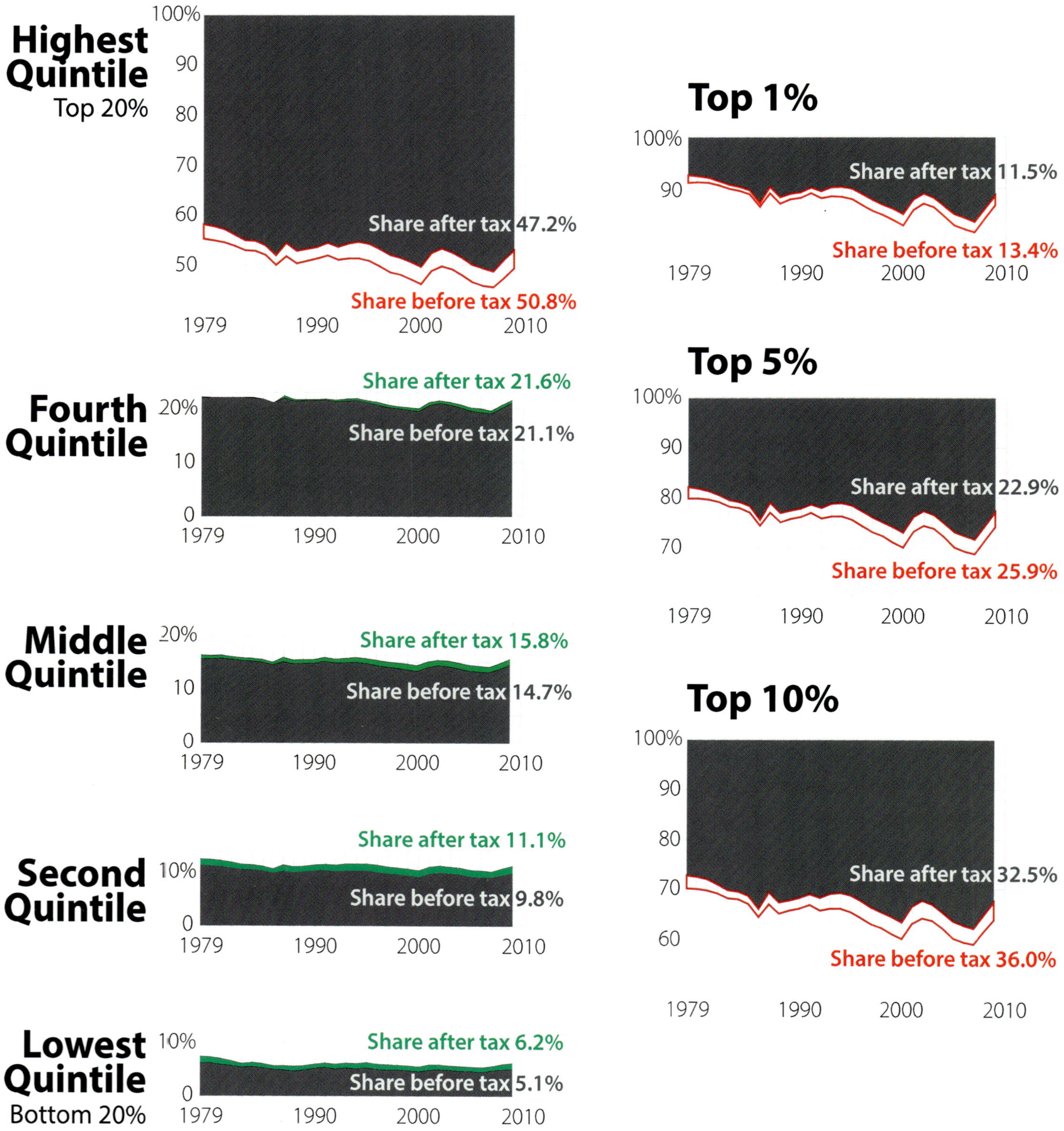

 Source: Congressional Budget Office, "The Distribution of Household Income and Federal Taxes, 2008 and 2009"

CBO

2009

Average Income: Before and After Federal Taxes

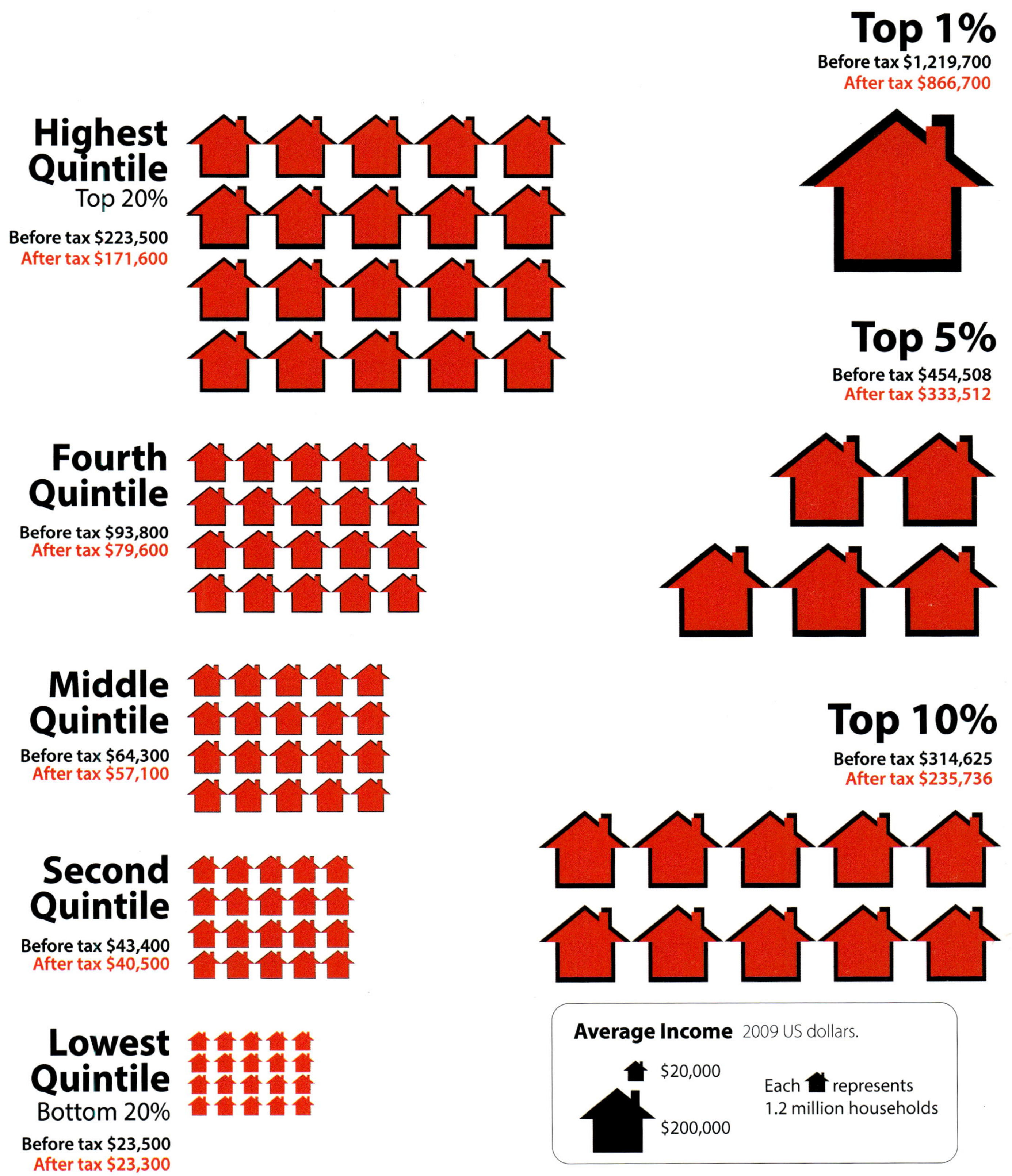

Source: Congressional Budget Office, "The Distribution of Household Income and Federal Taxes, 2008 and 2009"

1913–2011 Top Tax Rates

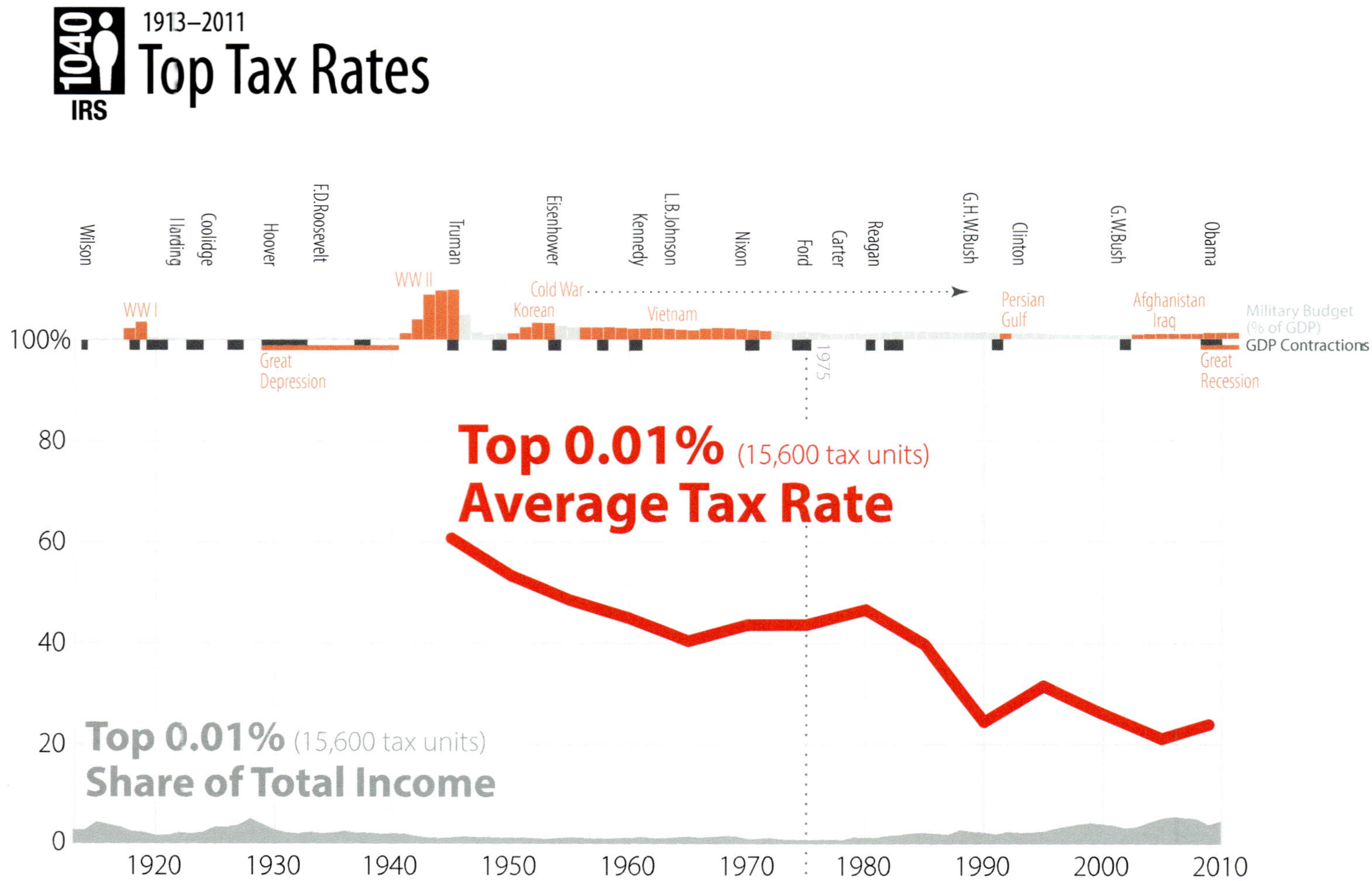

Marginal Tax Rates

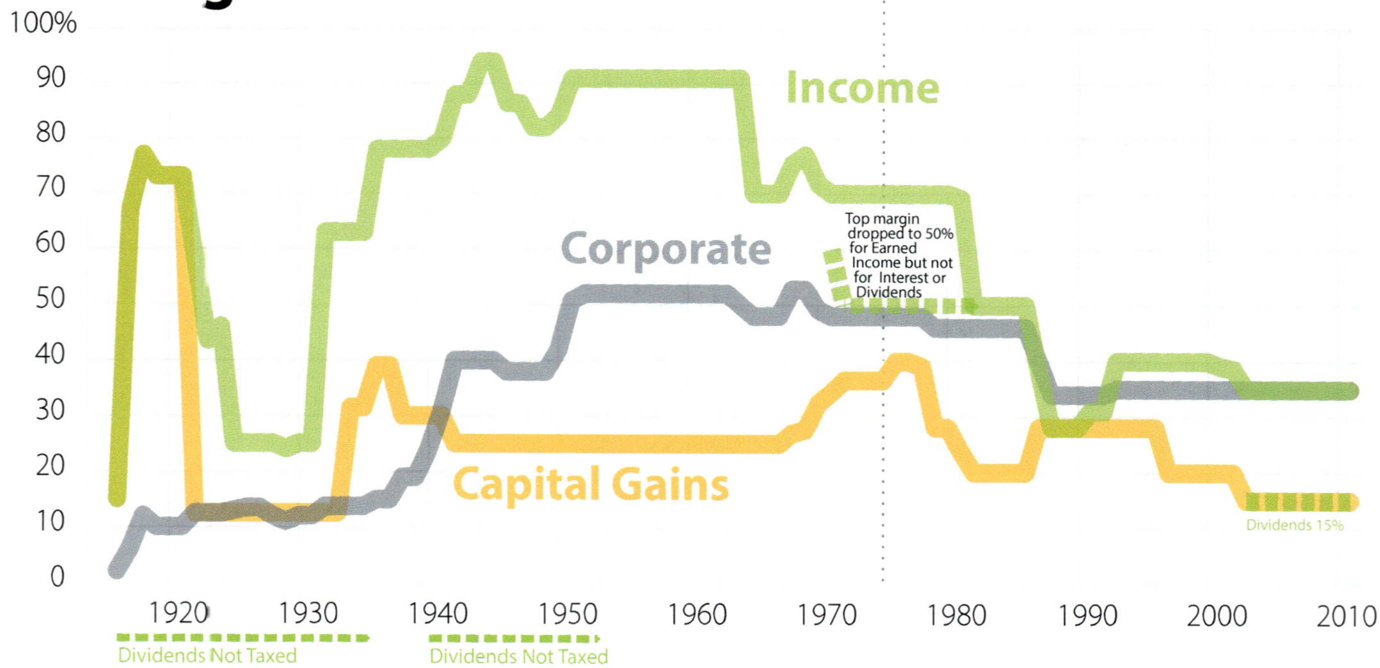

 Sources: TaxPolicyCenter.org, TaxFoundation.org, and Citizens for Tax Justice (ctj.org) • World Top Incomes Database, March 2012 (Compiled from data collected by IRS)

DEMOGRAPHICS

Even if the share of income going to the top 1% were unchanged, inequality would still have increased for the bottom 99% of income earners because of changes in household structure. For example, since the 1970s, there are more two-income families than one-income families. Two incomes are common in households earning more than $80,000 a year.

Census 1890–2010 Population Growth

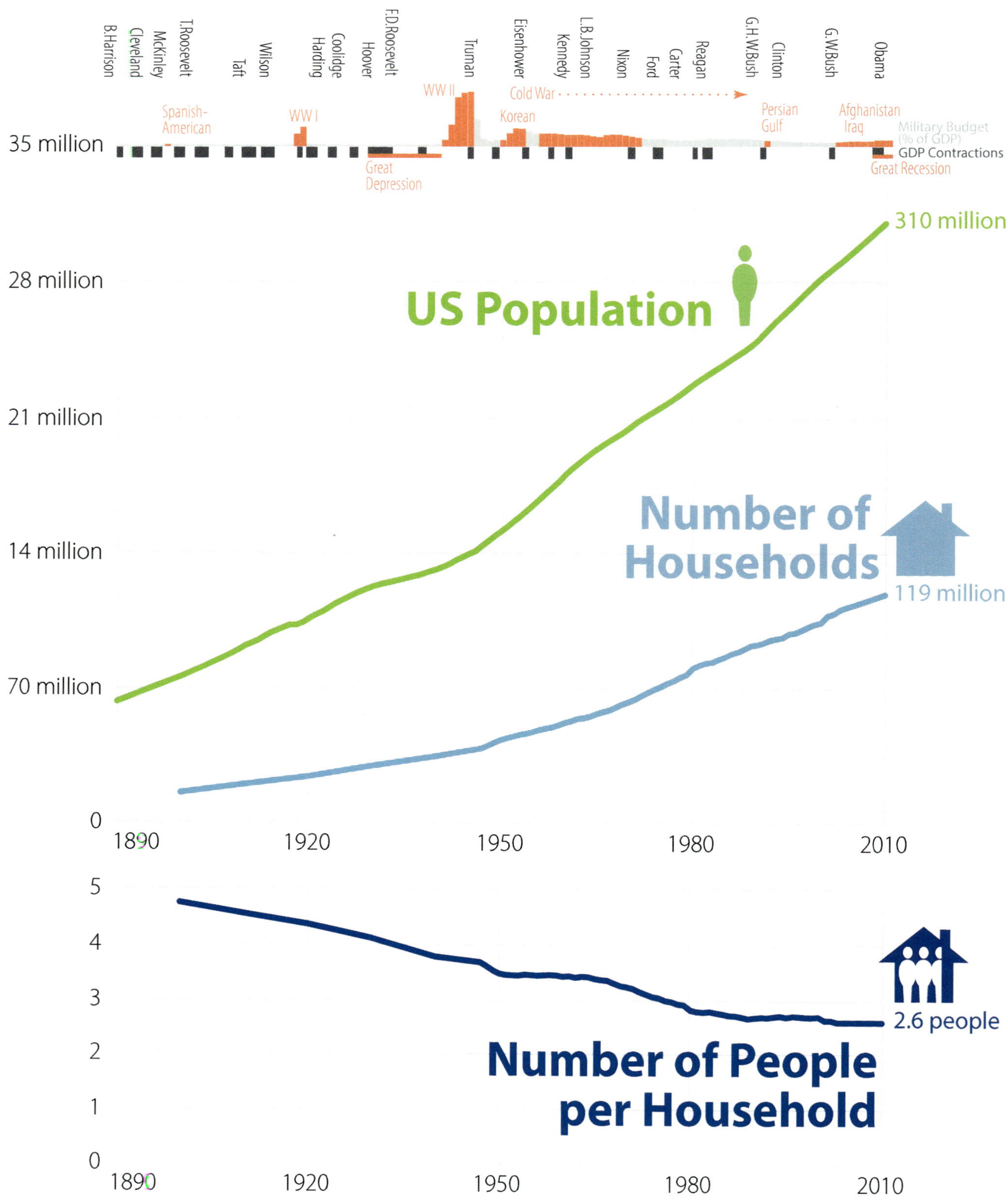

 Source: US Census Bureau

Over the last decades, the number of households has diverged from the number of families as more people lived together before marriage and more single adults lived alone.

Number of Households

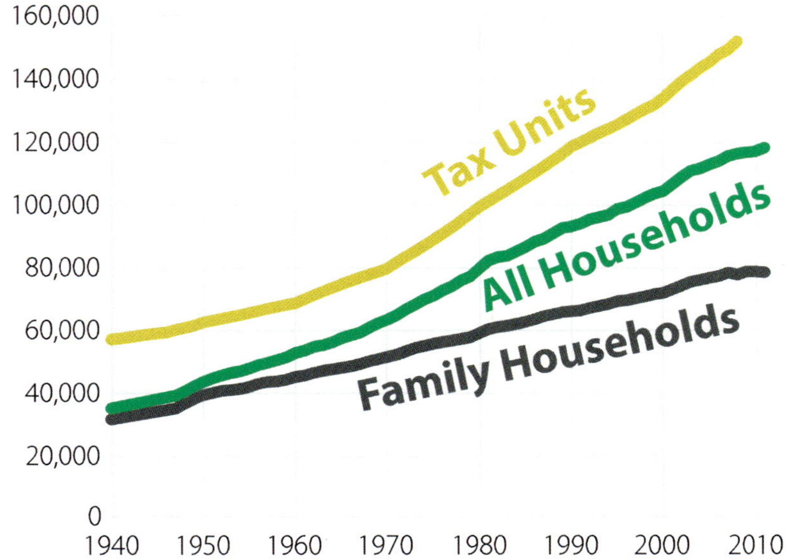

Share of All Households

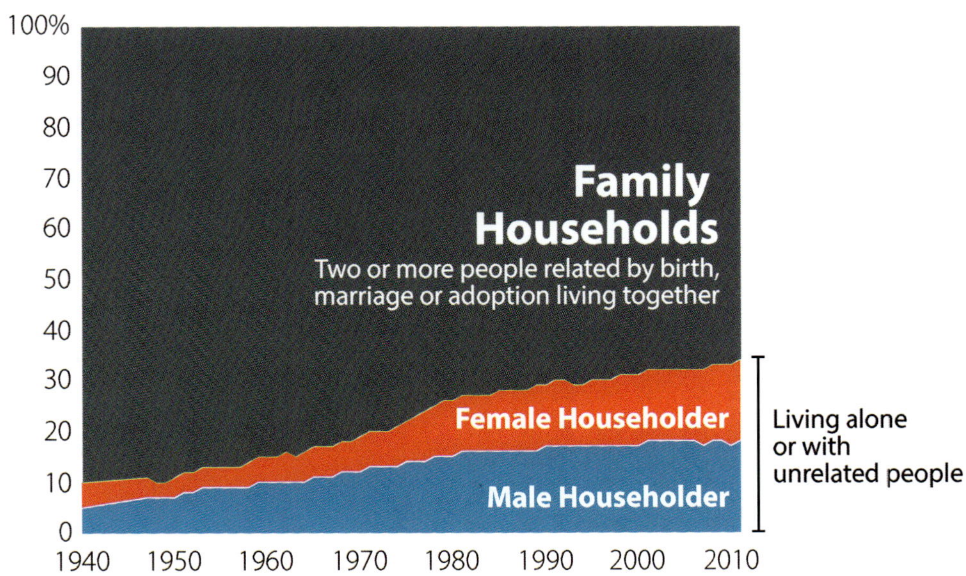

The percent of all households that are family households has dropped from 90% to 66% since the 1940s.

Source: US Census Bureau

20˙0

Household Income of Bottom 99%

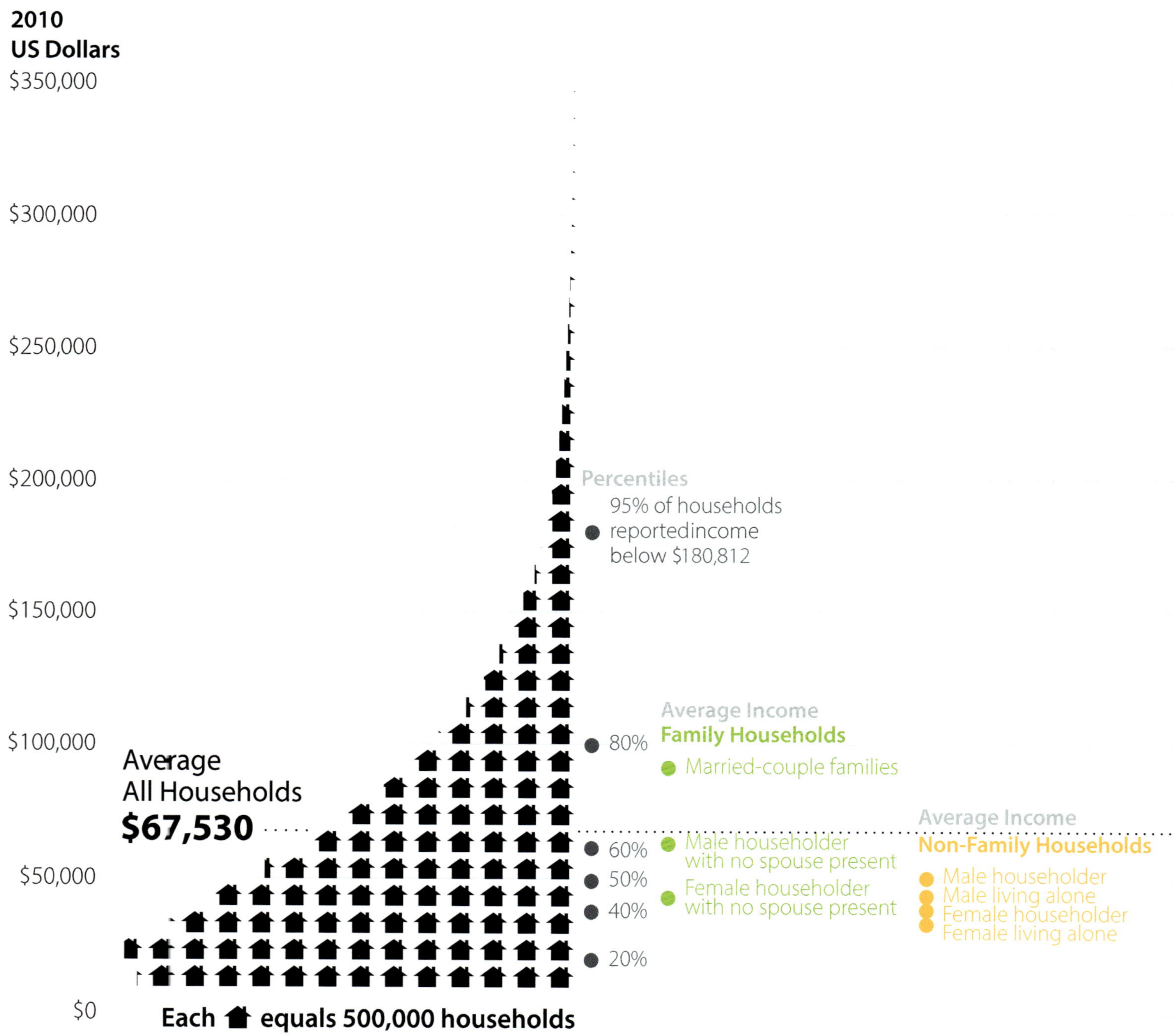

 Source: US Census Bureau, 2006–2010 American Community Survey

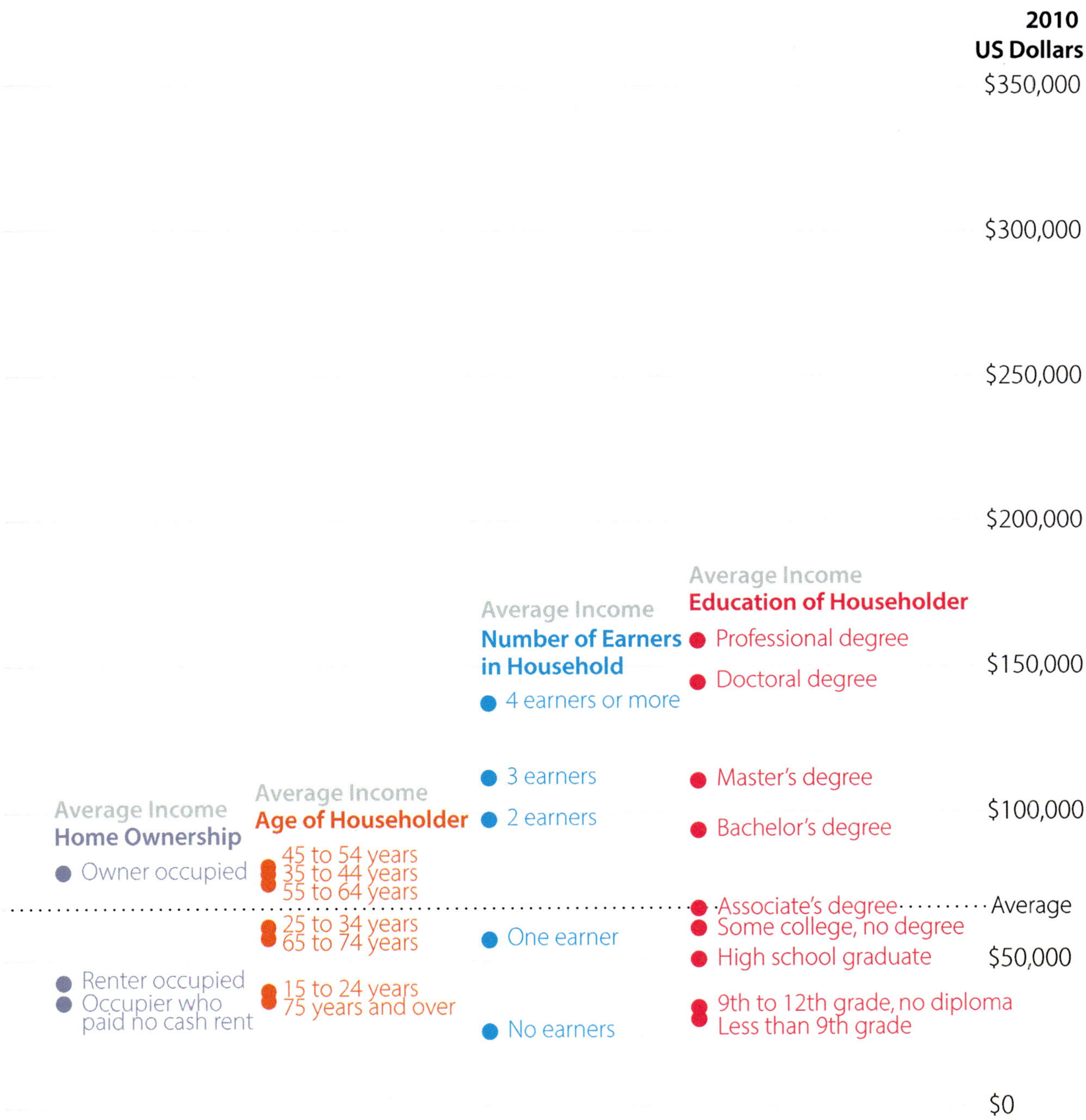

2010
US Dollars
$350,000
$300,000
$250,000
$200,000
$150,000
$100,000
$50,000
$0
Average
Average Income
Home Ownership
Owner occupied
Renter occupied
Occupier who paid no cash rent
Average Income
Age of Householder
45 to 54 years
35 to 44 years
55 to 64 years
25 to 34 years
65 to 74 years
15 to 24 years
75 years and over
Average Income
Number of Earners in Household
4 earners or more
3 earners
2 earners
One earner
No earners
Average Income
Education of Householder
Professional degree
Doctoral degree
Master's degree
Bachelor's degree
Associate's degree
Some college, no degree
High school graduate
9th to 12th grade, no diploma
Less than 9th grade

Census

2010

Demographics of All Incomes

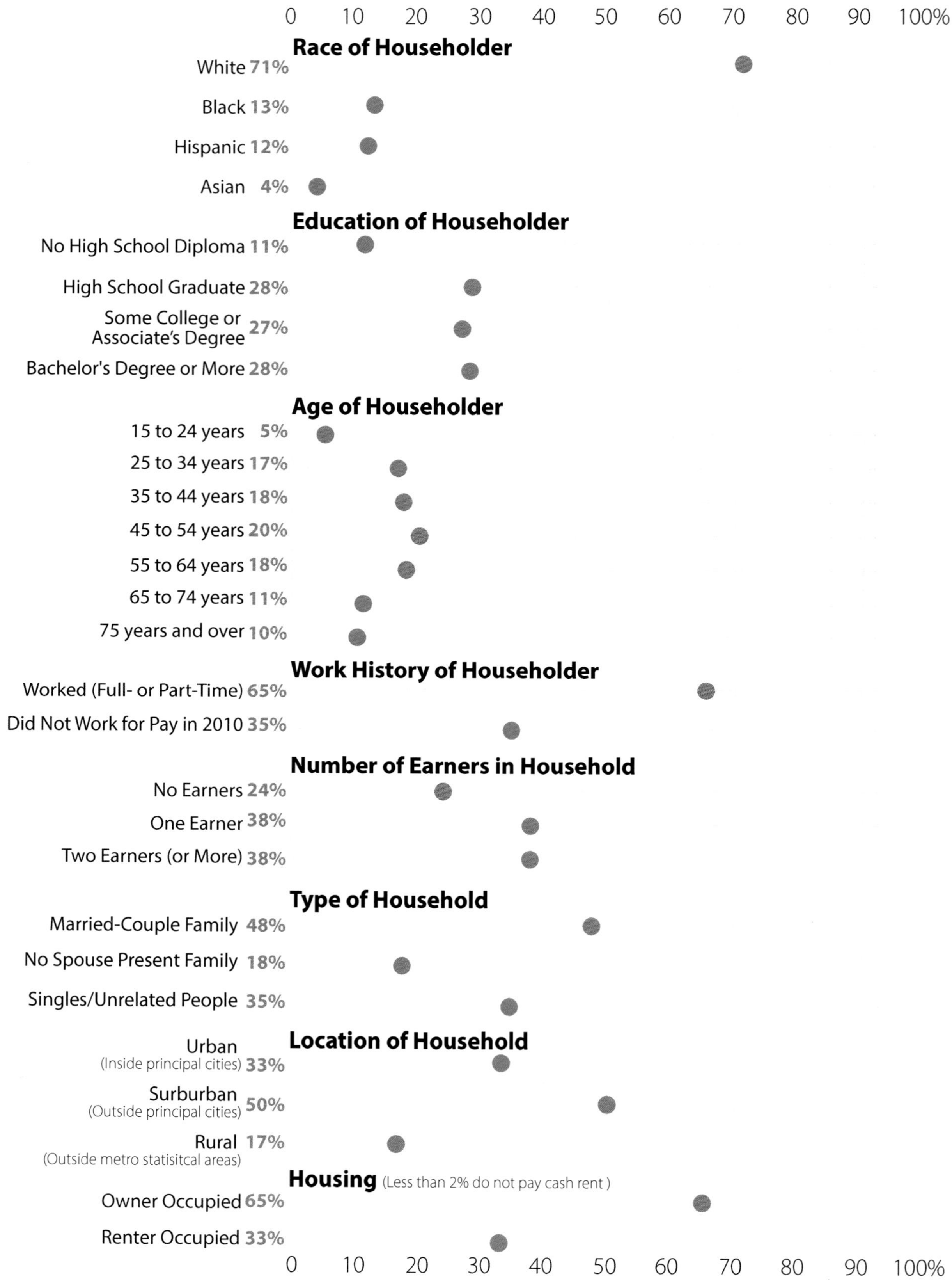

 Source: US Census Bureau, 2006–2010 American Community Survey

Census

2010

Demographics of Incomes below $30,000

Source: US Census Bureau, 2006–2010 American Community Survey

2010

Demographics of Incomes $30,000–$80,000

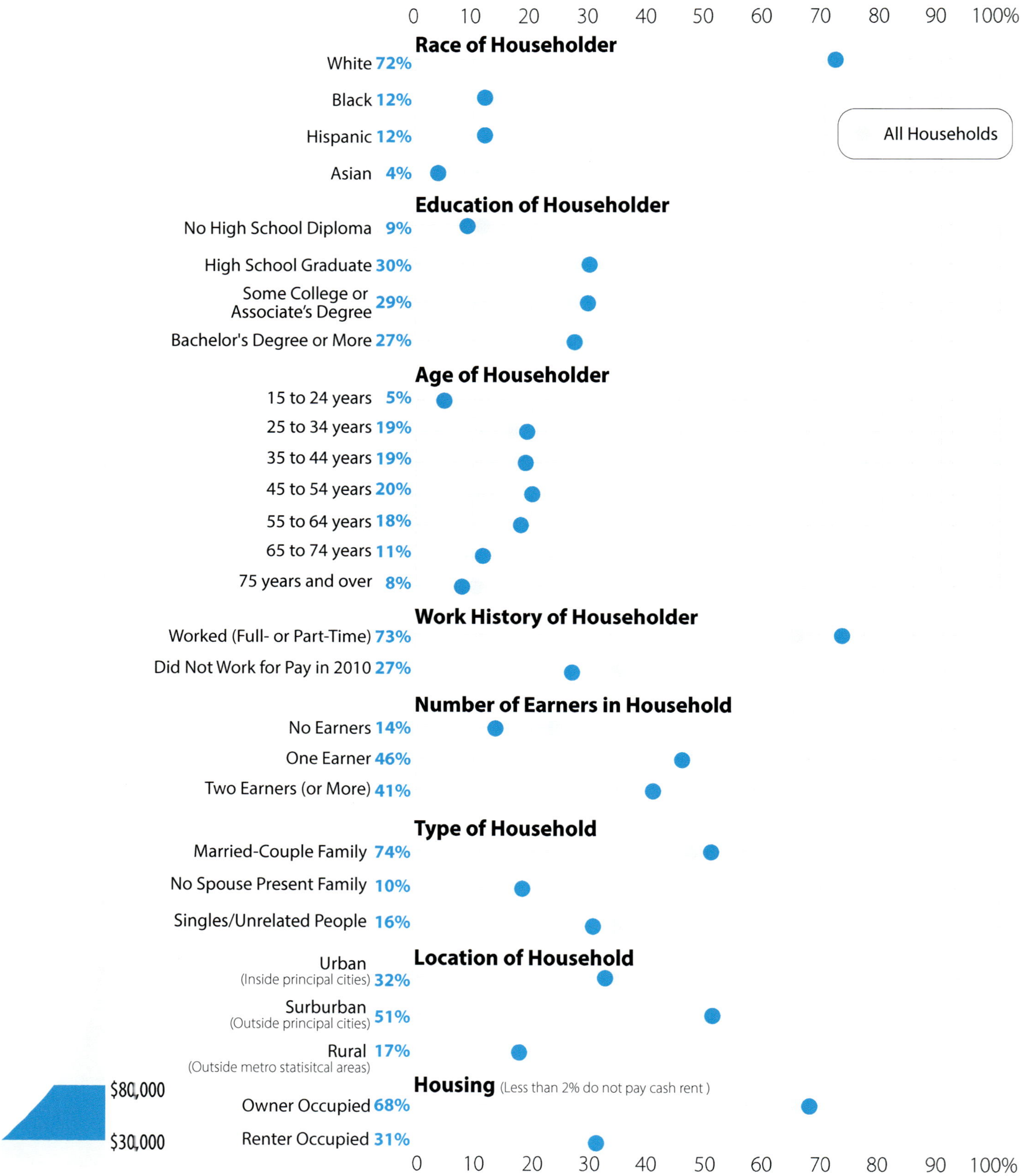

 Source: US Census Bureau, 2006–2010 American Community Survey

2010

Demographics of Incomes above $80,000

Census

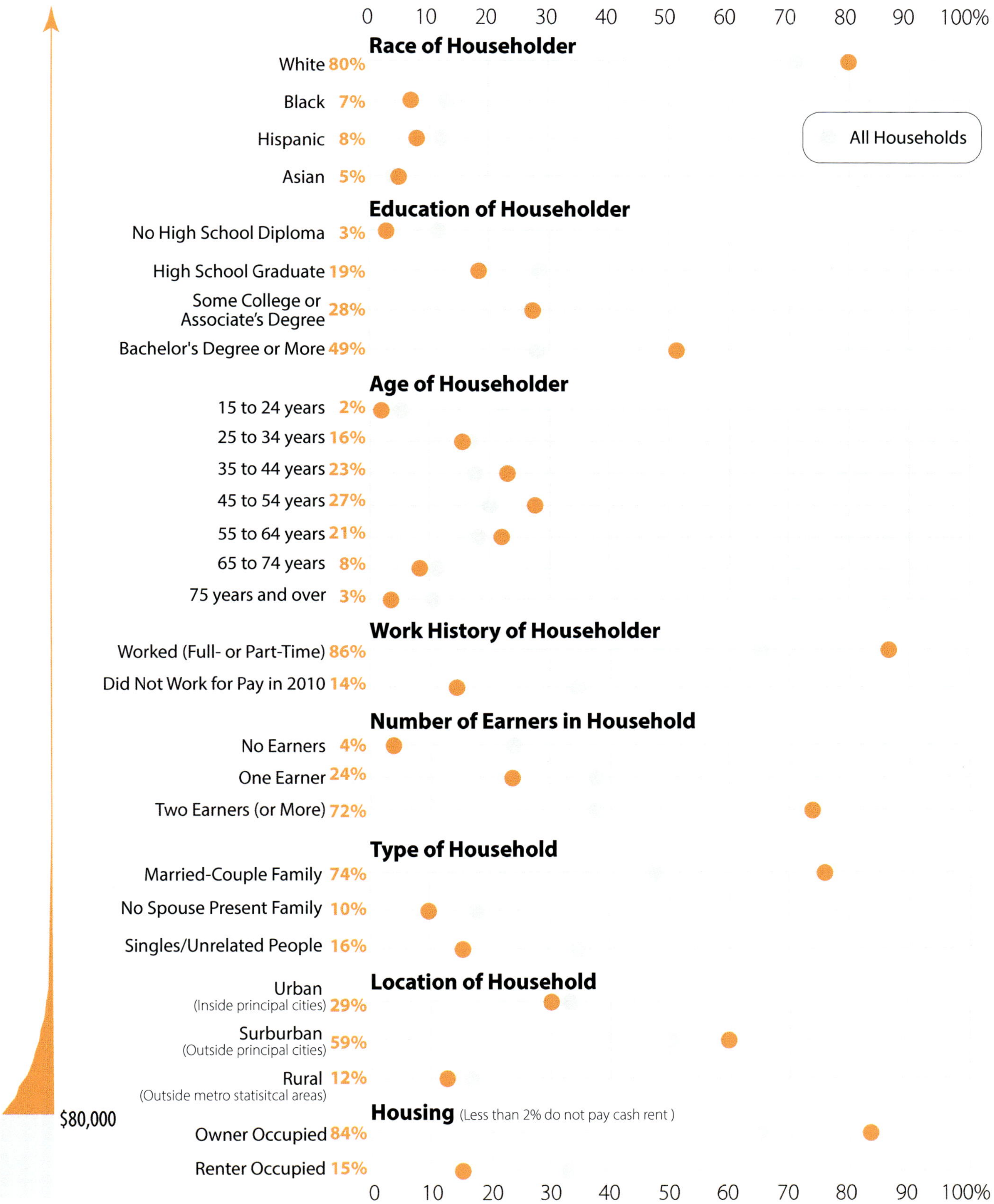

Source: US Census Bureau, 2006–2010 American Community Survey

Share of Family Households by Income Group

1945–2010

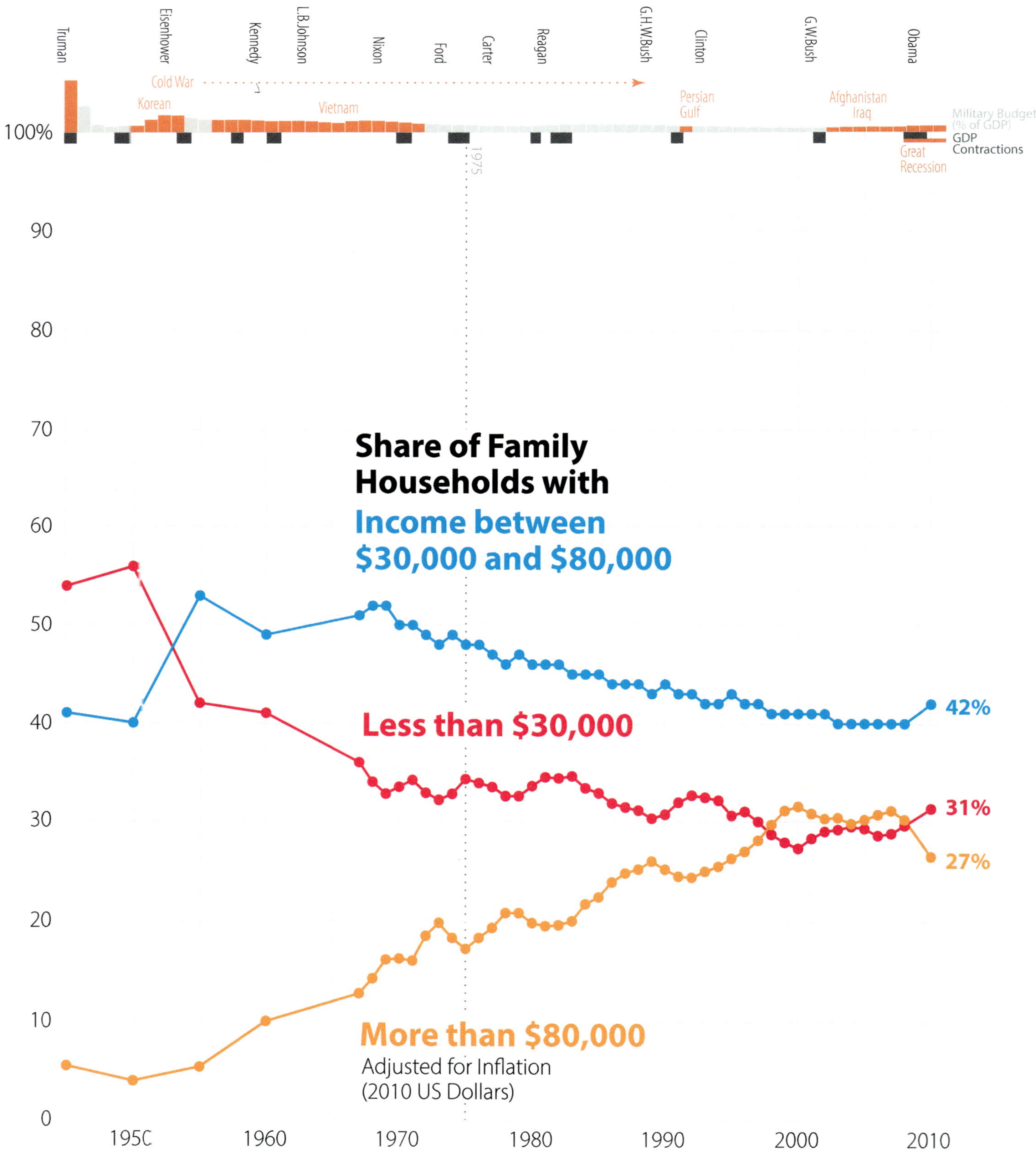

Source: US Census Bureau, 2006–2010 American Community Survey

Households with income but no earners include retired people who are receiving a pension, as well as people who are living on savings or receiving some form of financial support, such as unemployment insurance, Social Security, or money from family or friends.

Income Earners are individuals who receive wages, salaries, profits, interest payments, rents, and other forms of monetary compensation in exchange for work. They may be self-employed or work for someone else.

The **householder** is the person who owned, rented, or maintained the housing unit. If there is no such person, any adult member, excluding roomers, boarders, and paid employees, may be considered the householder. If the house is owned or rented jointly by a couple, the householder may be either of them.

2010 Distribution of Income by Number of Income Earners

Census

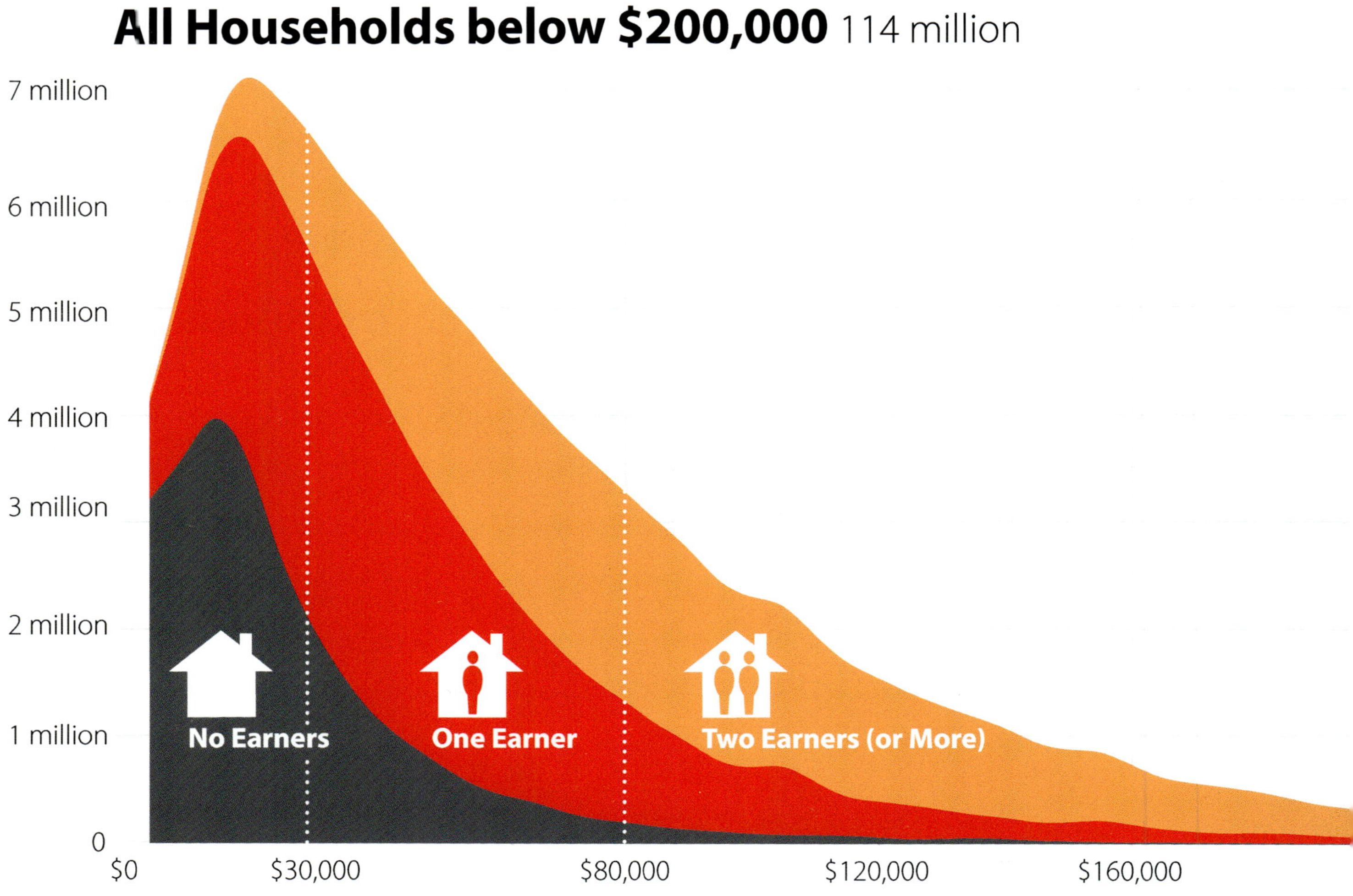

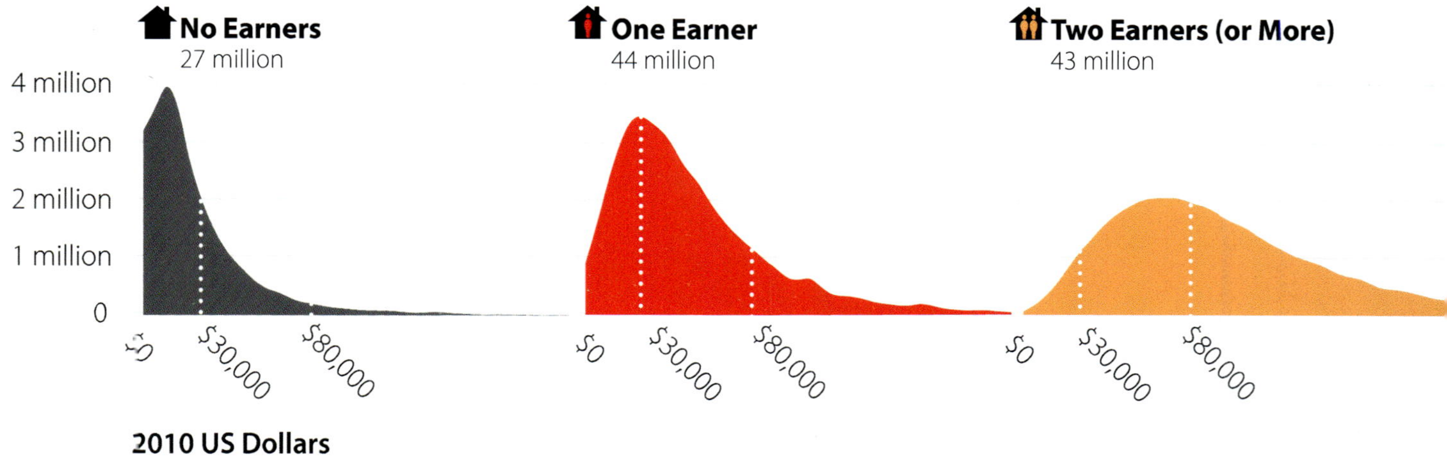

 Source: US Census Bureau, 2006–2010 American Community Survey

1947–2010

All Households by Number of Income Earners

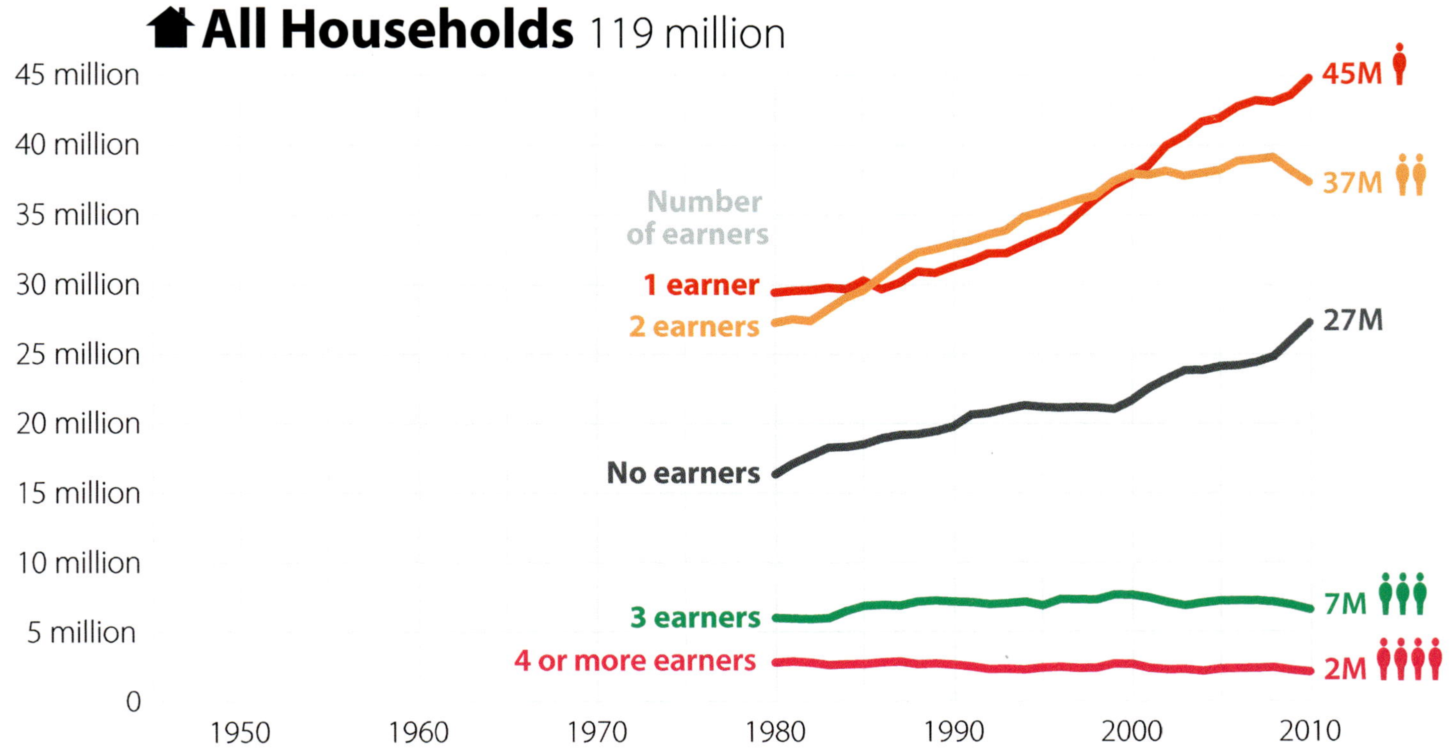

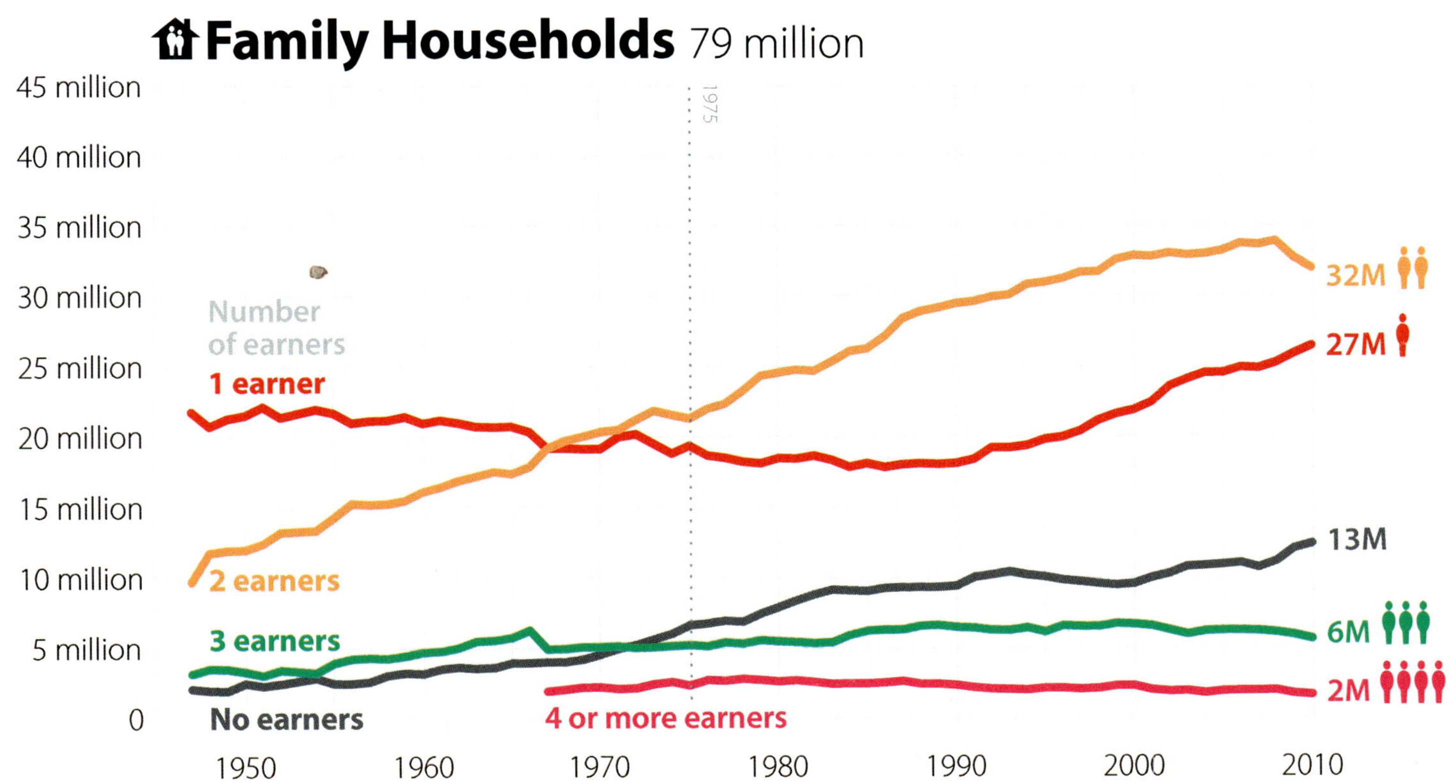

Source: US Census Bureau

1945–2010

Growth of Household Income by Number of Earners

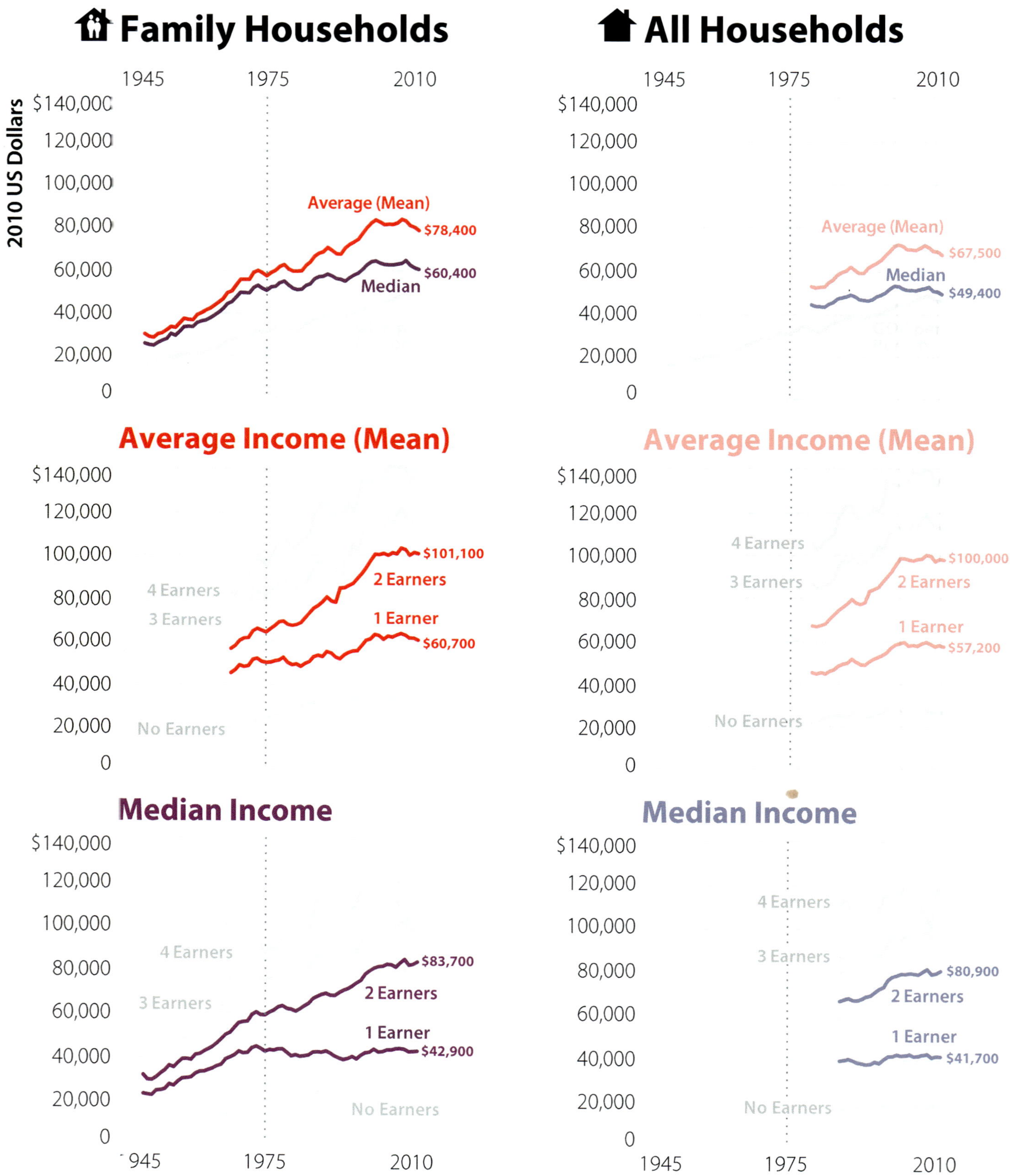

 Sources: US Census Bureau • US Bureau of Economics Analysis

Increasingly higher incomes, which produce the "long tail," can shift average income without affecting the median income.

Average is calculated by adding everyone's income together and then dividing by the total number of people (or households or tax returns). This is also called the "mean."

Changes at the lower end of the income distribution will move the median more than the average.

Median is the value at which half of the people (or households or tax returns) make less and half make more. This is also referred to as the "50th percentile."

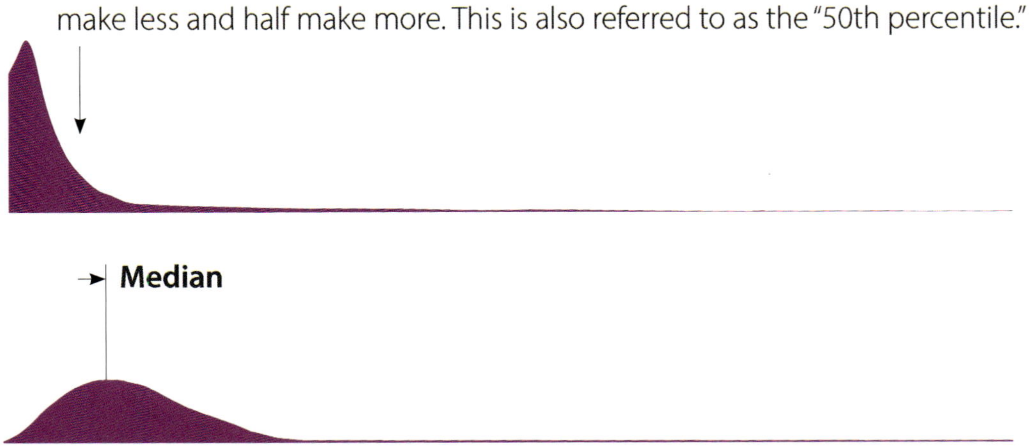

Census 1955–2010

Change in Income Ratio of Women/Men

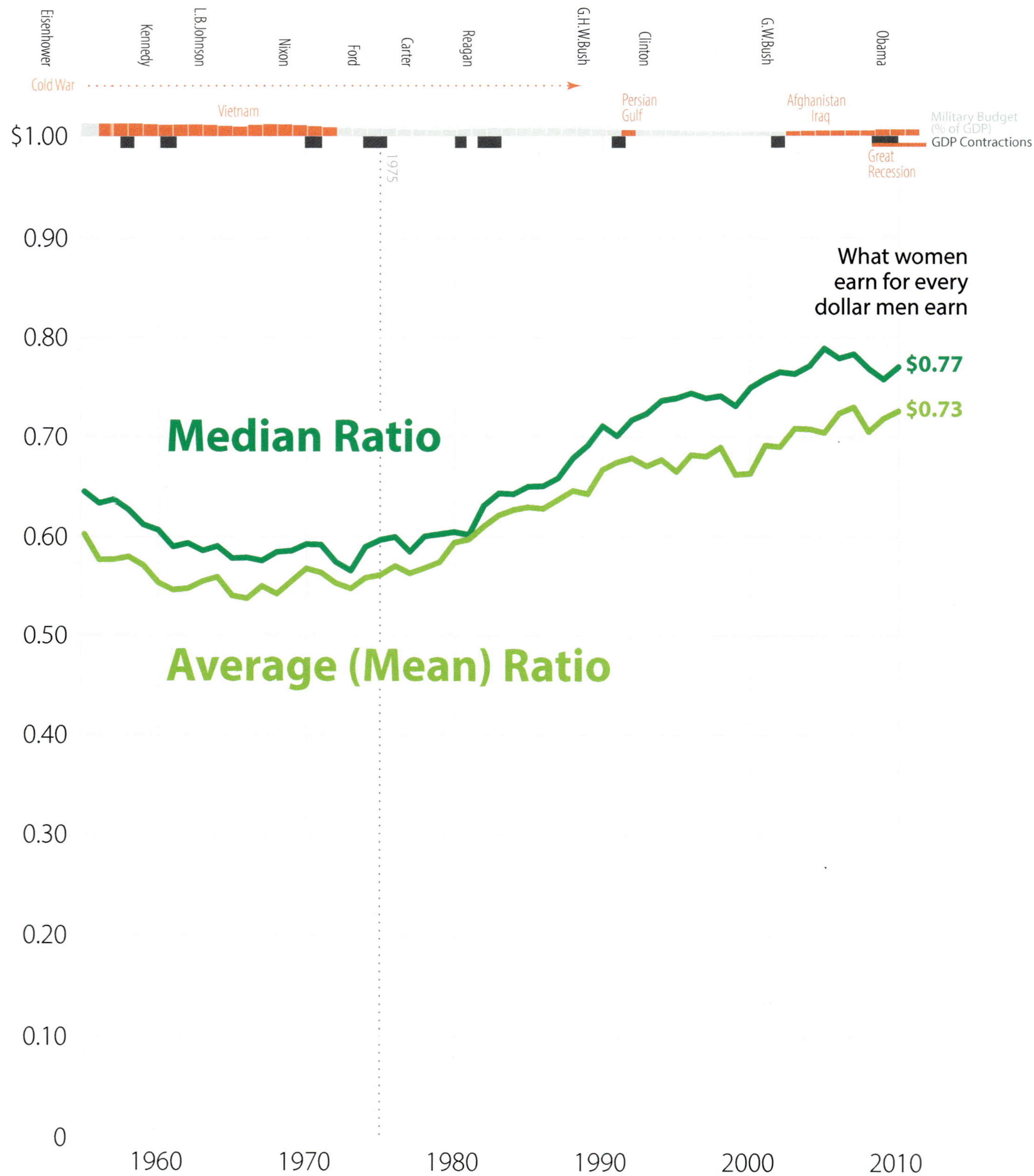

 Source: US Census Bureau

Although the income ratio between women and men has remained in men's favor, the gap between men's average income and men's median income has increased significantly since the 1970s. Income inequality among men has grown over the same period more than among women. This pattern of an increasing gap between average income and median income is most noticeable when looking at white men.

Census

1945–2010

Income by Sex: Average vs Median

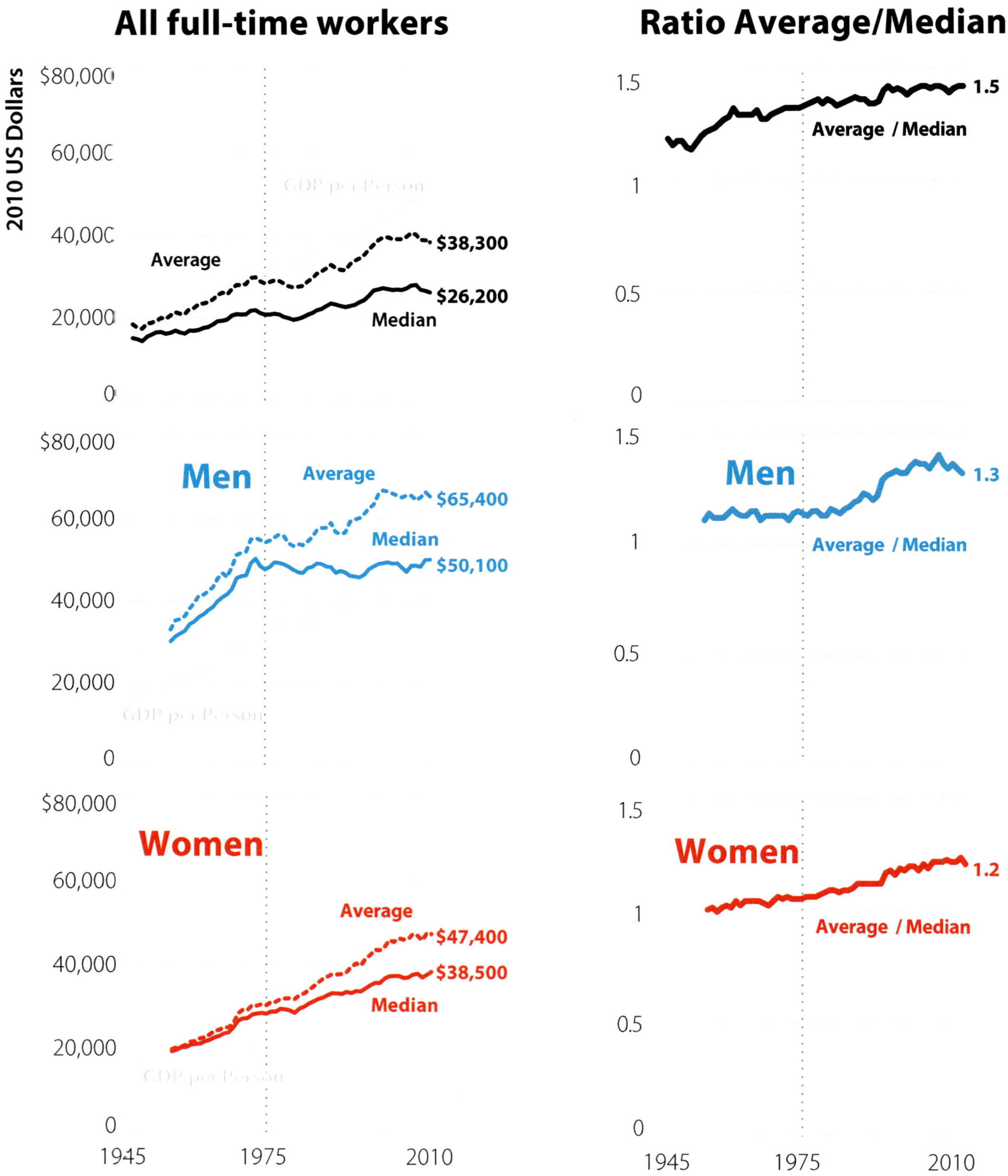

 Sources: US Census Bureau • US Bureau of Economics Analysis (BEA)

Census 1945–2010

Income Growth by Sex and Race

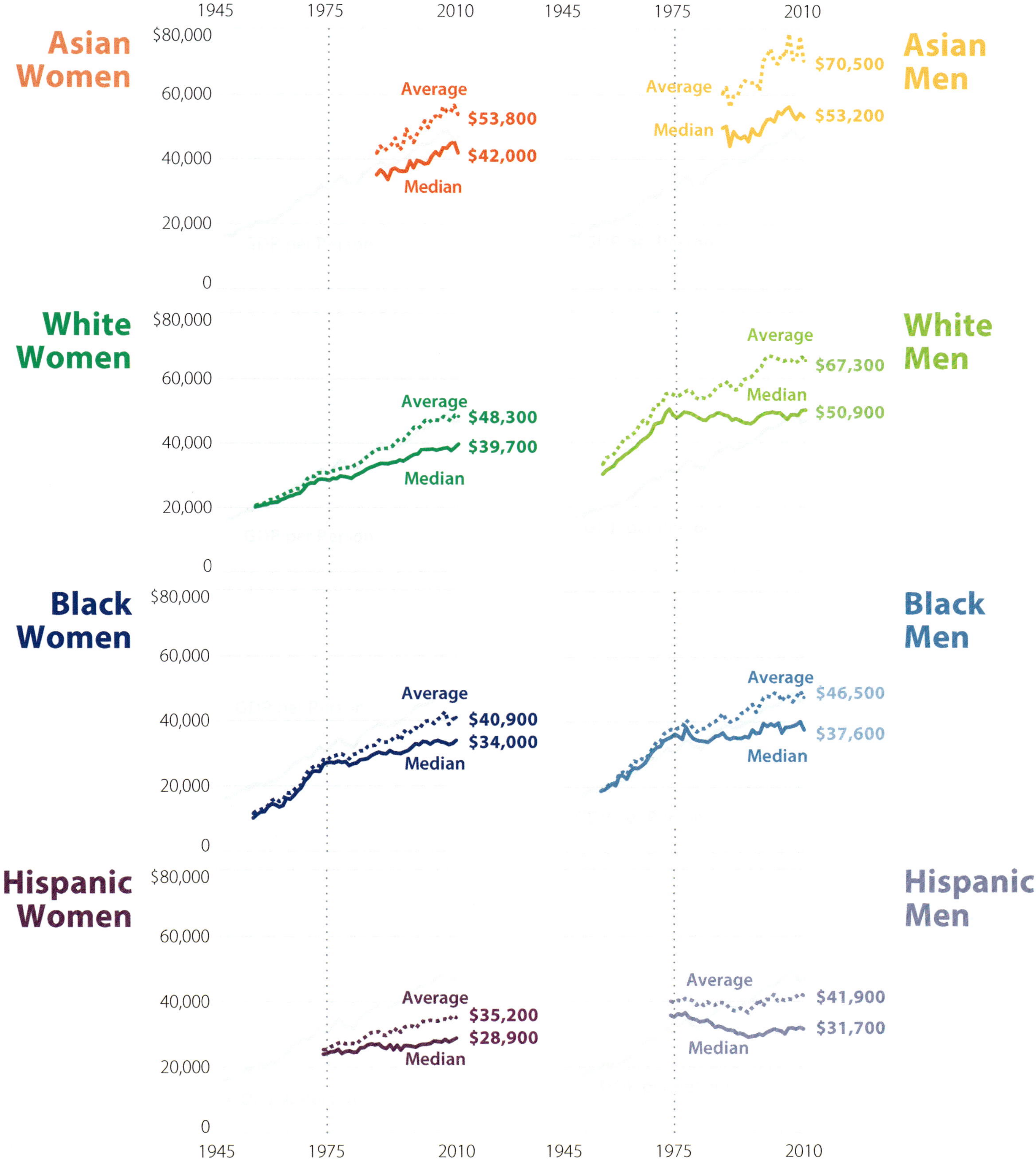

Source: US Census Bureau

1910–2010

Education of Population by Sex and Race

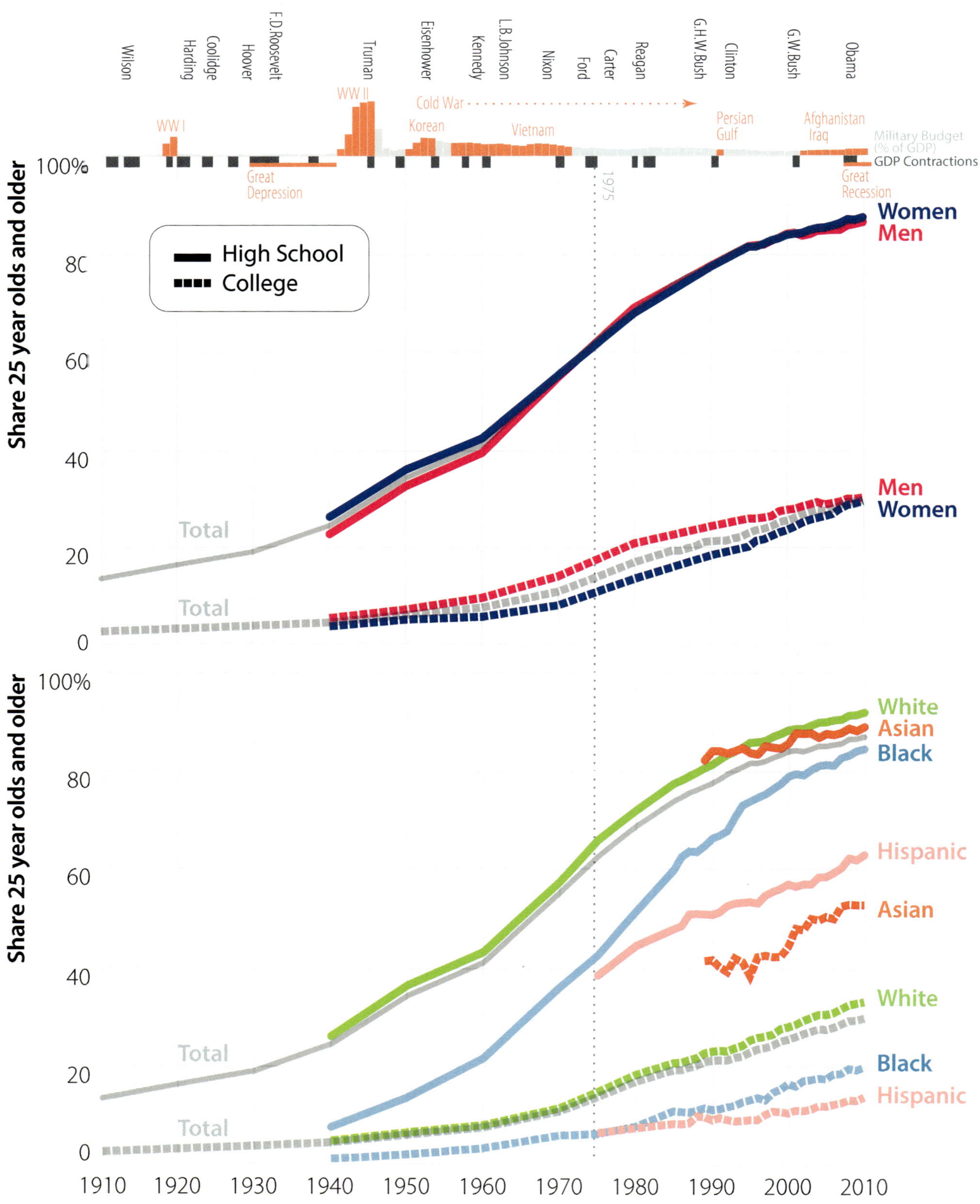

 Source: National Center for Education Statistics, Digest of Education Statistics 2010

Over the 20th century, the number of high school graduates increased dramatically. Today, nearly one-third of adults over age 25 also hold a college degree.

There is no difference between the number of men and women holding a college degree, but there is a significant difference by race. More than half of the Asian population has a college degree, but less than 20% of the Hispanic population has one.

High school—graduated with a diploma or completed high school through an equivalency program, such as a GED program. Before 1993, this refers to four or more years of high school.

College—a bachelor's degree or higher. Before 1993, this refers to four or more years of college.

Census 2010

Men's vs. Women's Earnings by Education

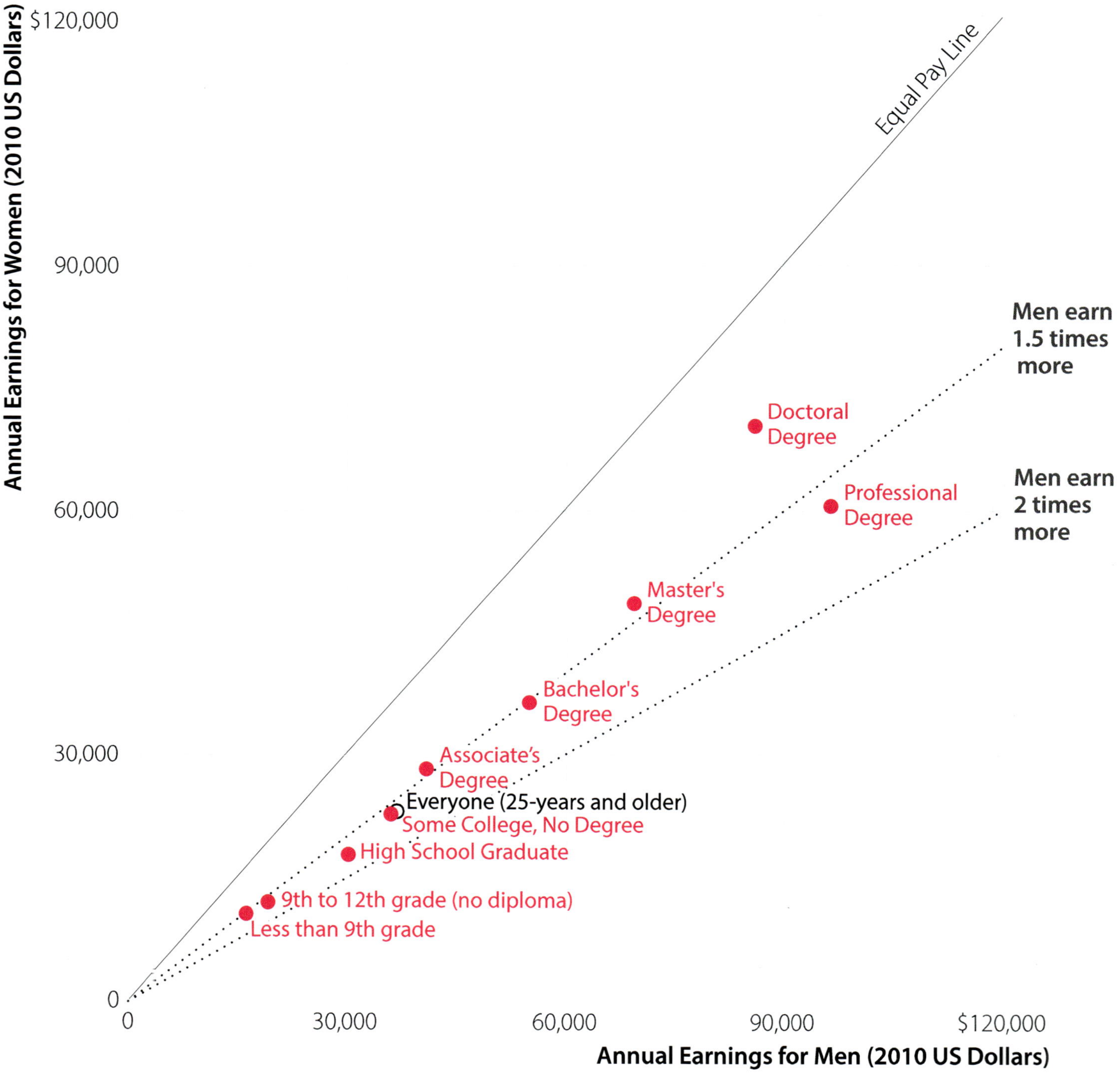

 Source: US Census Bureau

GEOGRAPHY

Cities and their surrounding urban areas tend to have higher incomes, especially coastal cities in the Northeast and in California. Some states have greater income inequality, such as New York, while others have less inequality, such as Utah. Although New York State has a higher GDP per person, Utah's median income of $57,000 is higher than New York's at $50,000.

2010
US Household Density

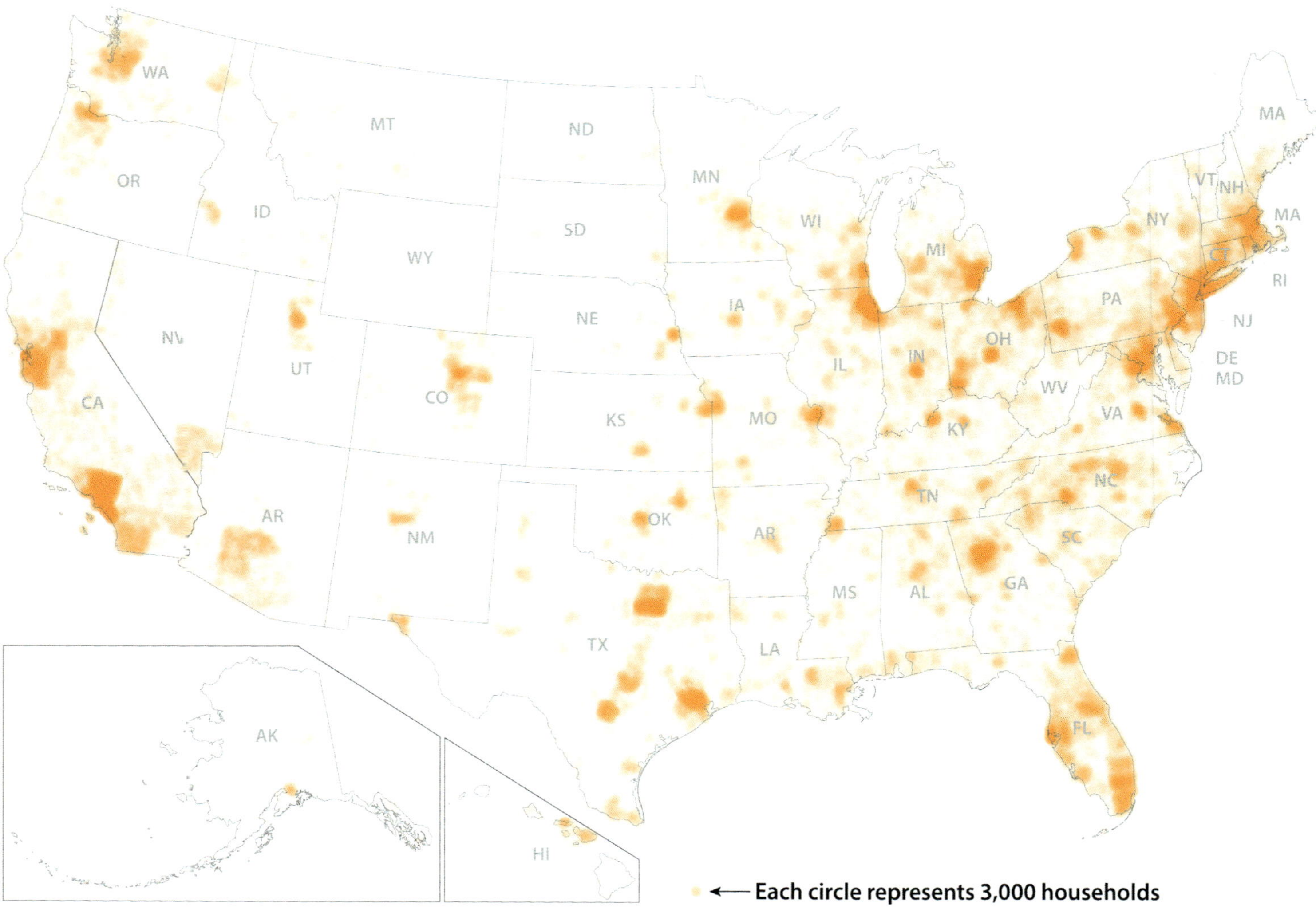

 Source: US Census Bureau

Census

2010

Average Household Income by US Counties

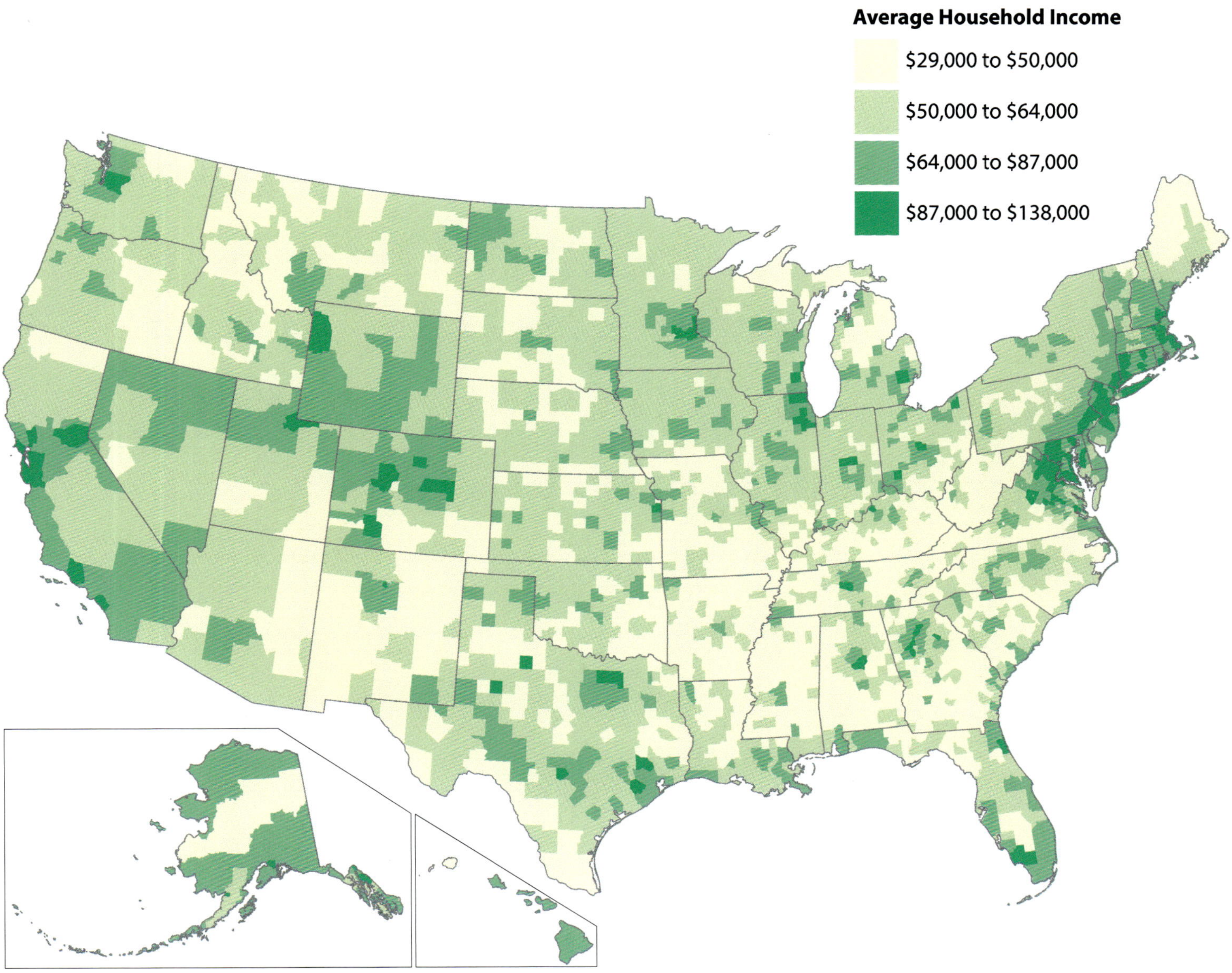

Source: US Census Bureau, 2006–2010 American Community Survey

2010

Poverty Rate by US Counties

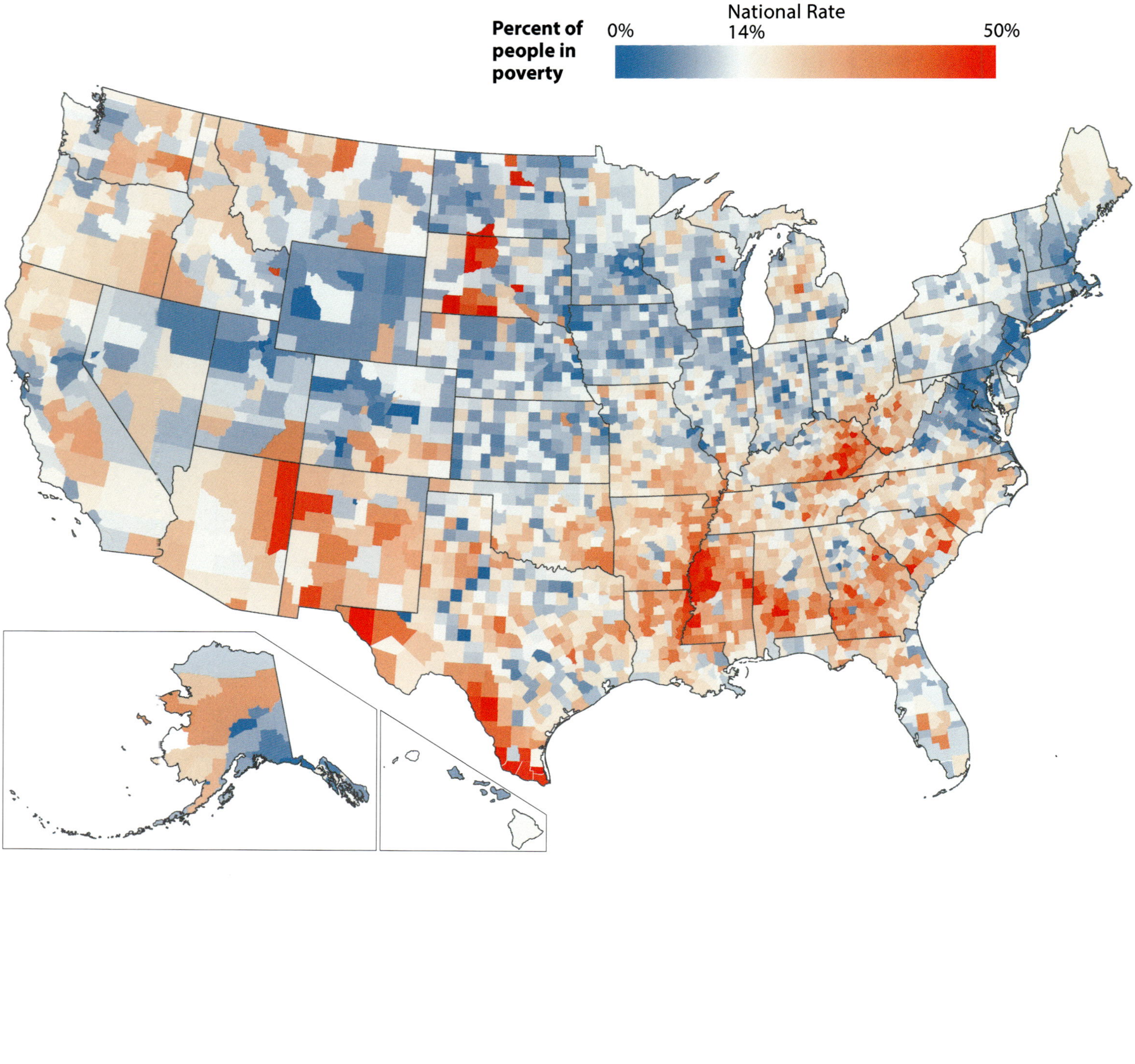

 Source: US Census Bureau, 2006–2010 American Community Survey

Census

2010

High-Income Households by US Counties

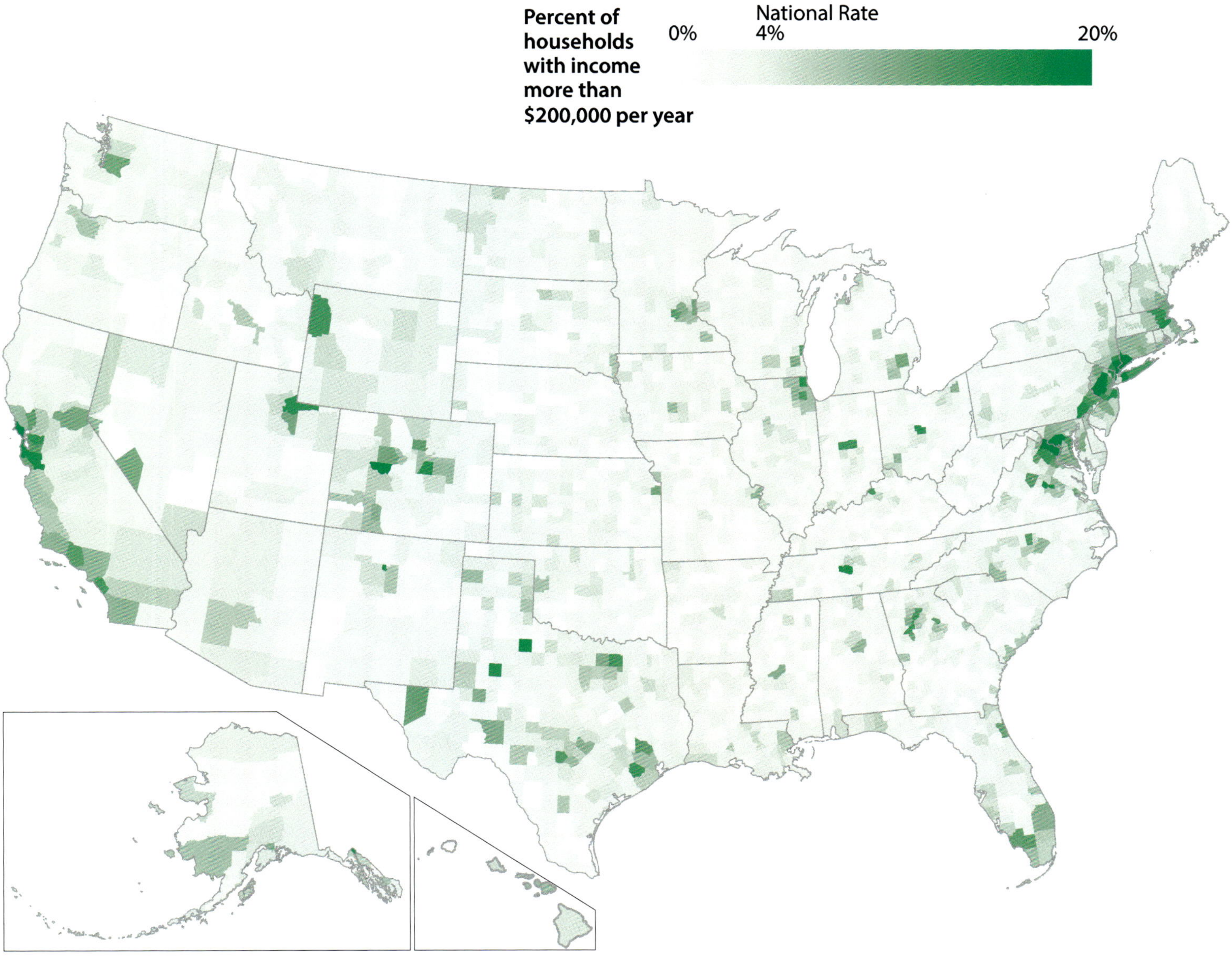

Source: US Census Bureau, 2006–2010 American Community Survey

Census

1934–2010

Household Income by State

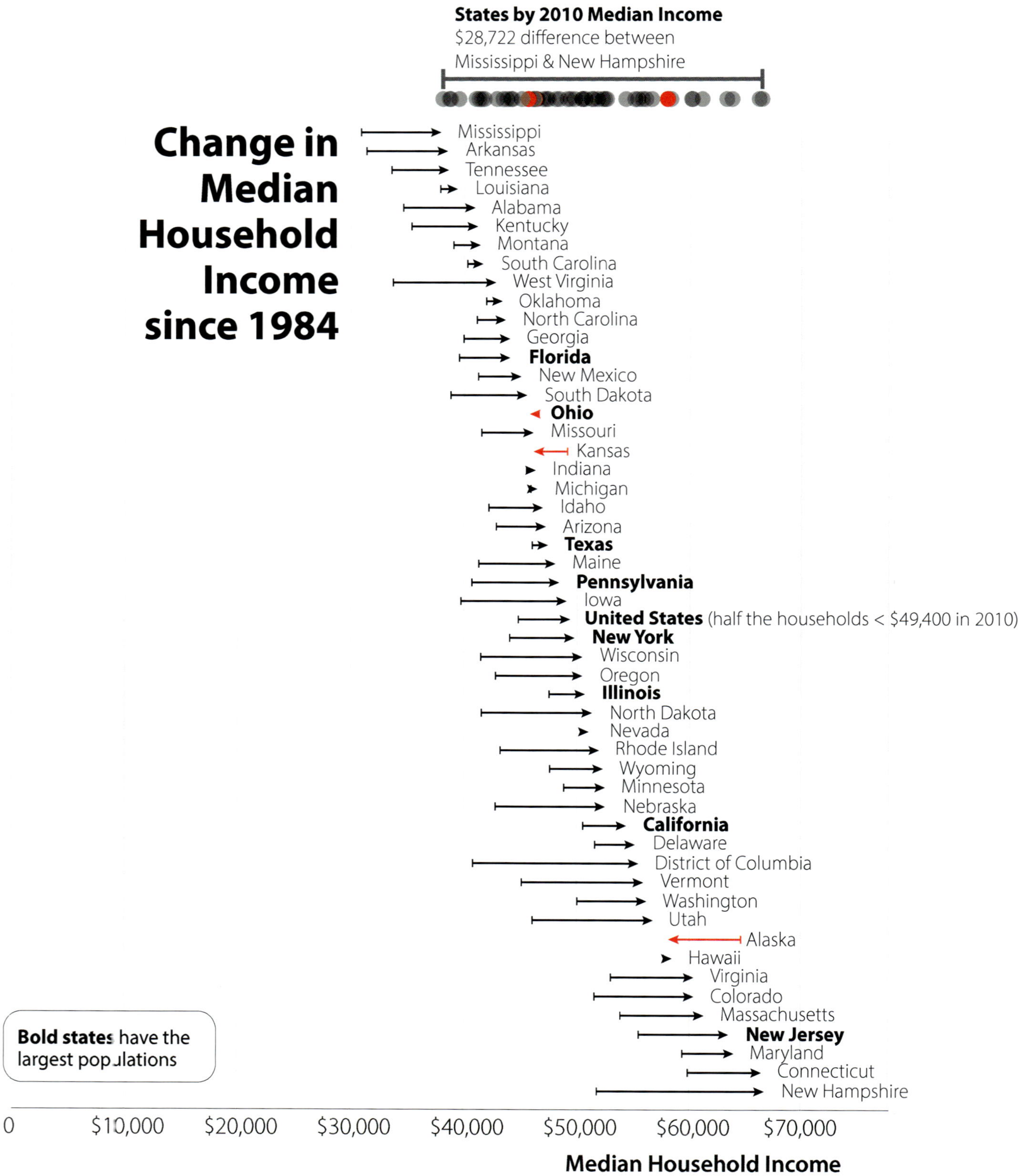

 Source: US Census Bureau, 2006–2010 American Community Survey

Six out of 220 countries make up half of the world's GDP.

Of the 12 countries with more than 100 million people, the United States is the richest.

Eight out of 50 states make up half of the United States' GDP.

If California were a country, it would be one of the top 10 largest economies in the world.

Purchasing power parity (PPP) translates other currencies into US dollars and is preferred to exchange rates when comparing living conditions in different countries.

GDP (gross domestic product) measures the amount of wealth that a country creates over the course of a year. Often calculated by measuring the production of goods and services, it can also be calculated from employee compensation, interest payments, and profits.

GDP per person (per capita) is a country's GDP divided by the population (assuming that everyone gets an equal share).

The **Gini index** measures the degree of income inequality using the distribution of family income. The more equal a country's income distribution, the lower its Gini index.

CIA

2010

GDP of the United States

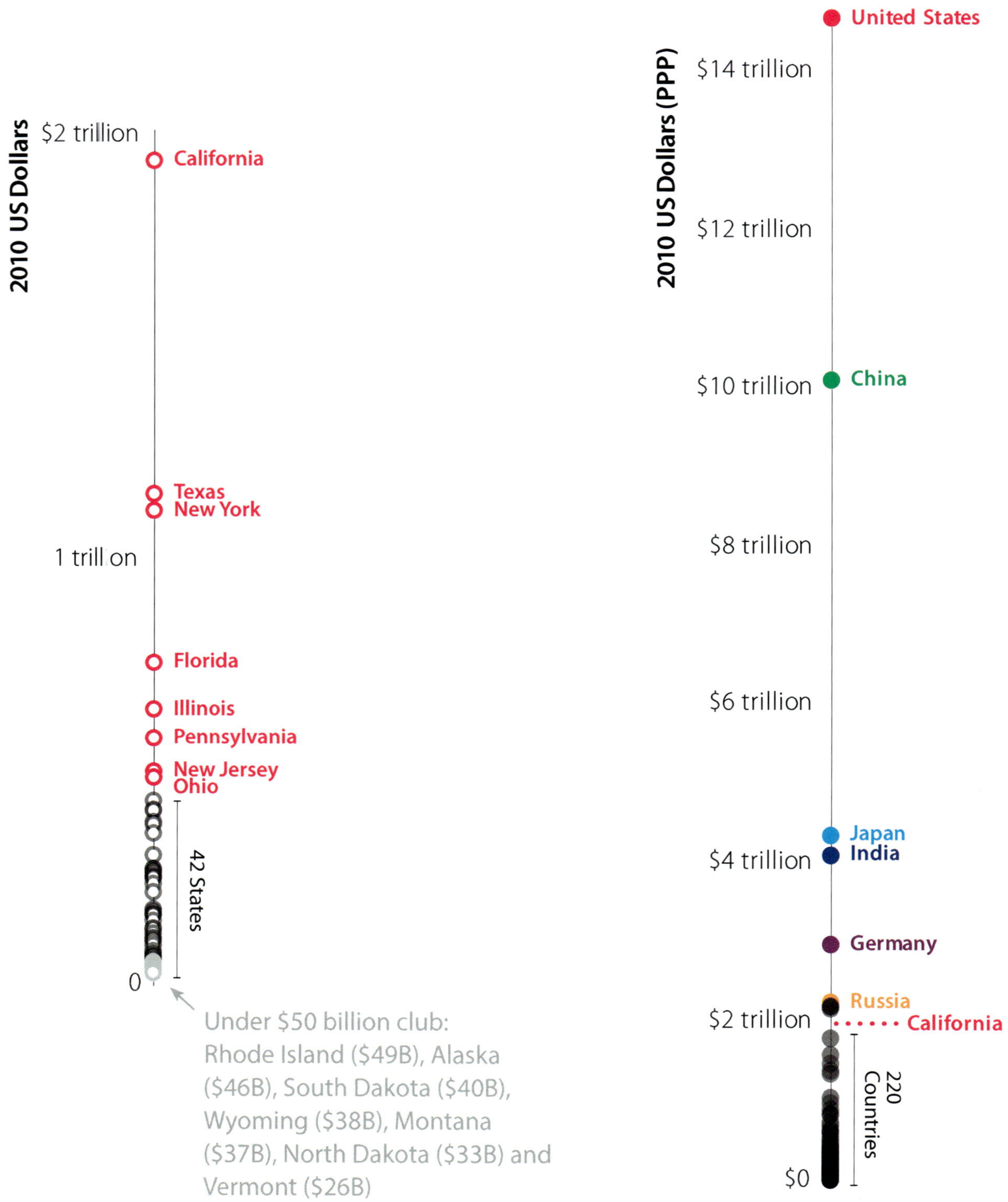

 Source: CIA World Factbook, July 2011

2010 Income and Inequality by State

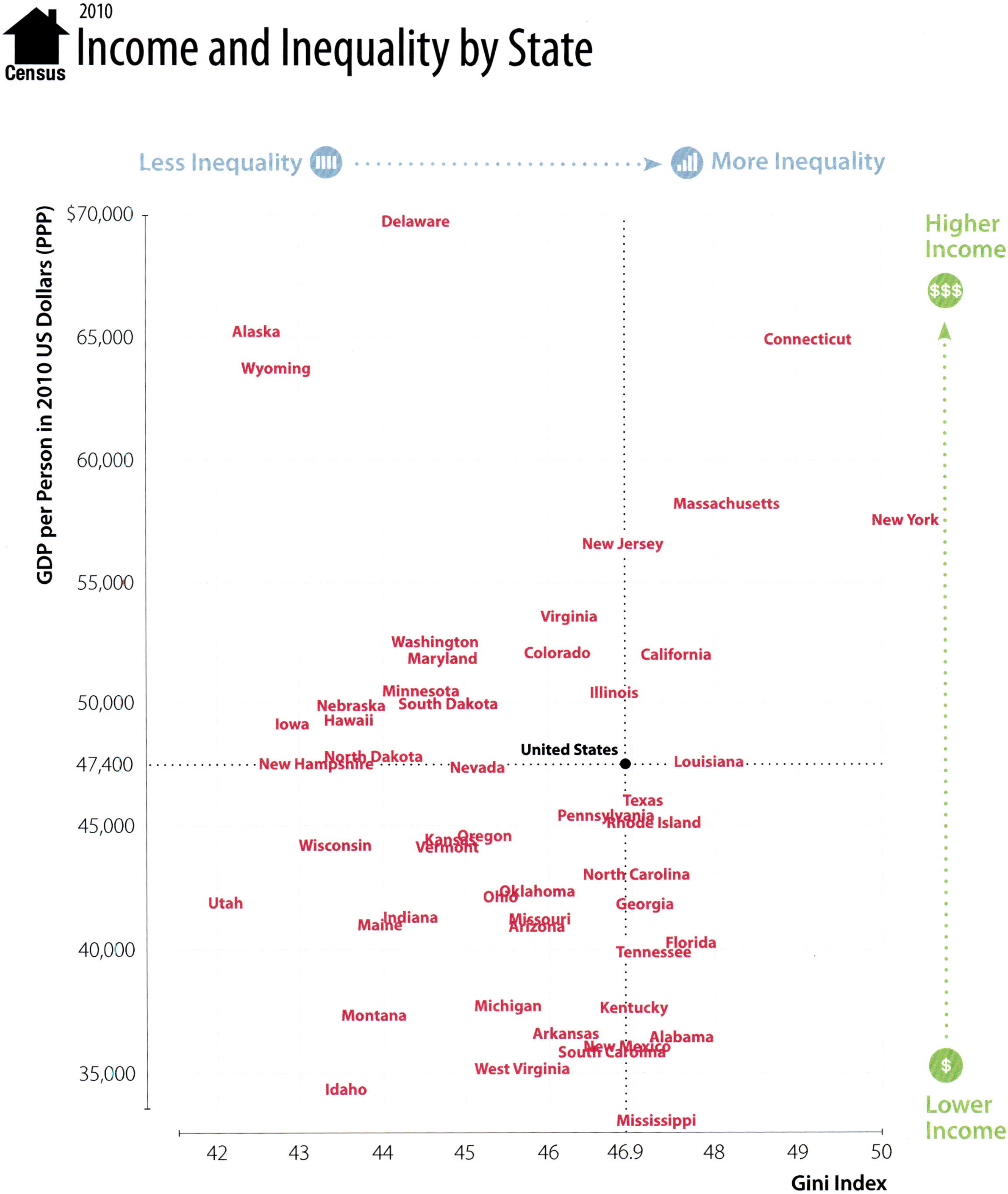

Sources: US Census Bureau, 2006–2010 American Community Survey • US Bureau of Economic Analysis

CIA

2010

Income and Inequality by Country

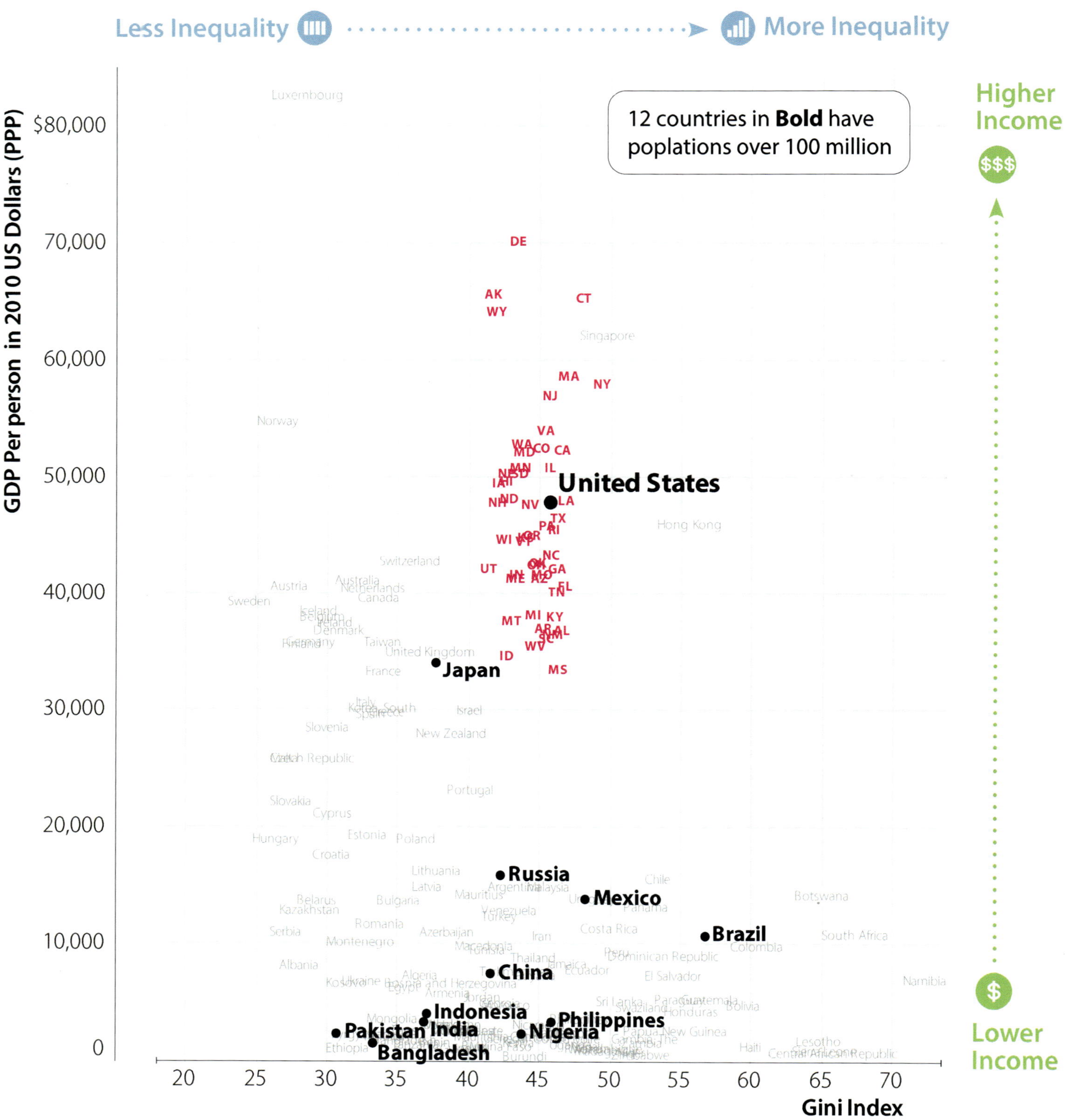

 Sources: CIA World Factbook, July 2011 • US Census Bureau, 2006–2010 American Community Survey • US Bureau of Economic Analysis

Over the last 500 years, the world economy has seen spectacular growth. The focus historically has been on Western Europe and the United States, but recently, China and India have surged forward. The distribution of wealth varies greatly, not only within but also among countries. The United States stands out as both very rich (high GDP per person) and very unequal (high Gini index).

The **international dollar** (1990 Int$), also known as the "Geary-Khamis dollar," is a hypothetical unit of currency that has the same purchasing power as the US dollar in 1990. It is based on purchasing power parity (PPP), as well as average international prices of commodities.

1500-2000

Past 500 Years of World GDP

World GDP Growth

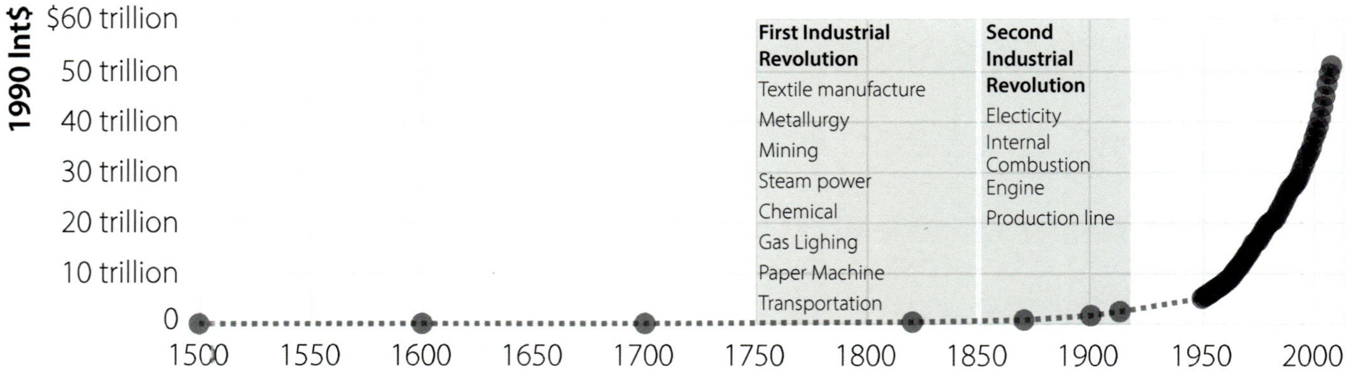

Share of World GDP

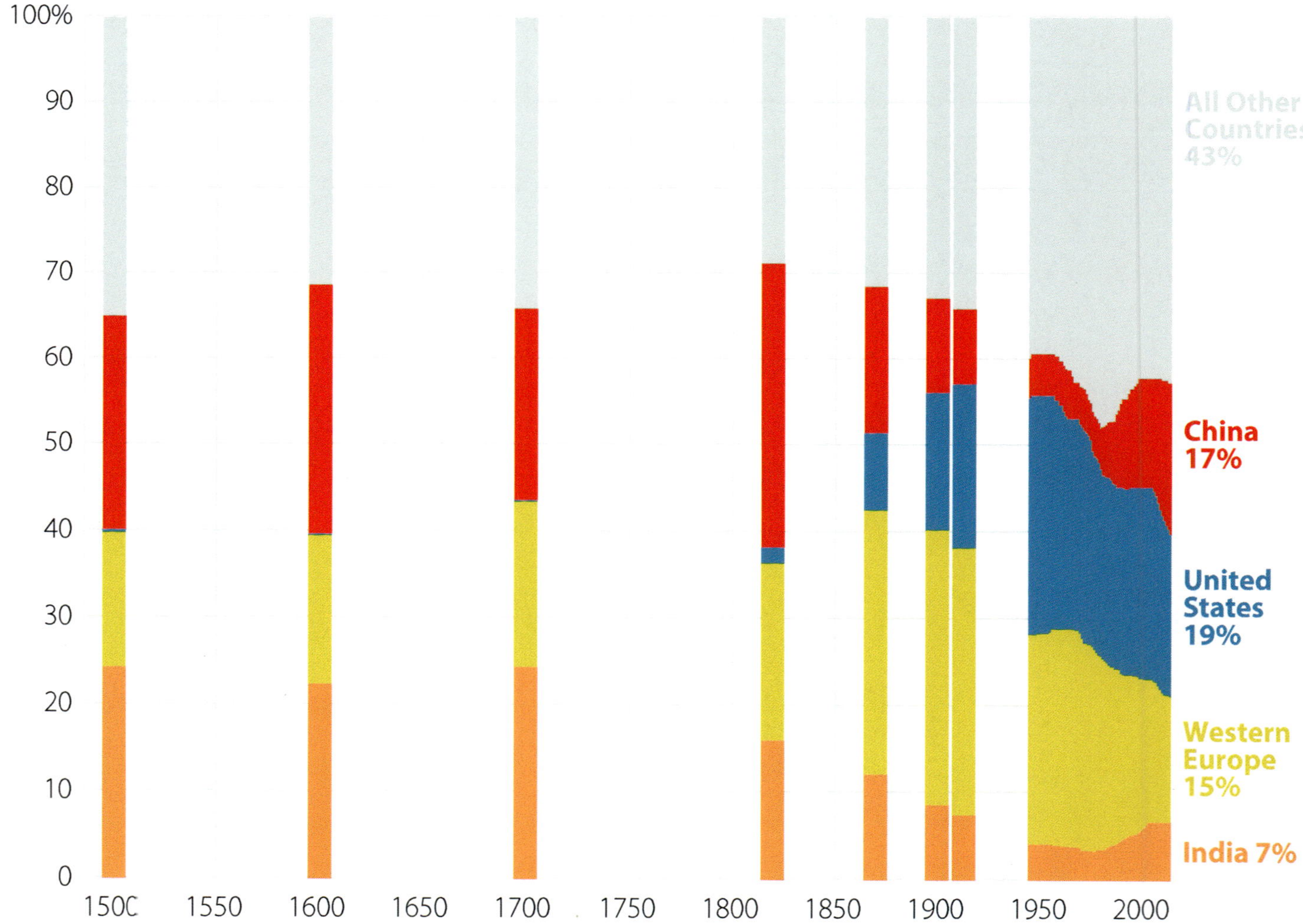

 Source: Angus Maddison, "Statistics on World Population, GDP and Per Capita GDP, 1–2008 AD"

WAGES

Median wages have stagnated since the mid-1970s, and in some occupations, wages have fallen. At the same time, the number of people of working age and their participation rate in the labor force has increased.

2011

Texas Public Employees: Salaries below $250,000

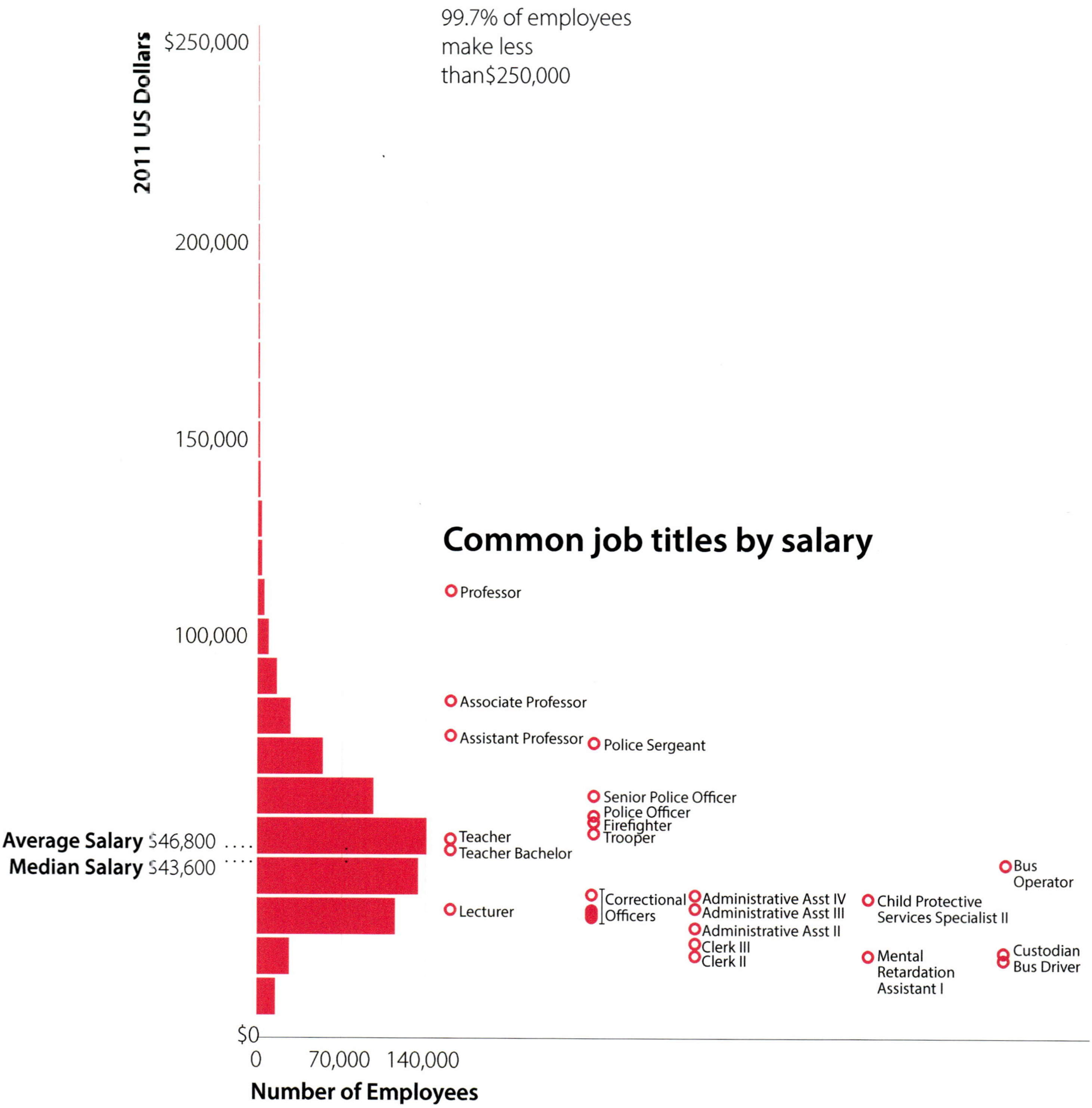

 Source: *The Texas Tribune,* Government Employee Salaries, June 2011

2011

Texas Public Employees: All Salaries

As of June 2011,
659,692 people worked for the state of Texas for a total **$31 billion** in salaries.

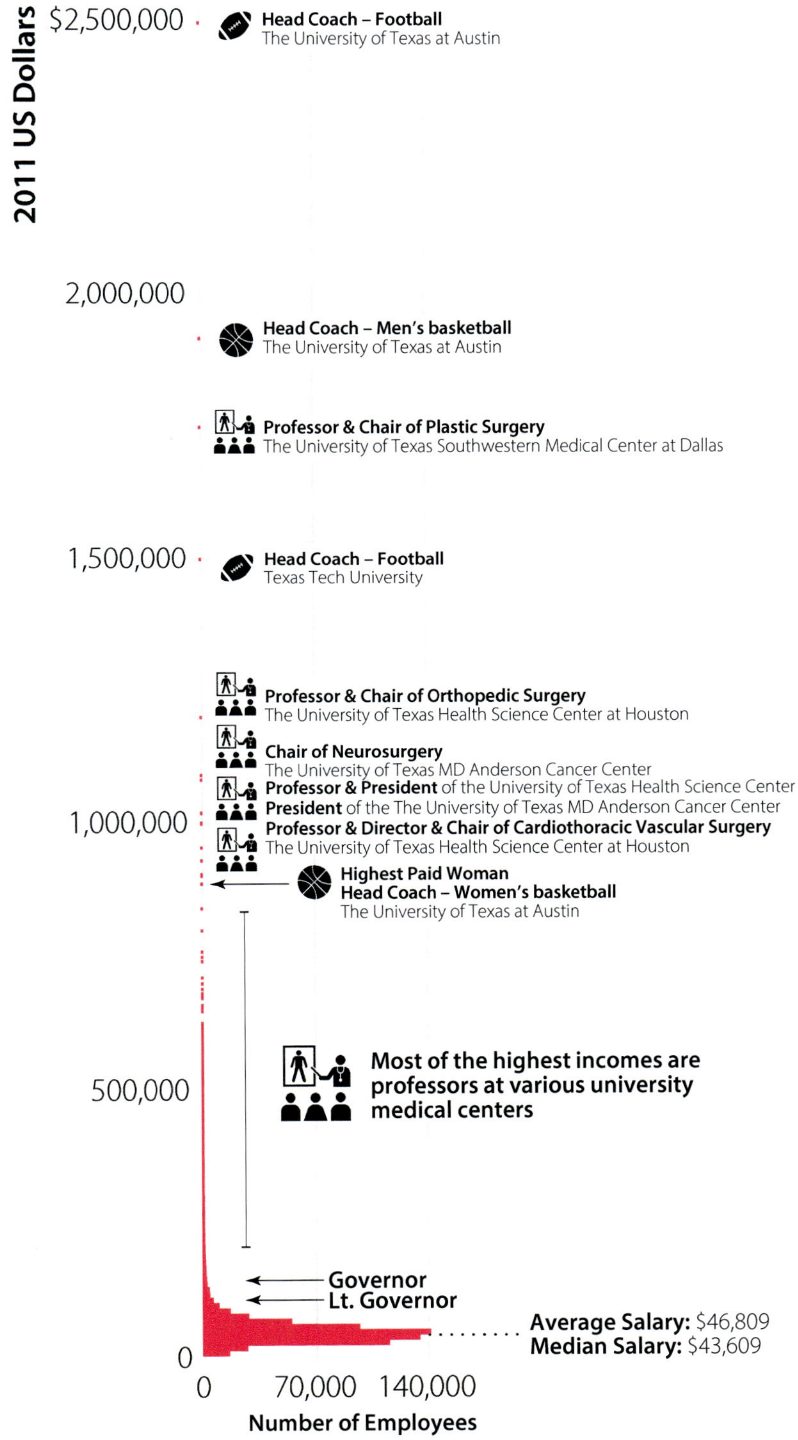

Bonuses were given to coaches based on their team's performance, which doubled the income for the football coach of the University of Texas at Austin.

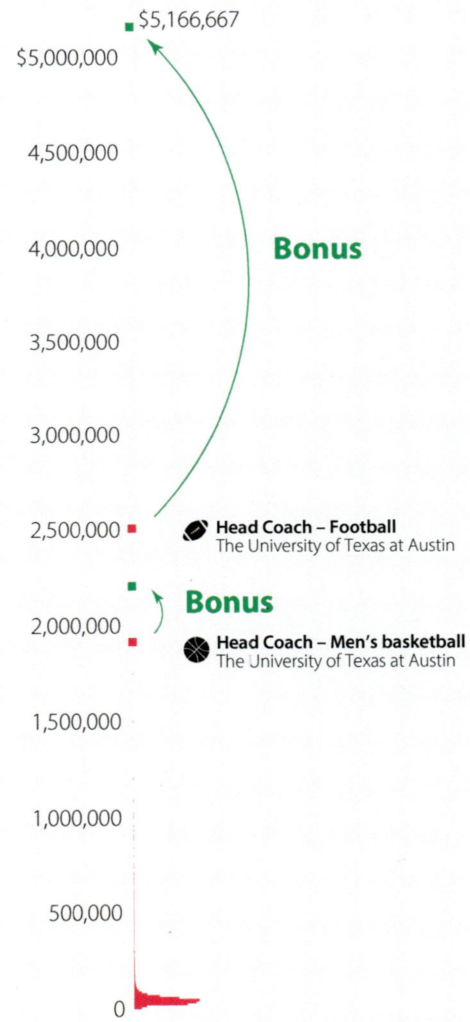

Source: *The Texas Tribune,* Government Employee Salaries, June 2011

Various

2011

Texas Public Employees: Income Share

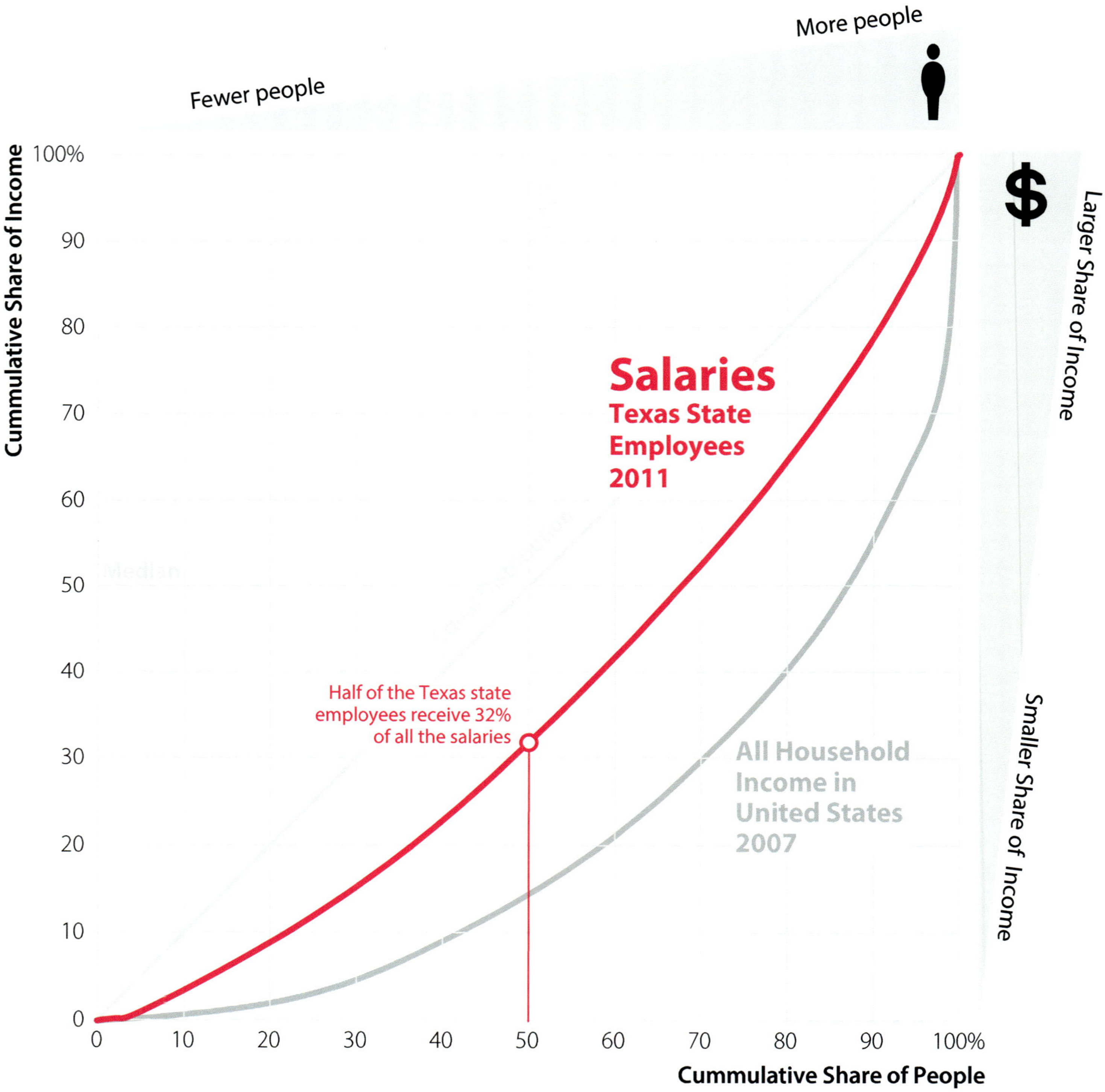

 Sources: *The Texas Tribune,* Government Employee Salaries, June 2011 • Congressional Budget Office, "Trends in the Distribution of Household Income Between 1979 and 2007," October 2011

Military basic pay is augmented by allowances for housing based on pay grade and number of dependents, family separation and subsistence, and clothing.

Incentive and special pay is available for circumstances such as hazardous duty, imminent danger or hostile fire, diving, parachuting, working on a flight deck, demolition duty (which sometimes is tied to pay grade), and submarine or sea duty (which is tied to pay grade and years of service).

Aviation careers, career enlisted flyers, and medical and dental officers receive additional pay based on years of service.

2011 Active Duty US Military Personnel

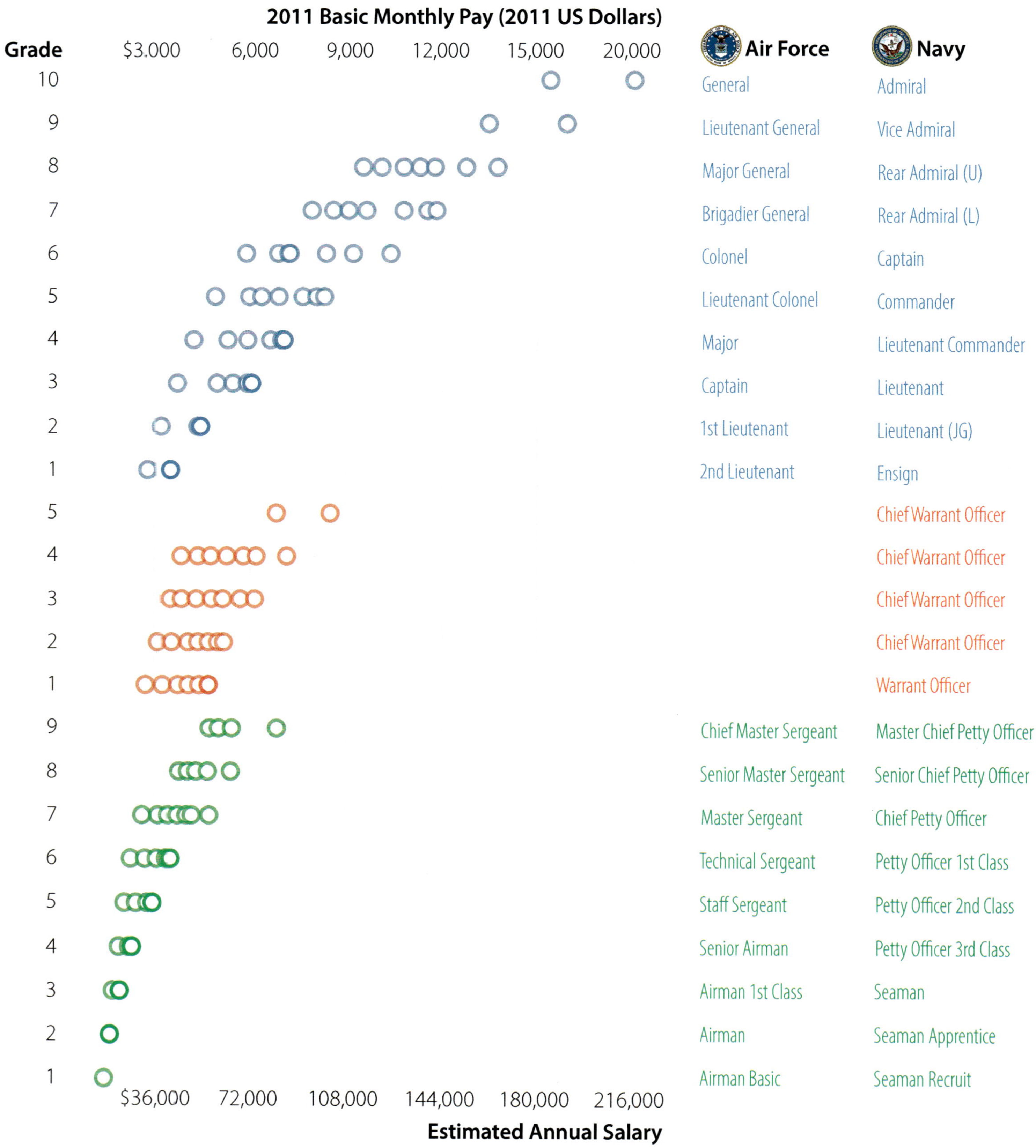

 Source: US Department of Defense, Defense Finance and Accounting Service

Army	Marine Corps
General	General
Lieutenant General	Lieutenant General
Major General	Major General
Brigadier General	Brigadier General
Colonel	Colonel
Lieutenant Colonel	Lieutenant Colonel
Major	Major
Captain	Captain
1st Lieutenant	1st Lieutenant
2nd Lieutenant	2nd Lieutenant
Chief Warrant Officer	Chief Warrant Officer
Chief Warrant Officer	Chief Warrant Officer
Chief Warrant Officer	Chief Warrant Officer
Chief Warrant Officer	Chief Warrant Officer
Warrant Officer	Warrant Officer
Sergeant Major	Sergeant Major/ Master Gunnery Sergeant
1st Sergeant/Master Sergeant	1st Sergeant/Master Sergeant
Sergeant First Class	Gunnery Sergeant
Staff Sergeant	Staff Sergeant
Sergeant	Sergeant
Corporal	Corporal
Private First Class	Lance Corporal
Private	Private 1st Class
Private	Private

Employment

≈ 20,000 people

Commissioned officers 212,749 people

Warrant officers 19,860 people

Enlisted personnel 1,226,337 people

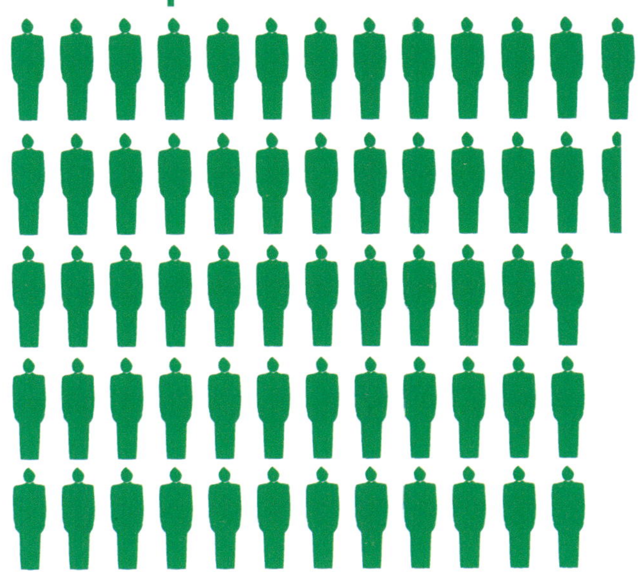

The range of salaries differs by industry, by geographic region, and by the experience and expertise of the job holder.

Income in some occupations is limited, however, and will never reach the highest income levels (e.g., dental assistants), whereas other occupations span both the lowest and the highest income levels (e.g., actors).

For example, 80% of dental assistants make between $11 and $23 per hour, while 80% of actors make between $8 and $48 per hour.

2011

Wages of Common Occupations

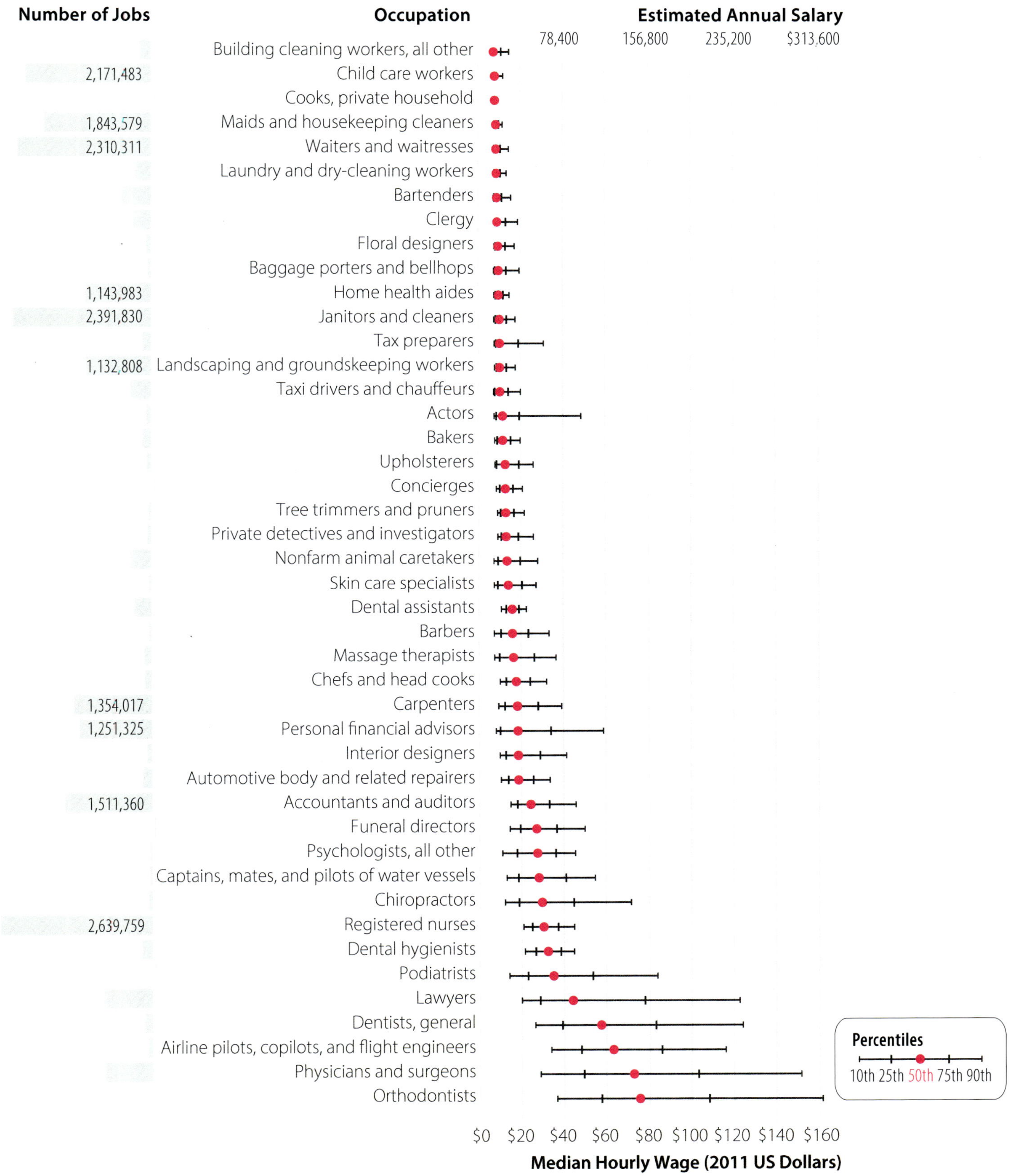

Source: EMSI EconomicModeling.com (Compiled from data collected by BLS, BEA and US Census Bureau)

2011

Wages of All Occupations by Education

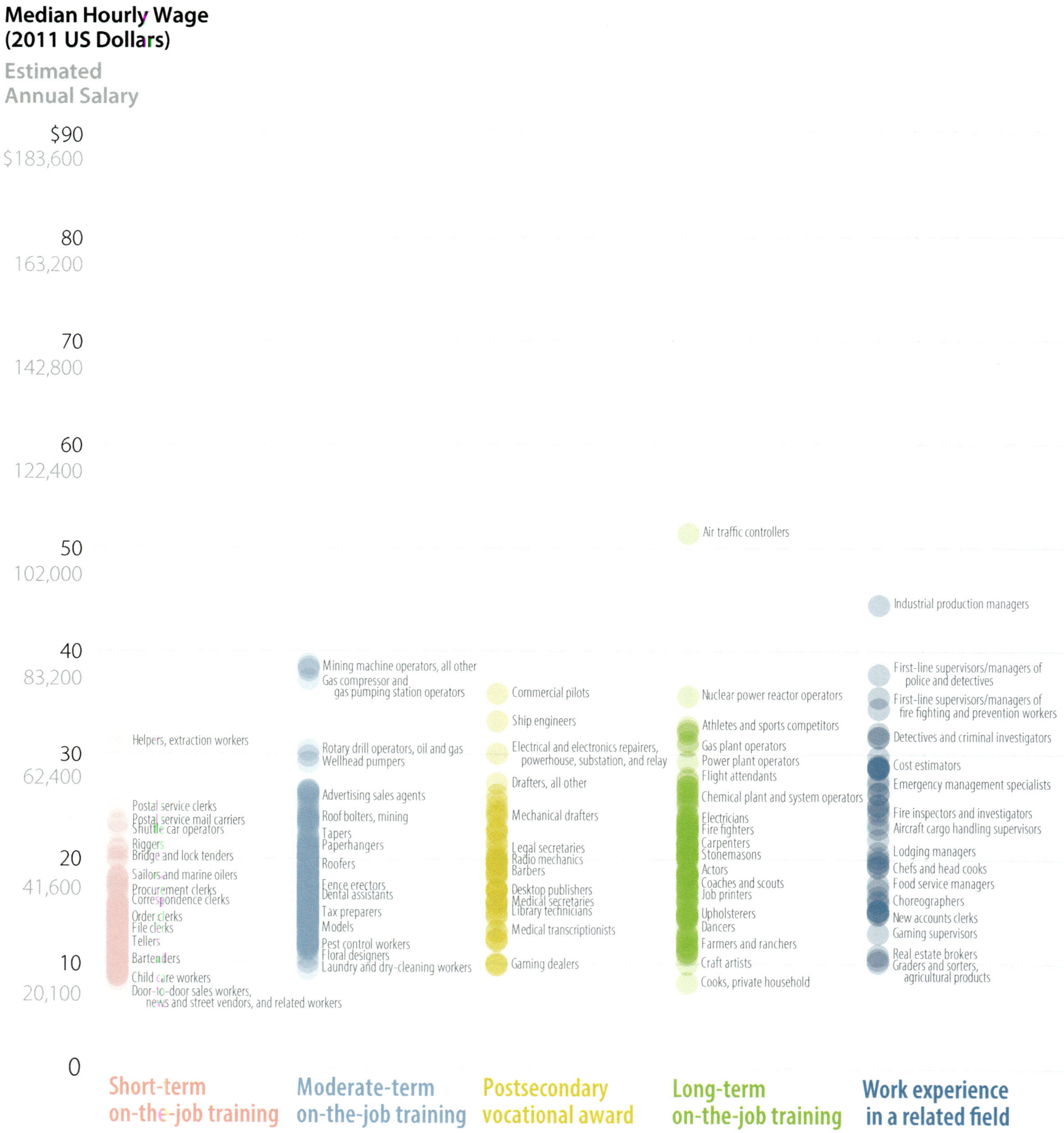

 Source: EMSI EconomicModeling.com (Compiled from data collected by BLS, BEA and US Census Bureau)

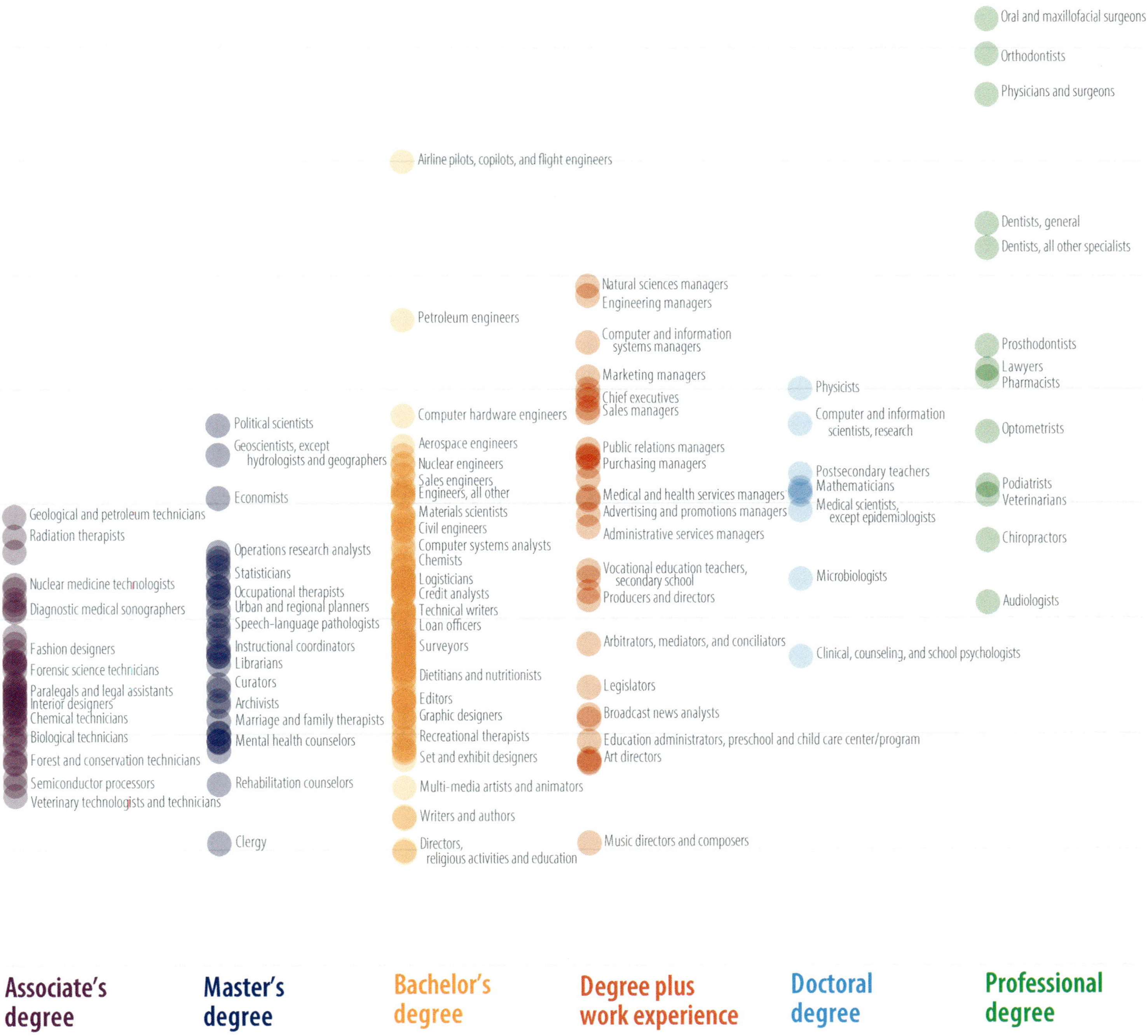
Oral and maxillofacial surgeons
Orthodontists
Physicians and surgeons
Airline pilots, copilots, and flight engineers
Dentists, general
Dentists, all other specialists
Natural sciences managers
Engineering managers
Petroleum engineers
Computer and information systems managers
Prosthodontists
Marketing managers
Lawyers
Pharmacists
Physicists
Chief executives
Sales managers
Computer hardware engineers
Political scientists
Computer and information scientists, research
Optometrists
Geoscientists, except hydrologists and geographers
Aerospace engineers
Public relations managers
Nuclear engineers
Purchasing managers
Postsecondary teachers
Sales engineers
Podiatrists
Mathematicians
Engineers, all other
Economists
Medical and health services managers
Veterinarians
Medical scientists, except epidemiologists
Geological and petroleum technicians
Materials scientists
Advertising and promotions managers
Radiation therapists
Civil engineers
Administrative services managers
Chiropractors
Operations research analysts
Computer systems analysts
Chemists
Statisticians
Vocational education teachers, secondary school
Microbiologists
Nuclear medicine technologists
Logisticians
Occupational therapists
Credit analysts
Producers and directors
Audiologists
Urban and regional planners
Diagnostic medical sonographers
Technical writers
Speech-language pathologists
Loan officers
Arbitrators, mediators, and conciliators
Instructional coordinators
Surveyors
Fashion designers
Clinical, counseling, and school psychologists
Librarians
Forensic science technicians
Dietitians and nutritionists
Curators
Legislators
Paralegals and legal assistants
Interior designers
Editors
Archivists
Chemical technicians
Marriage and family therapists
Graphic designers
Broadcast news analysts
Biological technicians
Mental health counselors
Recreational therapists
Education administrators, preschool and child care center/program
Forest and conservation technicians
Set and exhibit designers
Art directors
Rehabilitation counselors
Semiconductor processors
Multi-media artists and animators
Veterinary technologists and technicians
Writers and authors
Clergy
Music directors and composers
Directors, religious activities and education
Associate's degree
Master's degree
Bachelor's degree
Degree plus work experience
Doctoral degree
Professional degree

Occupations can be grouped by job duties or by industry. Some jobs, such as farmers and ranchers, are concentrated in a few industries, whereas others, such as CEOs, are found in all industries.

The Bureau of Labor Statistics uses the Standard Occupational Classification (SOC) system to classify workers into 840 occupations and 23 major occupation groups based on the similarity of job duties. Employees who perform essentially the same tasks are grouped in the same occupation, even if they work in different industries.

The BLS also gathers information about education and training requirements for each occupation.

2011

Major Occupation Sectors

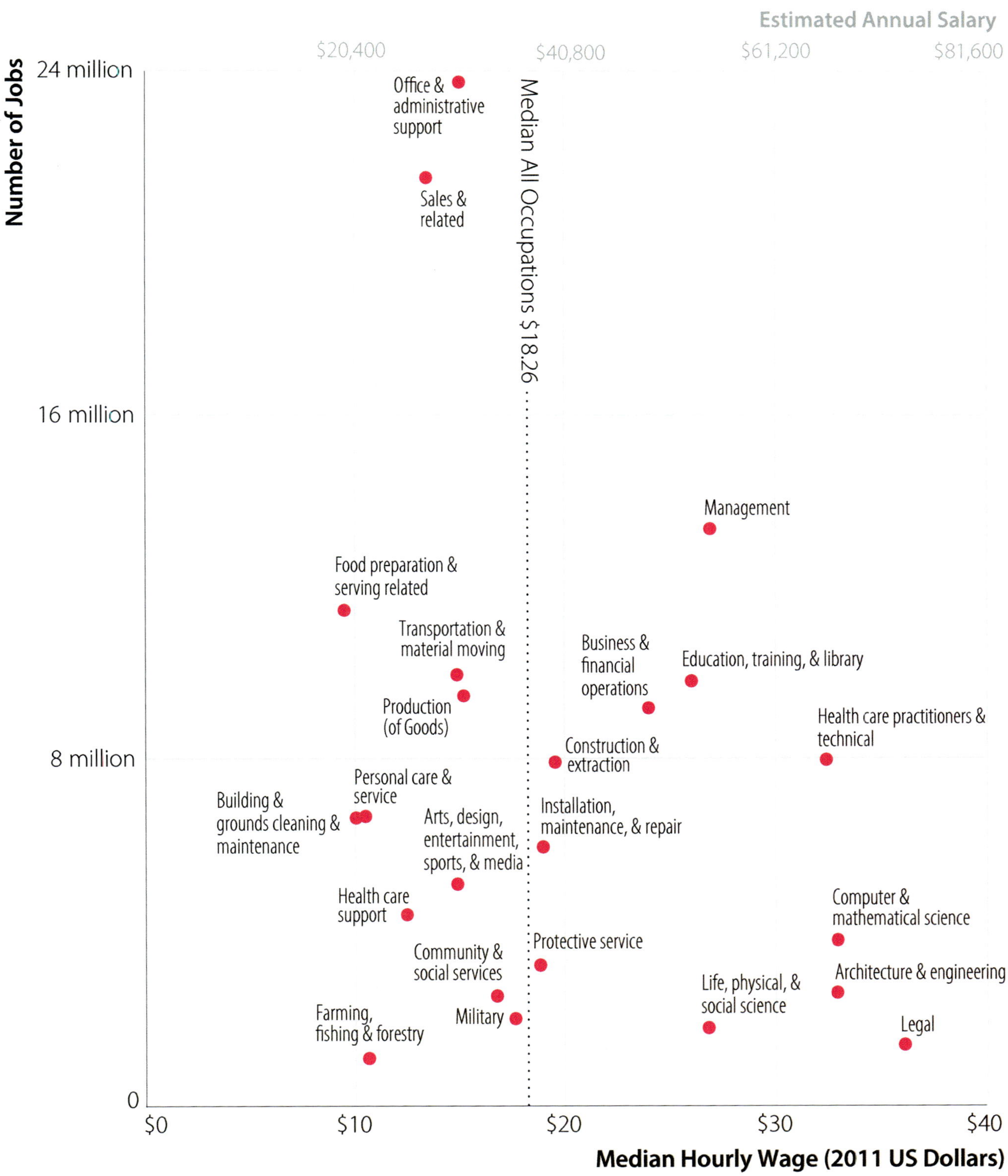

Source: EMSI EconomicModeling.com (Compiled from data collected by BLS, BEA and US Census Bureau)

2011

The Market for Labor

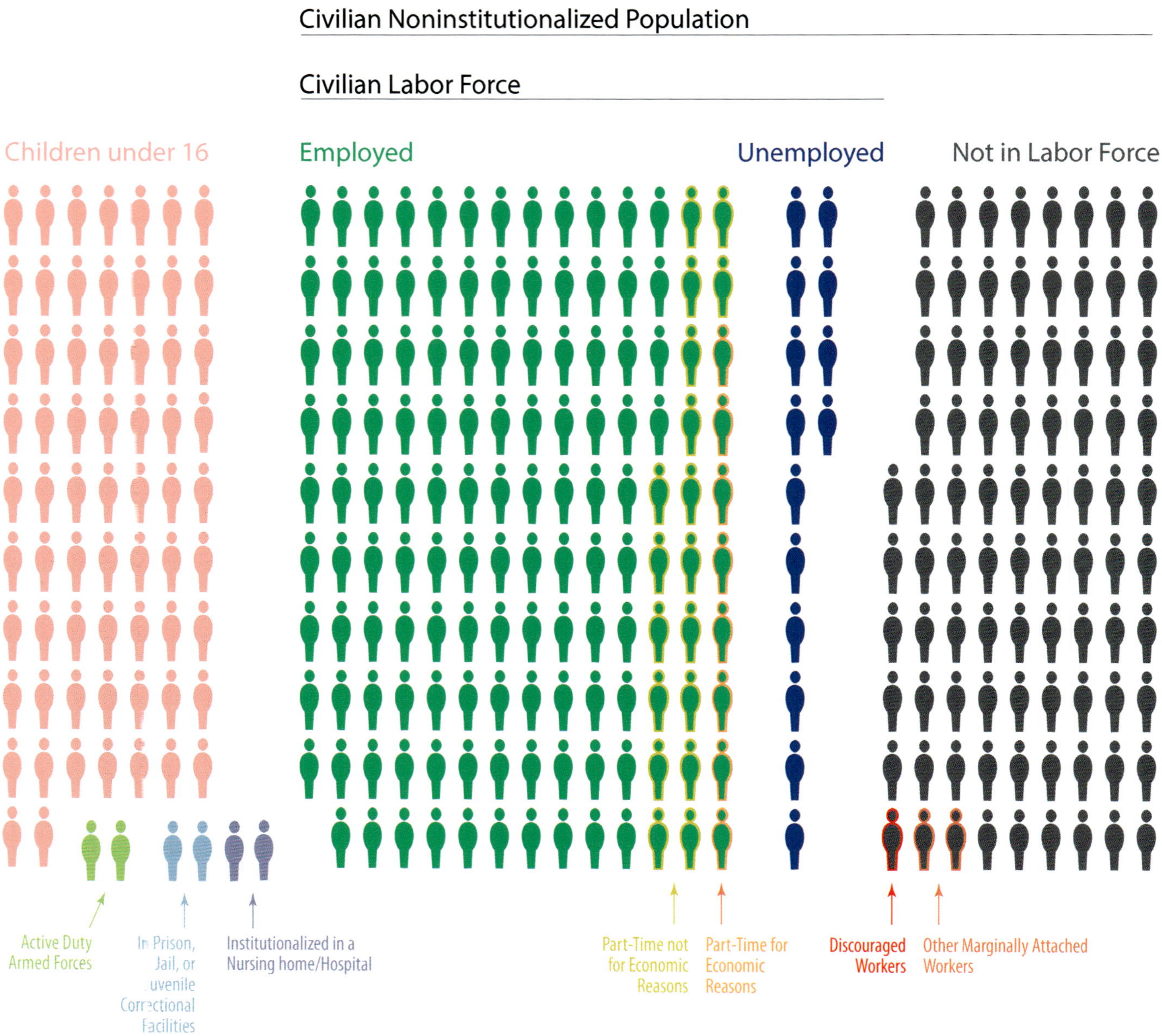

310,000,000 people in the United States
= 1,000,000 people

 Sources: US Bureau of Labor Statistics • US Census Bureau

Defining the Labor Force

Are you 16 years of age or older?

Not in the active military service?

Not in prison, juvenile correctional facility, a mental hospital, or a nursing home?

Then you are in the *civilian noninstitutional population*. If you meet the definition of either Employed or Unemployed, then you are in the Civilian Labor Force.

Employed

You are counted as Employed if you are in the *civilian noninstitutional population* and can answer yes to one of the following questions:

Did you do any work for pay or profit during the last week?

Did at least 15 hours of unpaid work in a family-owned enterprise (like a farm) operated by someone in your household?

Are self-employed?

Were temporarily absent from your regular jobs because of illness, vacation, bad weather, industrial dispute, or various personal reasons, whether or not you were paid for the time off?

Part-time for economic reasons

Do you want a full-time job but worked less than 35 hours during the last week primarily due to slack work (a reduction in hours in response to unfavorable business conditions) or the inability to find full-time work?

Unemployed

You are counted as Unemployed if you are in the *civilian noninstitutional population,* do not meet the definition of Employed, but searched for work in the preceding 4

Not in Labor Force

All persons in the *civilian noninstitutional population* who are defined as neither Employed nor Unemployed. Common reasons given for not seeking paid work include: retired, a student, taking care of children or other family members.

Marginally Attached Workers

If you are neither working nor looking for work but have indicated that you want and are available for a job and have looked for work sometime in the past 12 months. You are not counted as Unemployed if you have not searched for work in the preceding 4 weeks.

Discouraged Workers

You meet the definition of a Marginally Attached Worker. In addition you have indicated you are not currently looking for work because you believed no jobs were available or there were none for which you would qualify.

Measuring Unemployment

As of July 2011

U-1 5.3%

Unemployed
15 weeks or longer
÷
Civilian Labor Force

U-2 5.4%

Unemployed
Job losers (including anyone who completed a temporary job)
÷
Civilian Labor Force

Official Unemployment Rate

U-3 9.2%

Total Unemployed
Job losers + People who have quit their job + People entering the workforce (i.e. recent graduates)
÷
Civilian Labor Force

U-4 9.8%

Total Unemployed + Discouraged Workers
÷
Civilian Labor Force + Discouraged Workers

U-5 10.7%

Total Unemployed + Discouraged Workers + Other Marginally Attached Workers
÷
Civilian Labor Force + Discouraged Workers + Other Marginally Attached Workers

U-6 16.1%

Total Unemployed + Discouraged Workers + Other Marginally Attached Workers + Employed Part-Time for Economic Reasons
÷
Civilian Labor Force + Discouraged Workers + Other Marginally Attached Workers

Sources: US Bureau of Labor Statistics • US Census Bureau

Various

1948–2010

Growth of GDP per Worker

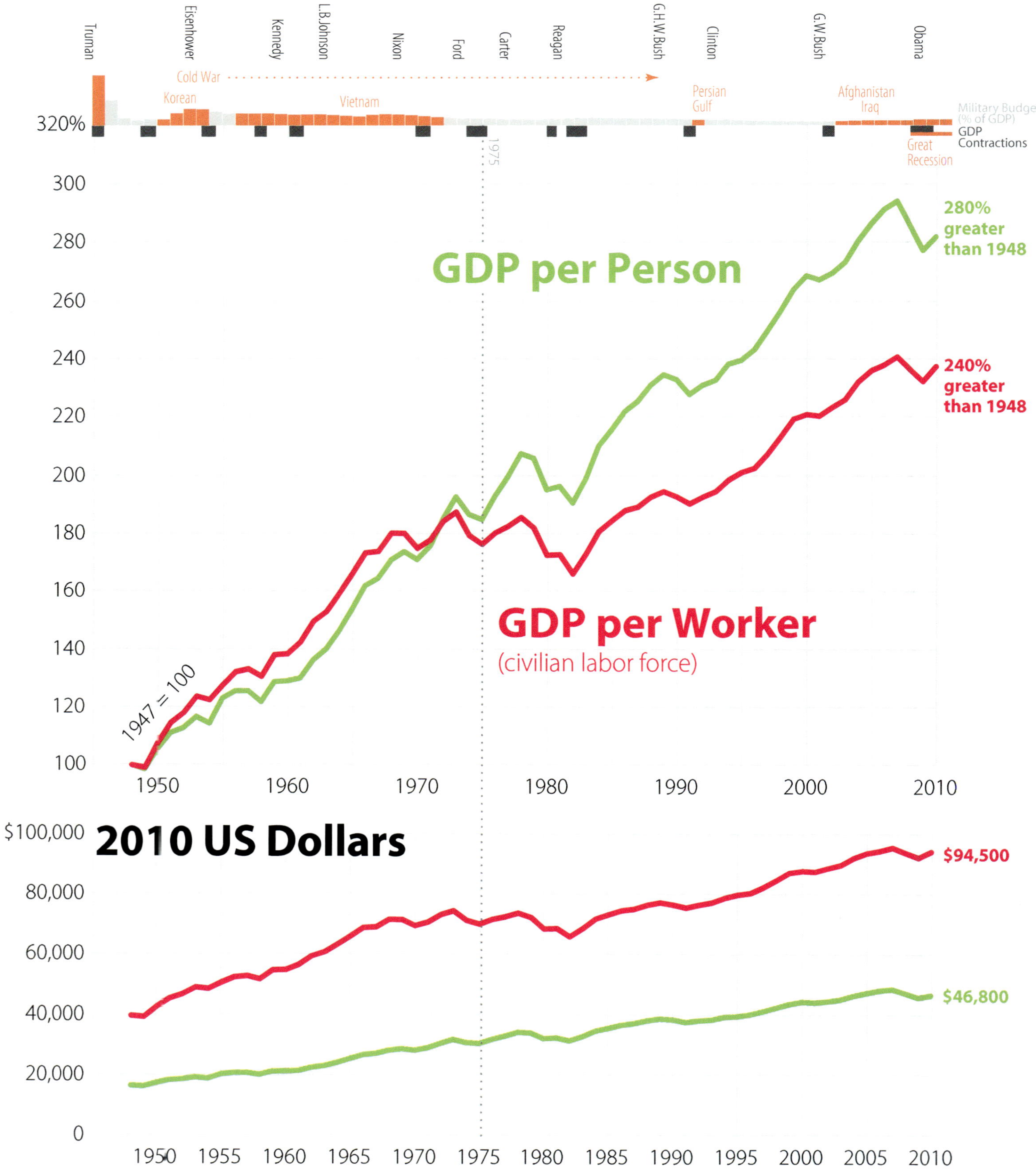

 Sources: US Bureau of Labor Statistics • US Bureau of Economics Analysis

1947–2011 Labor Force

BLS

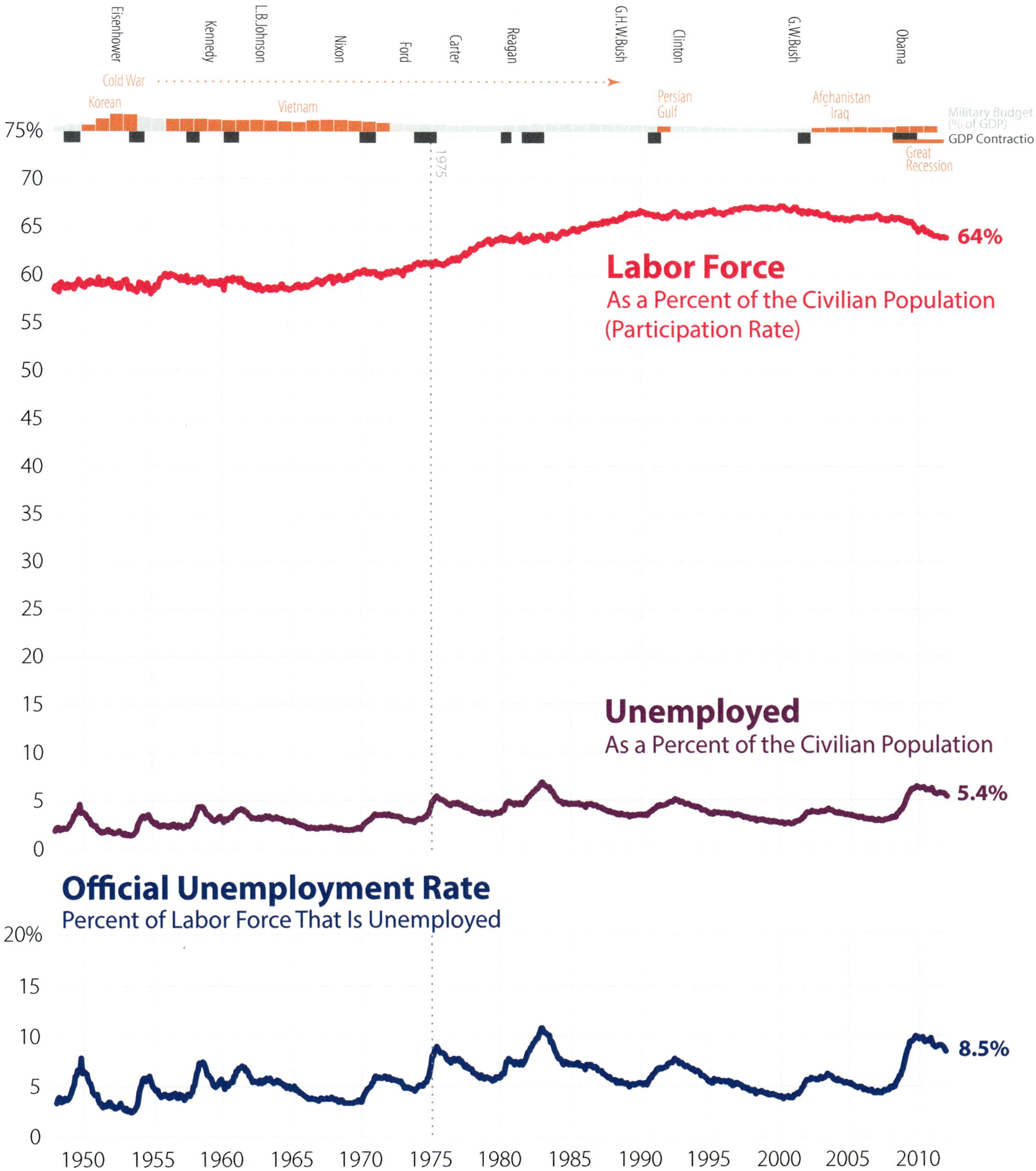

Sources: US Bureau of Labor Statistics

1790–2010 Average Unskilled Wages

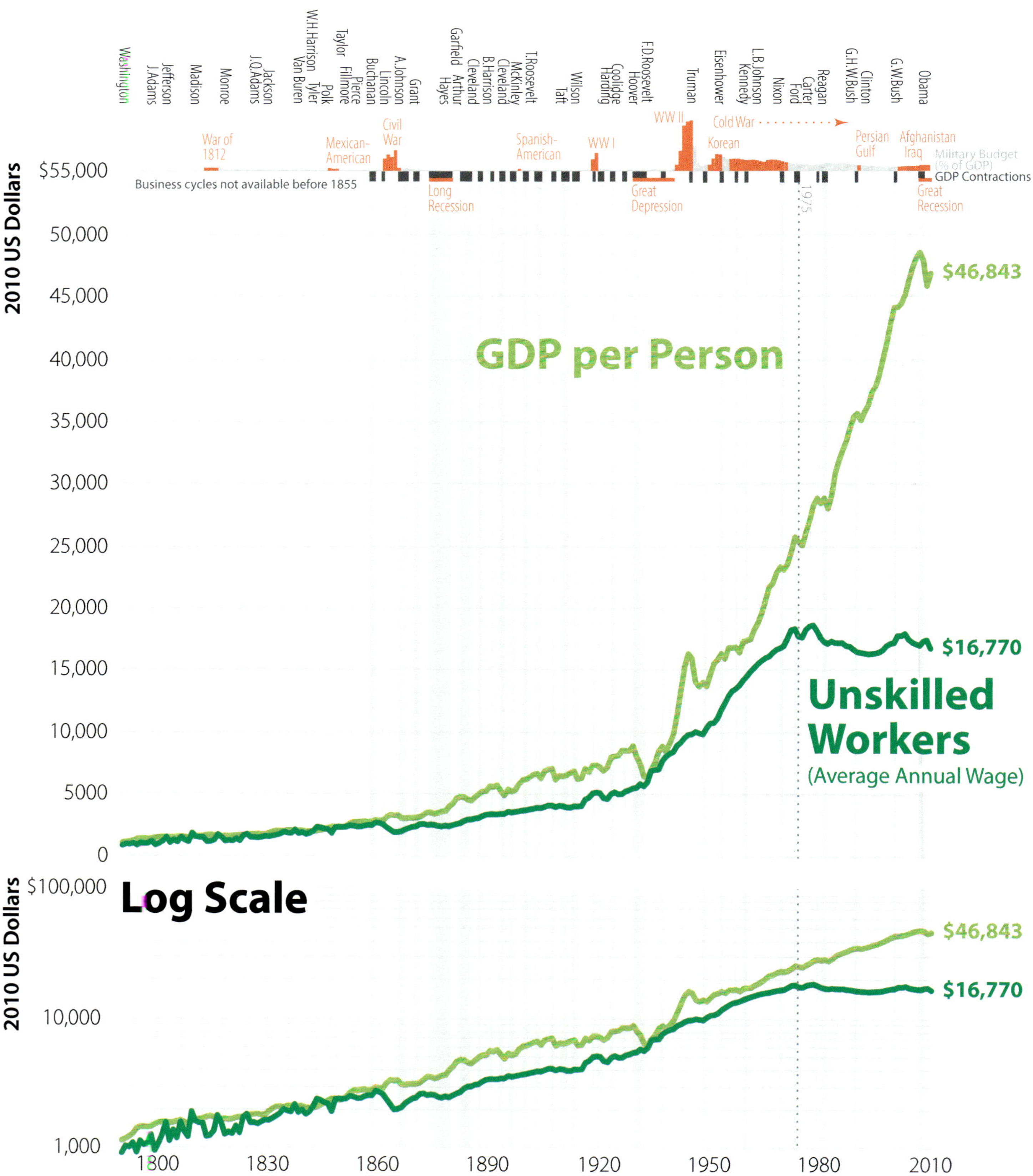

 Source: Lawrence H. Officer and Samuel H. Williamson, "Annual Wages in the United States, 1774–Present," MeasuringWorth.com, 2011

1774–2010

Production Workers' Wages

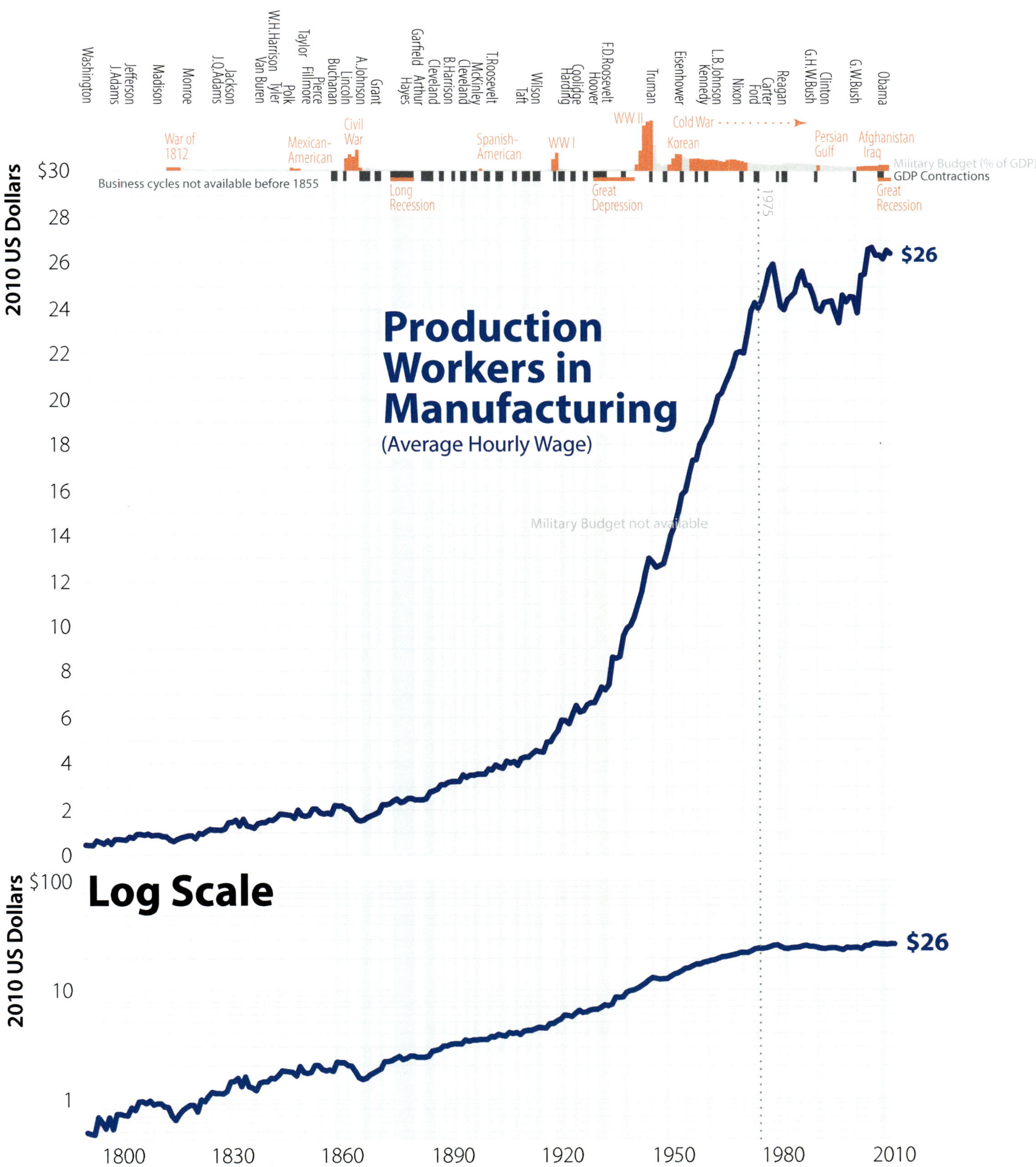

Source: Lawrence H. Officer and Samuel H. Williamson, "Annual Wages in the United States, 1774-Present," MeasuringWorth.com, 2011

1964–2011

Service-Providing Industries: Average Wages

BLS

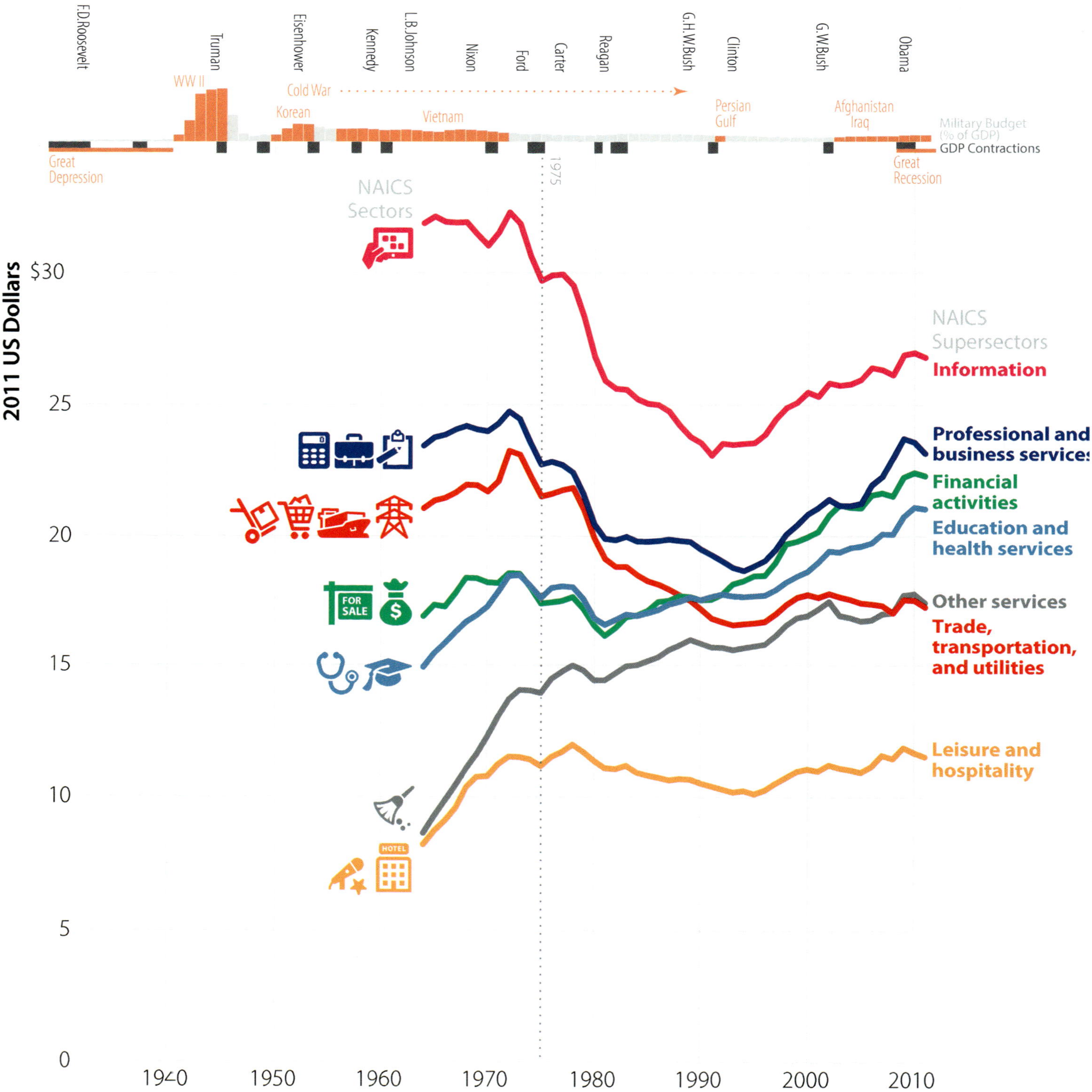

 Source: US Bureau of Labor Statistics

Four-digit Standard Industrial Classification (SIC) codes were established in 1937 to classify companies by industry. This scheme is now being replaced by the North American Industry Classification System (NAICS), a six-digit system designed to accommodate changes in the US economy attributable to new technologies and the growth of the service sector.

NAICS supersectors combine several industry sectors:

Education and Health Services = Educational Services + Health Care and Social Assistance

Financial Activities = Finance and Insurance + Real Estate and Rental and Leasing

Leisure and Hospitality = Arts, Entertainment, and Recreation + Accommodation and Food Services

Trade, Transportation, and Utilities = Wholesale Trade + Retail Trade + Transportation and Warehousing + Utilities

Professional and Business Services = Professional, Scientific, and Technical Services + Management Companies and Enterprises + Administrative Support and Waste Management and Remediation Services

1939–2011 Goods-Producing Industries: Average Wages

BLS

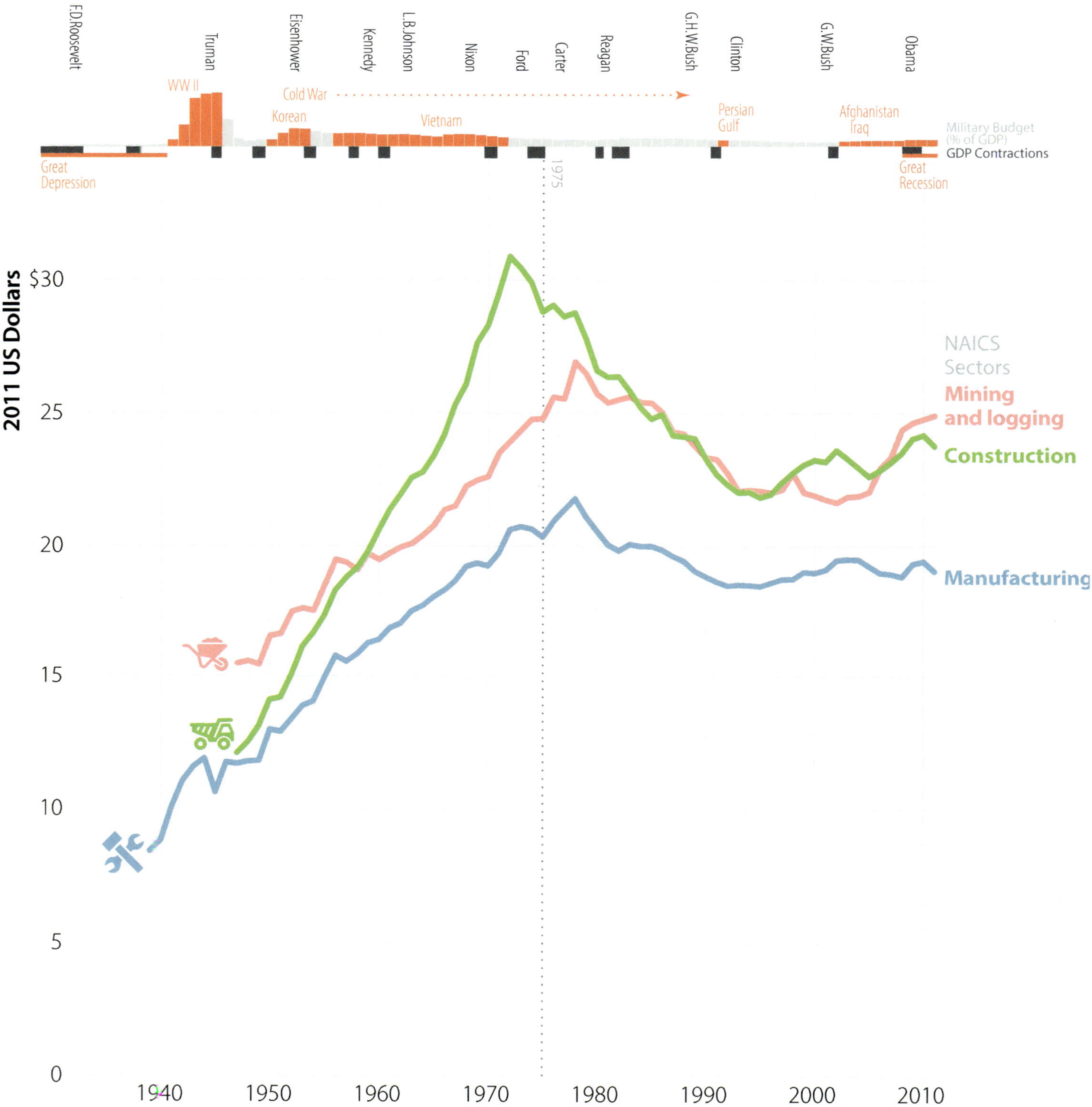

 Source: US Bureau of Labor Statistics

INDUSTRIES

One reason income inequality has increased is because of fewer jobs in goods-producing industries such as manufacturing and more jobs in both low-paid service industries such as accommodation and food services and high-paid ones such as finance and insurance. Although labor productivity has grown since the 1970s, wages have not kept pace with that growth.

1947–2010

Labor Productivity: All Businesses Except Farms

BLS

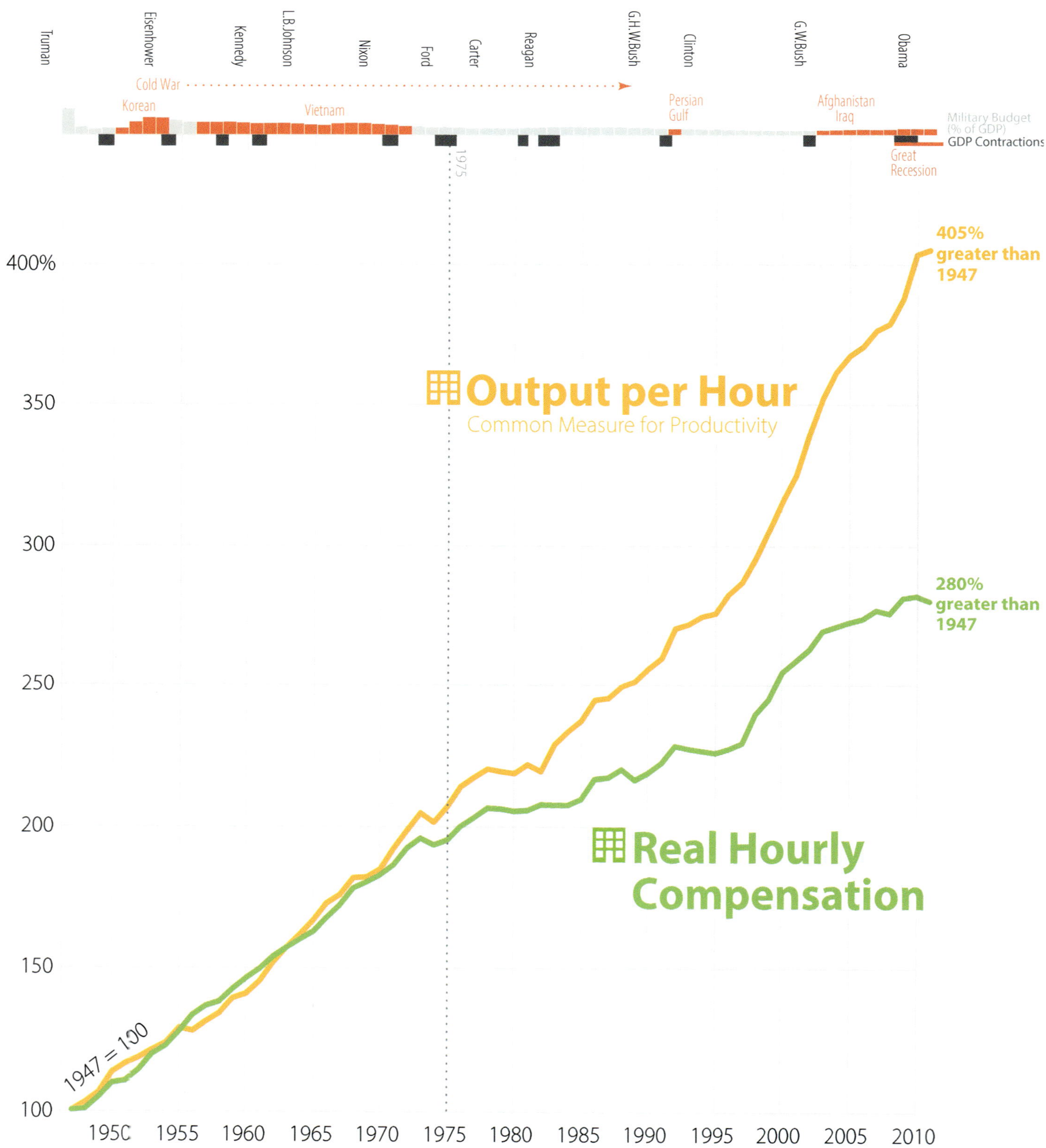

 Source: US Bureau of Labor Statistics

BLS

1986–2010

Labor Productivity: Manufacturing vs. All Businesses

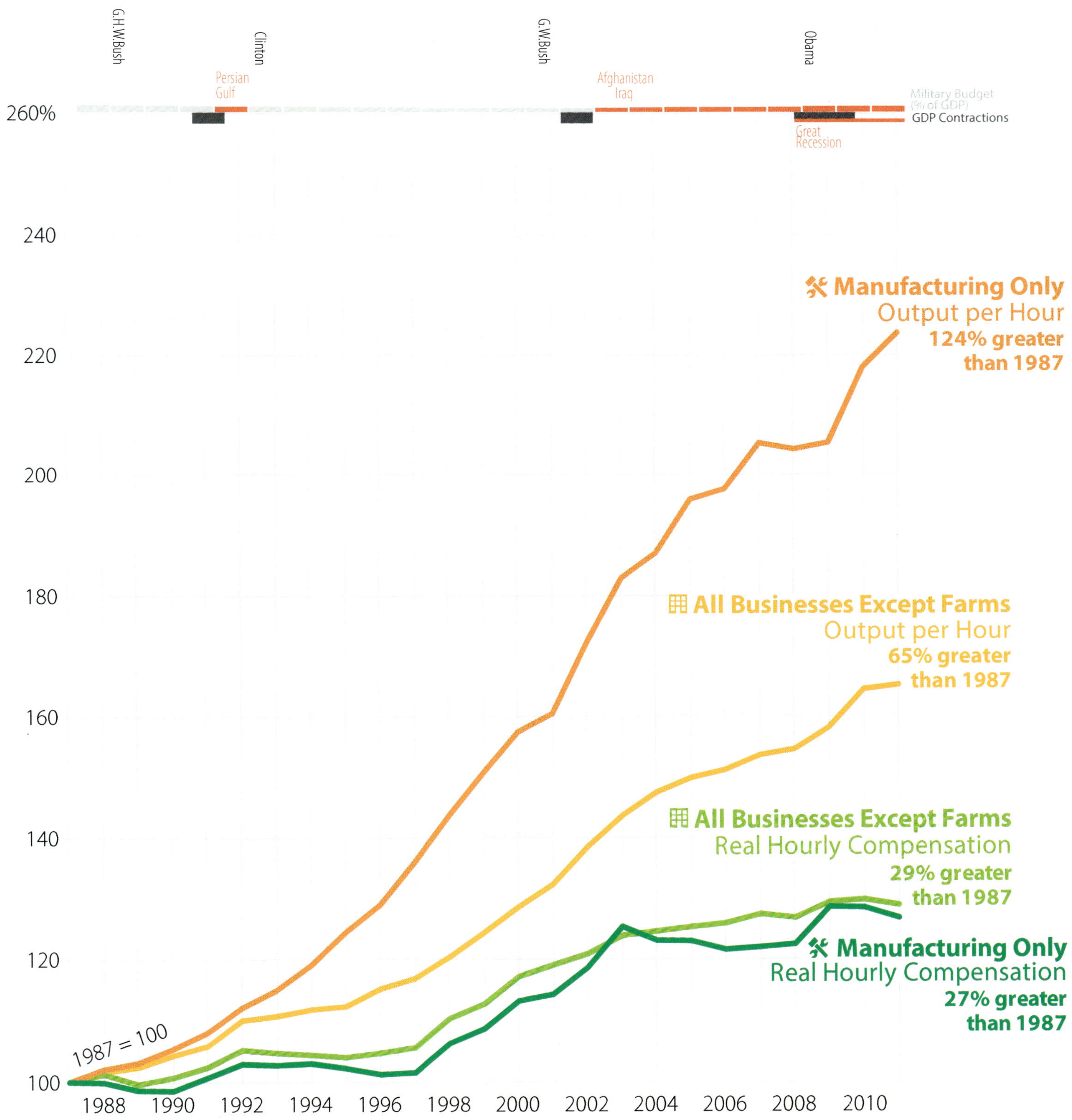

Source: US Bureau of Labor Statistics

Productivity is a measure of economic efficiency: How effectively are economic inputs such as labor and raw materials converted into outputs such as cars or bread or services such as health care?

Labor Productivity measures the output per hour of all workers. It is the productivity measure most often cited in the press.

All Businesses Except Farms excludes farms as well as activities for which it is difficult to measure productivity, such as government, nonprofit institutions, paid employees of private households, and the rental value of owner-occupied dwellings.

Value Added is the contribution that each industry makes to the GDP of the United States, but from the point of view of production rather than consumption. For example, a patient would not distinguish between paying for prescription drugs and the doctor who prescribes them—they are both "health care." But on the production side, the value added by doctors to the country's GDP is included in the health care industry, while the employees who manufacture drugs for a pharmaceutical company are working in the manufacturing industry.

Average Earnings is calculated by EMSI from wages, salaries, and proprietor earnings for pensions, insurance plans, profit-sharing plans, retirement plans, compensation plans, and supplemental unemployment benefit plans, as well as employer contributions to government social insurance.

2001–2011

Industry Job Growth vs. Income

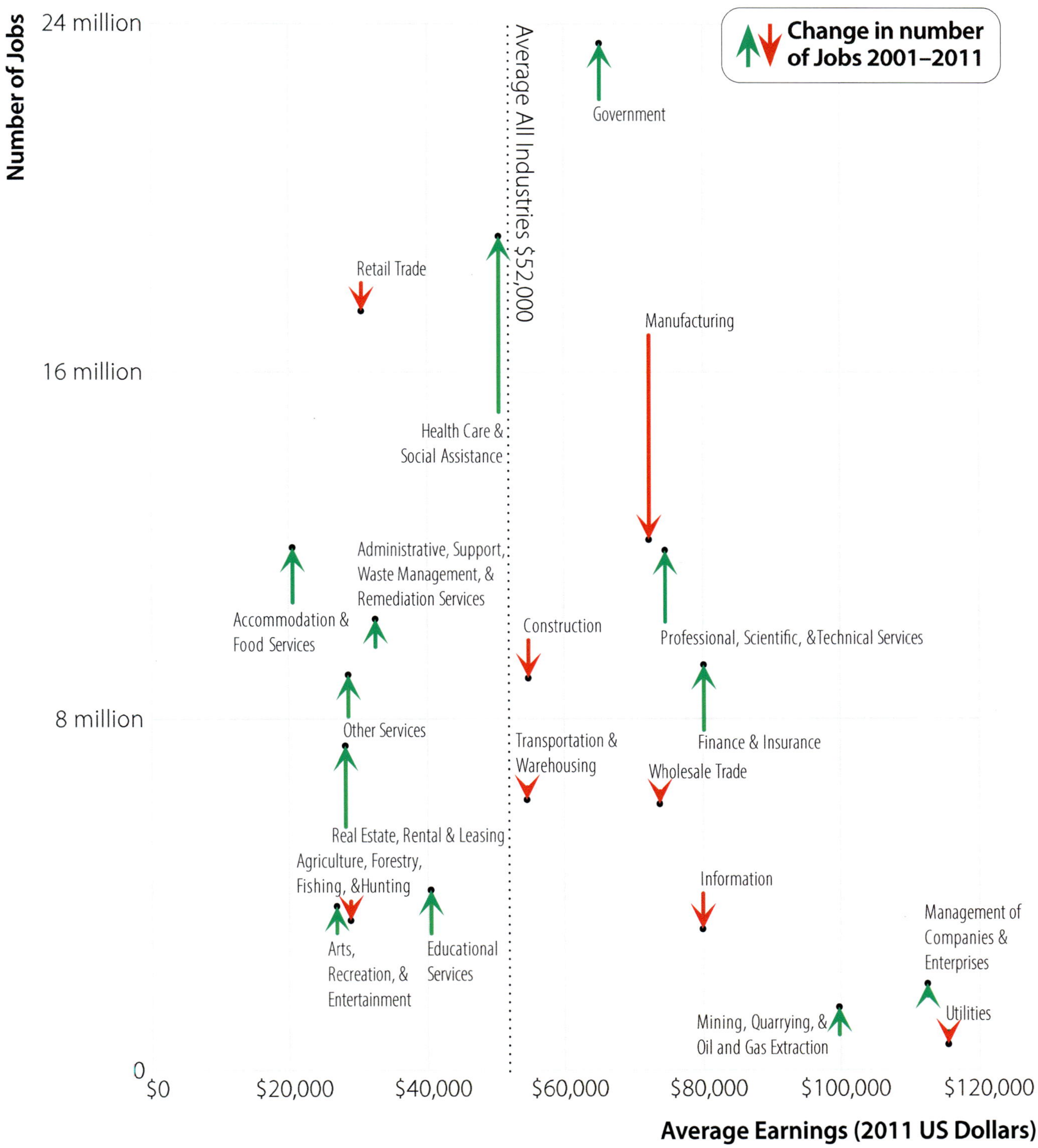

Source: EMSI EconomicModeling.com (Compiled from data collected by BLS, BEA and US Census Bureau)

1947–2010

Top 5 Industries' Share of GDP

BEA

Value added by these five industries in 2010

53.6%

50.1% in 1947

Government

Enacting laws
Civil and criminal courts
Writing and enforcing regulations
Taxation
National defense
Public order and safety
Immigration services
Foreign affairs
International assistance
Postal service
Activities that can be separated out (e.g., school and hospitals) are classified elsewhere

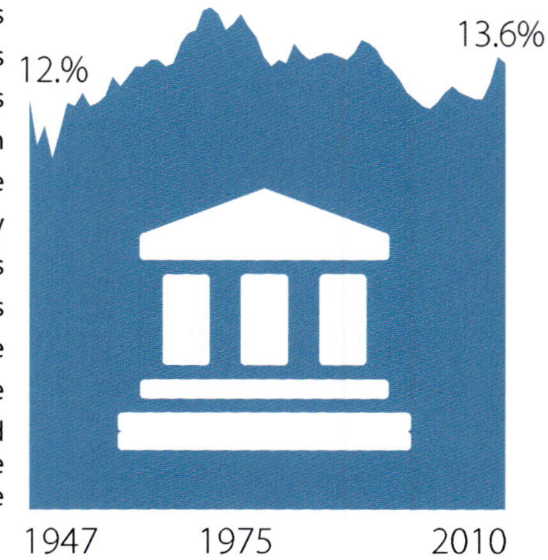

Manufacturing

Chemical plants
Steel mills
Bakeries
Food manufacturers
Apparel
Tailors
Electronics
Paper
Furniture
Machinery

Real estate and rental and leasing

Managing real estate, appraising, selling, renting and/or buying real estate for others
Real estate investment trusts (REITs)
Leasing motor vehicles, computers, and consumer goods
Leasing patents, trademarks, brand names, and/or franchise agreements

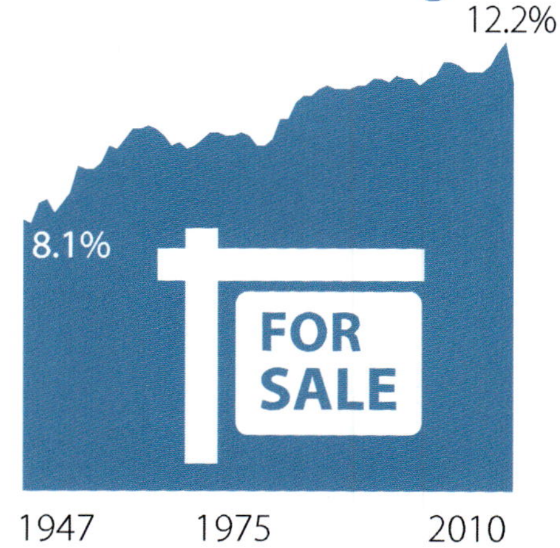

Finance and insurance

Taking deposits
Issuing securities
Underwriting insurance and annuities
Facilitating or supporting financial intermediation, insurance, and employee benefit programs
Monetary authorities
Central bank

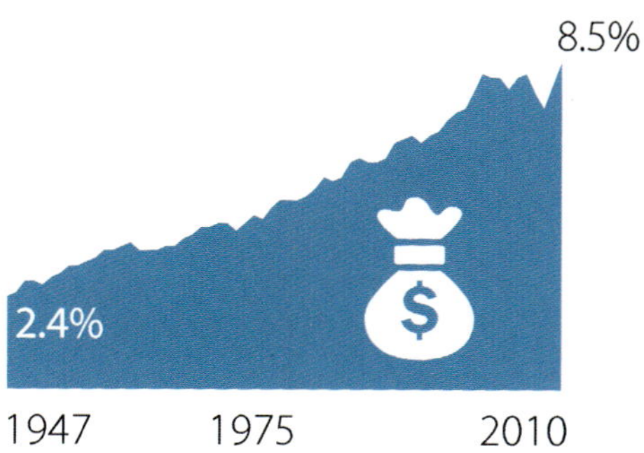

Health care and social assistance

Hospitals
Nursing and residential care facilities
Ambulatory health care
Community food, housing, and emergency help
Job counseling/training
Child day-care
Big brother/big sister
Alcoholic and drug addiction

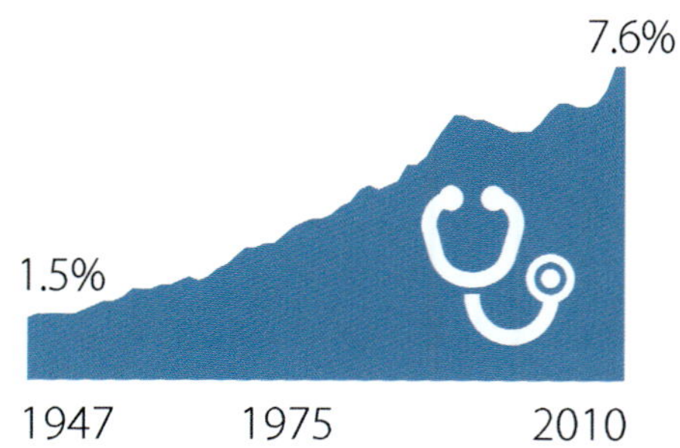

 Source: US Bureau of Economics Analysis

1947–2010

BEA

Upper 5 Industries' Share of GDP

Value added by these five industries in 2010

26.9%

23.6% in 1947

Professional, scientific, and technical services

Legal advice and representation
Accounting
Bookkeeping
Payroll
Architectural
Engineering
Consulting
Research
Advertising
Translation
Veterinary

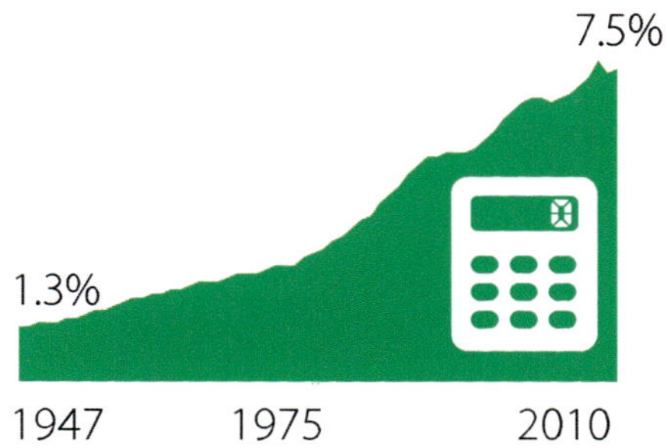

Retail trade

Selling merchandise in small quantities to the public
Retail stores
Broadcasting of "infomercials"
Direct-response advertising
Catalogs
Door-to-door solicitation
In-home demonstration
Selling from portable stalls (street vendors, except food)
Distribution through vending machines

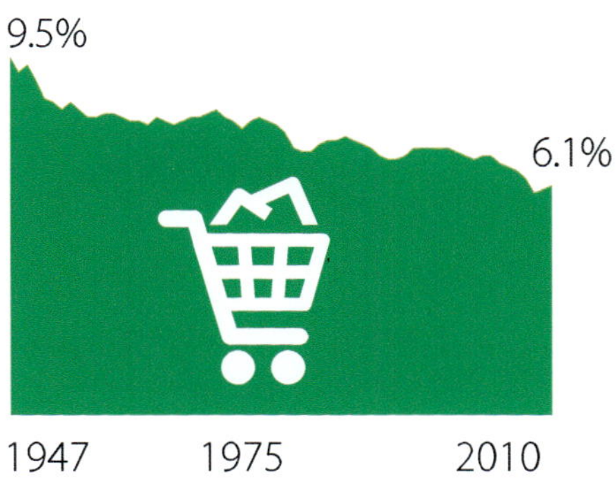

Wholesale trade

Organize or arrange the sale of merchandise for resale or parts, supplies, and raw materials used in production
Outputs of agriculture, mining, manufacturing, & publishing

Information

Newspaper, periodical, & book publishing
Software publishing
Motion picture
Sound recording industries
Broadcasting
Telecommunications
Web search portals
Data processing
Internet Hosting

Construction

Construction of buildings or engineering projects
Buildings
Highways
Utility systems
Preparation of sites for new construction
Subdividing land for sale as building sites

Source: US Bureau of Economics Analysis

BEA

1947–2010

Lower 5 Industries' Share of GDP

Value added by these five industries in 2010

12.9%

13.5% in 1947

Accommodation and food services

Hotels/motels
Resorts
RV parks and campgrounds
Hunting and fishing camps
Cafés
Bars
Restaurants
Caterers
Food trucks

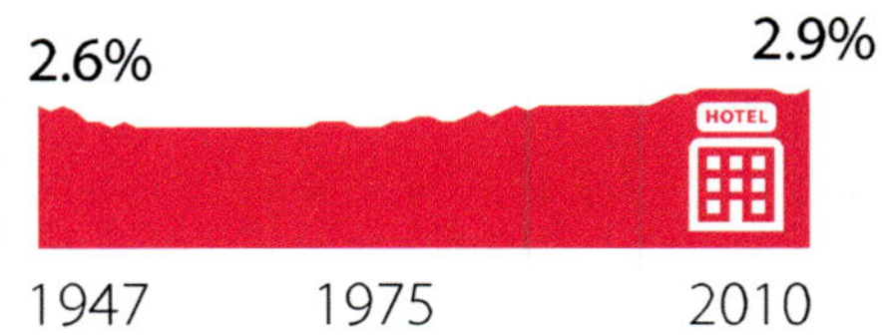

Administrative and waste management services

Hiring and placing personnel
Preparing documents
Taking orders from clients
Collecting payments for claims
Arranging travel
Providing security and surveillance
Cleaning buildings
Packaging and labeling products
Collection, treatment and disposal of waste material
Operation of material recovery facilities
Removal of pollution from environment
Cleaning of septic tanks

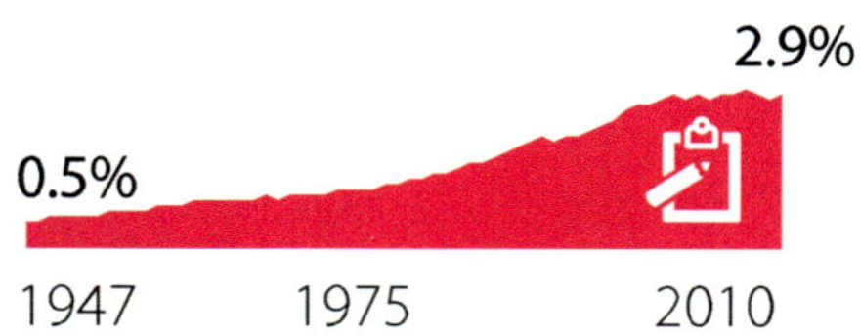

Transportation and warehousing

Transportation of passengers and cargo
Warehousing and storage for goods
Scenic and sightseeing transportation
Support activities (e.g., air traffic control)

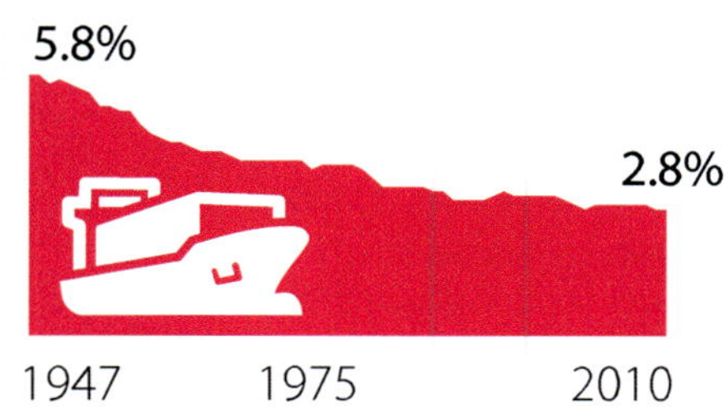

Other services

Auto mechanics
Repairing machinery and equipment
Funerals
Laundry
Pet care
Promoting religious activities
Grant-making
Advocating social and political causes
Cooks, maids, butlers, gardeners in private households

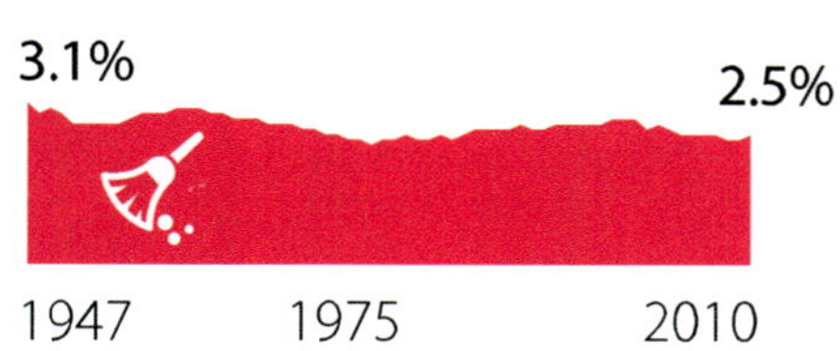

Management of companies and enterprises

Establishments owning a controlling interest or influencing management decisions of other companies
Holding companies
Head offices

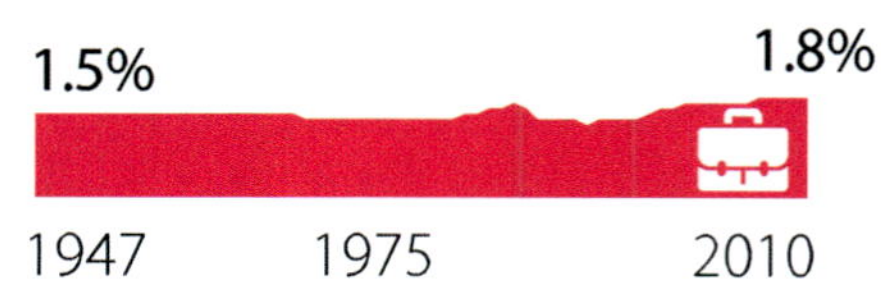

 Source: US Bureau of Economics Analysis

BEA

1947–2010

Bottom 5 Industries' Share of GDP

Value added by these five industries in 2010

6.6%

12.9% in 1947

Utilities

Electric power
Natural gas
Steam supply
Water supply
Sewage removal

Mining

Extract naturally occurring mineral solids, liquid minerals, and gases
Quarrying
Well operations
Beneficiating
Other preparation customarily performed at the mine site, or as a part of mining activity

Educational services

Providing instruction and training in a wide variety of subjects
Publicly or privately owned profit or nonprofit schools
Colleges & universities
Training centers

Agriculture, forestry, fishing, and hunting

Growing crops, raising animals, harvesting timber or fish
Farms
Ranches
Dairies
Greenhouses
Nurseries
Orchards
Hatcheries

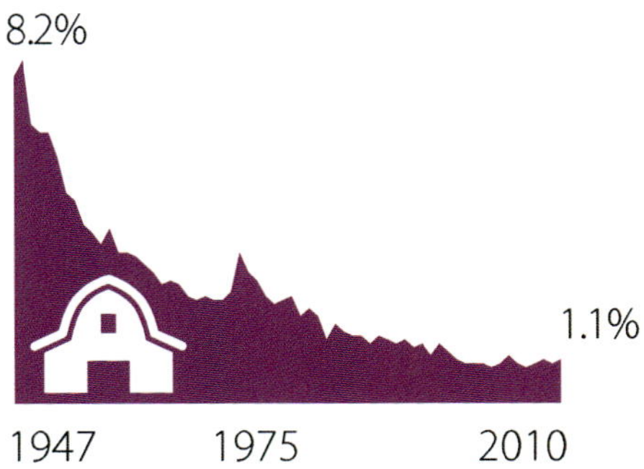

Arts, entertainment, and recreation

Performing arts
Spectator sports
Exhibiting objects, sites, & natural wonders of historical, cultural, and educational value
Amusement, gambling, and recreation

Source: US Bureau of Economics Analysis

Various

2000–2010

Share of GDP by Industry and Earnings per Worker

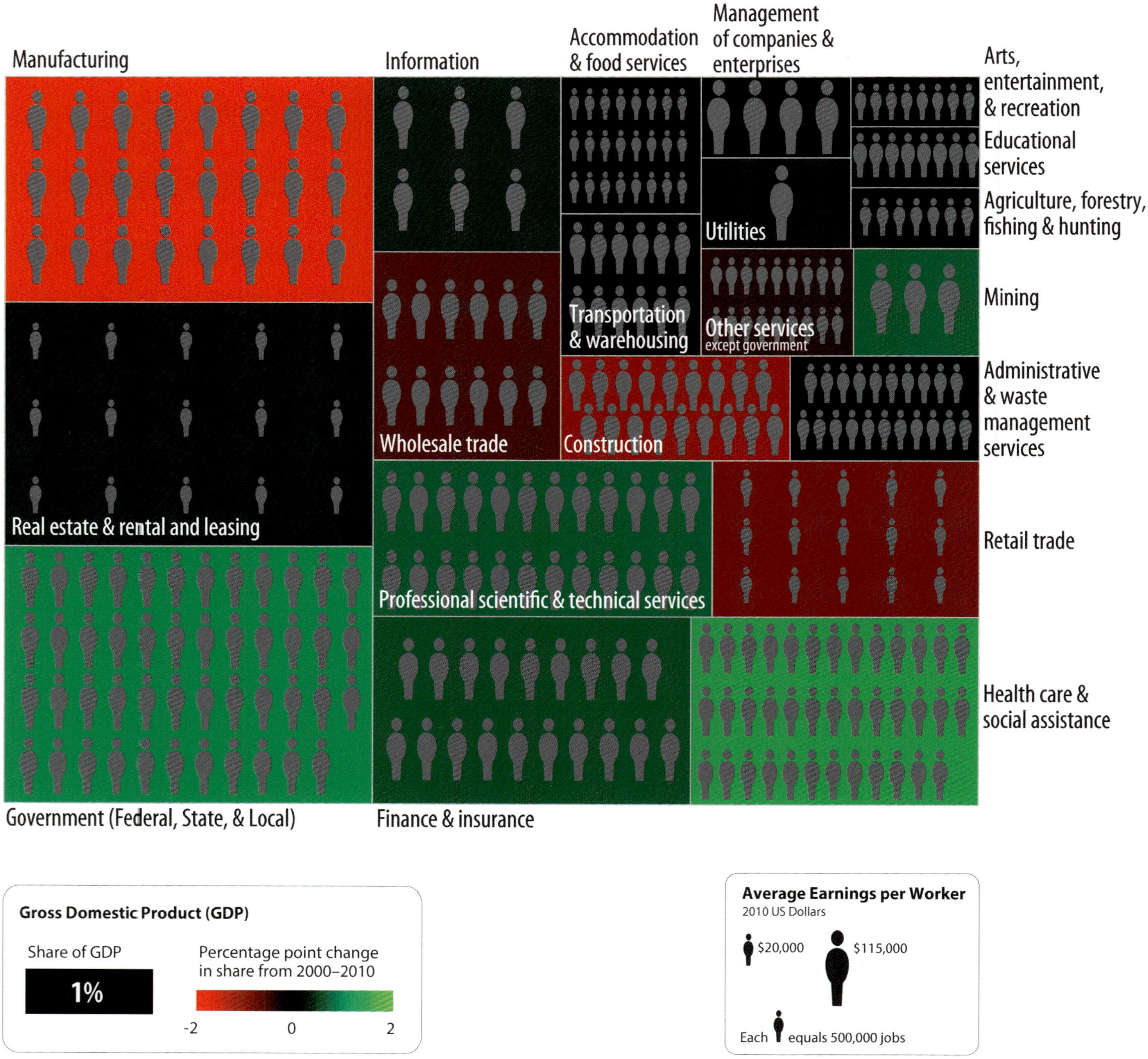

 Source: US Bureau of Economics Analysis • EMSI EconomicModeling.com (Compiled from data collected by BLS, BEA and US Census Bureau)

OCCUPATIONS BY INDUSTRIES

This section provides an overview of nearly 800 occupations. These "maps" take a bird's-eye view of the labor market by looking at patterns of income and job growth by industry and by education.

2001–2011

All Occupations by Industry: Income

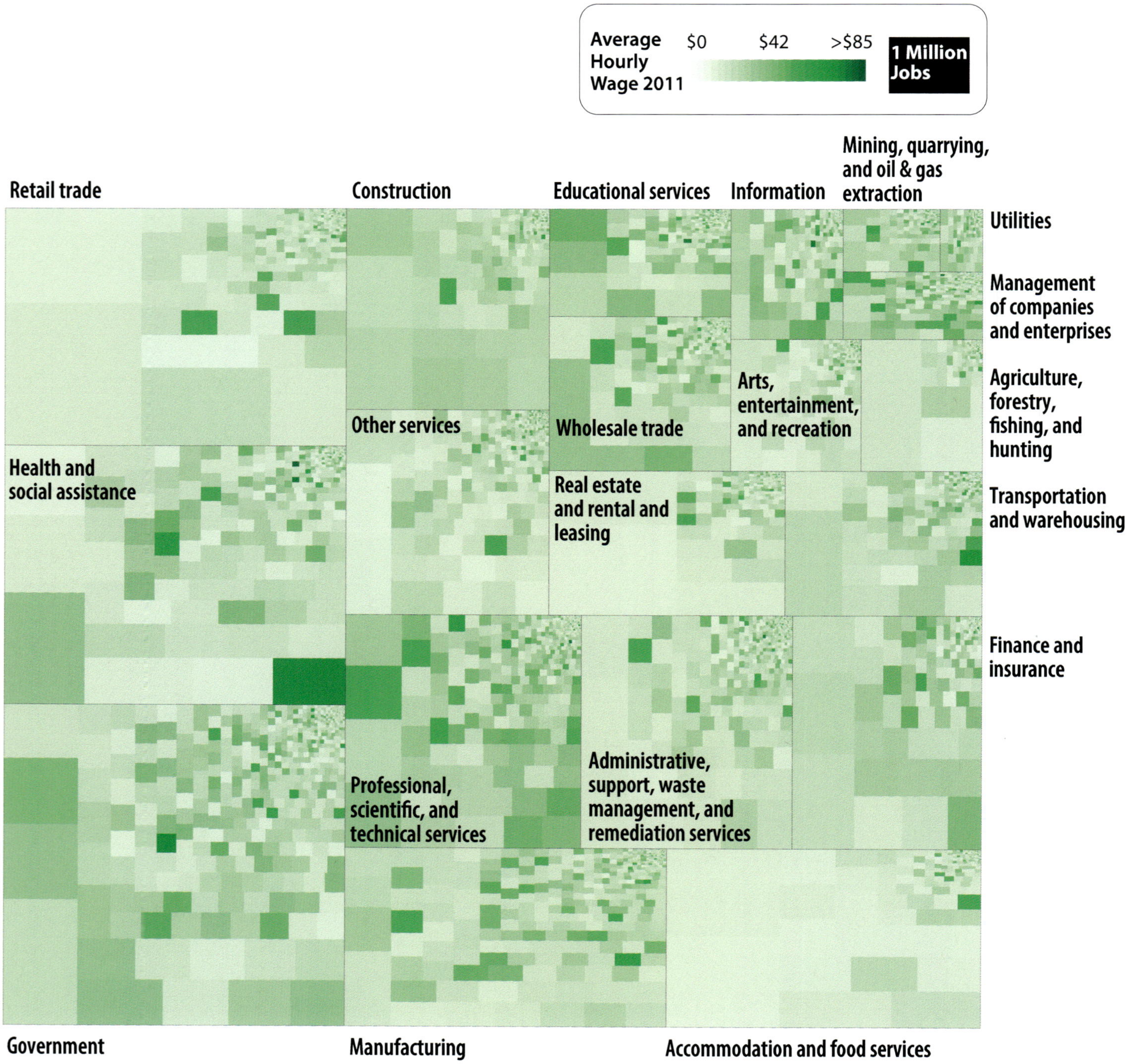

 Source: EMSI EconomicModeling.com (Compiled from data collected by BLS, BEA and US Census Bureau)

2001–2011

All Occupations by Industry: Job Growth

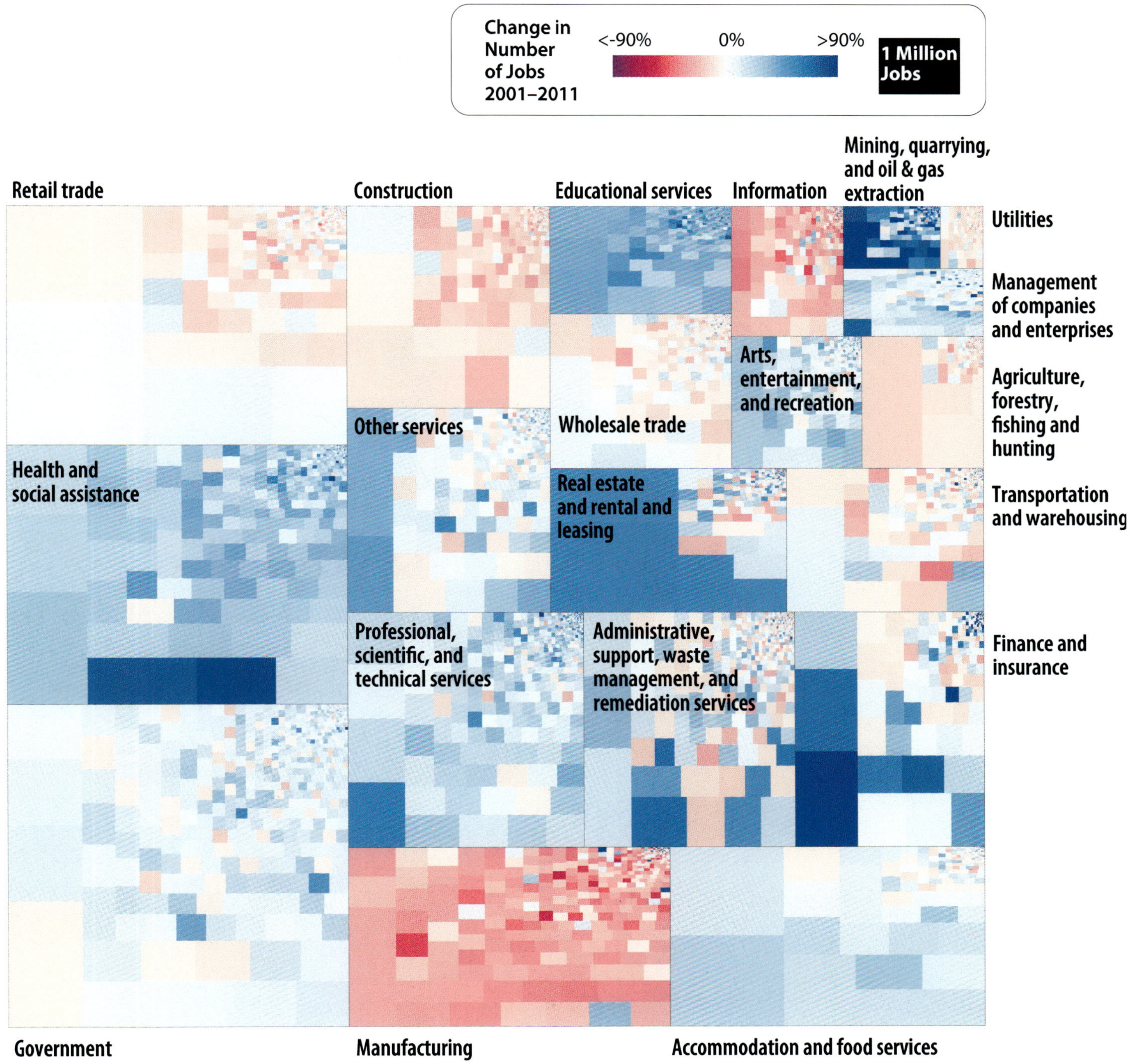

Source: EMSI EconomicModeling.com (Compiled from data collected by BLS, BEA and US Census Bureau)

All Occupations by Education: Income

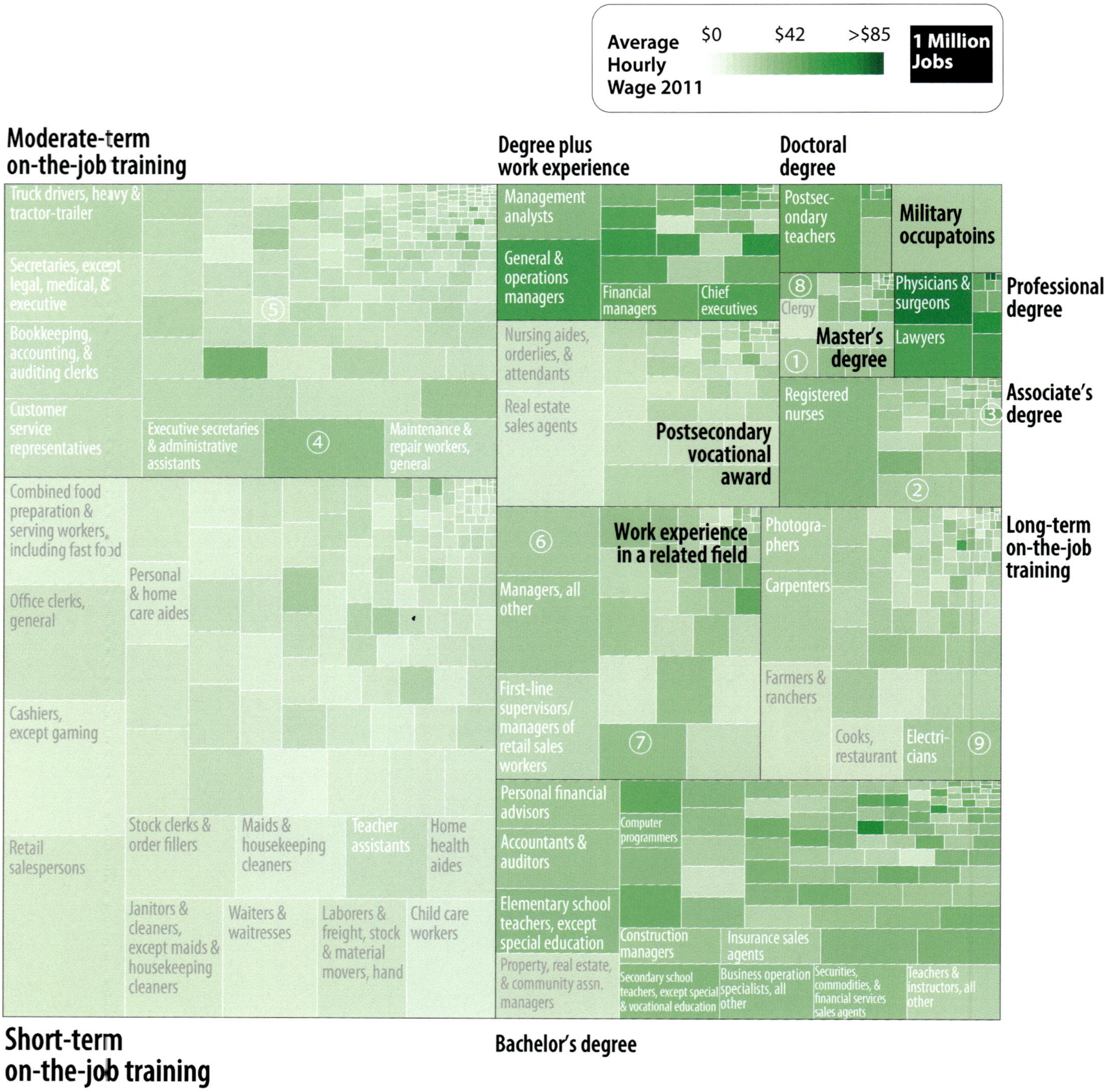

① School counselors
② Computer support specialists
③ Geological & petroleum technicians
④ Sales representatives, wholesale & manufacturing, except technical & scientific products
⑤ Sewing machine operators
⑥ First-line supervisors/ managers of office & administrative support workers
⑦ First-line supervisors/managers of production & operating workers
⑧ Physical therapists
⑨ Police & sheriff's patrol officers

 Source: EMSI EconomicModeling.com (Compiled from data collected by BLS, BEA and US Census Bureau)

2001–2011

All Occupations by Education: Job Growth

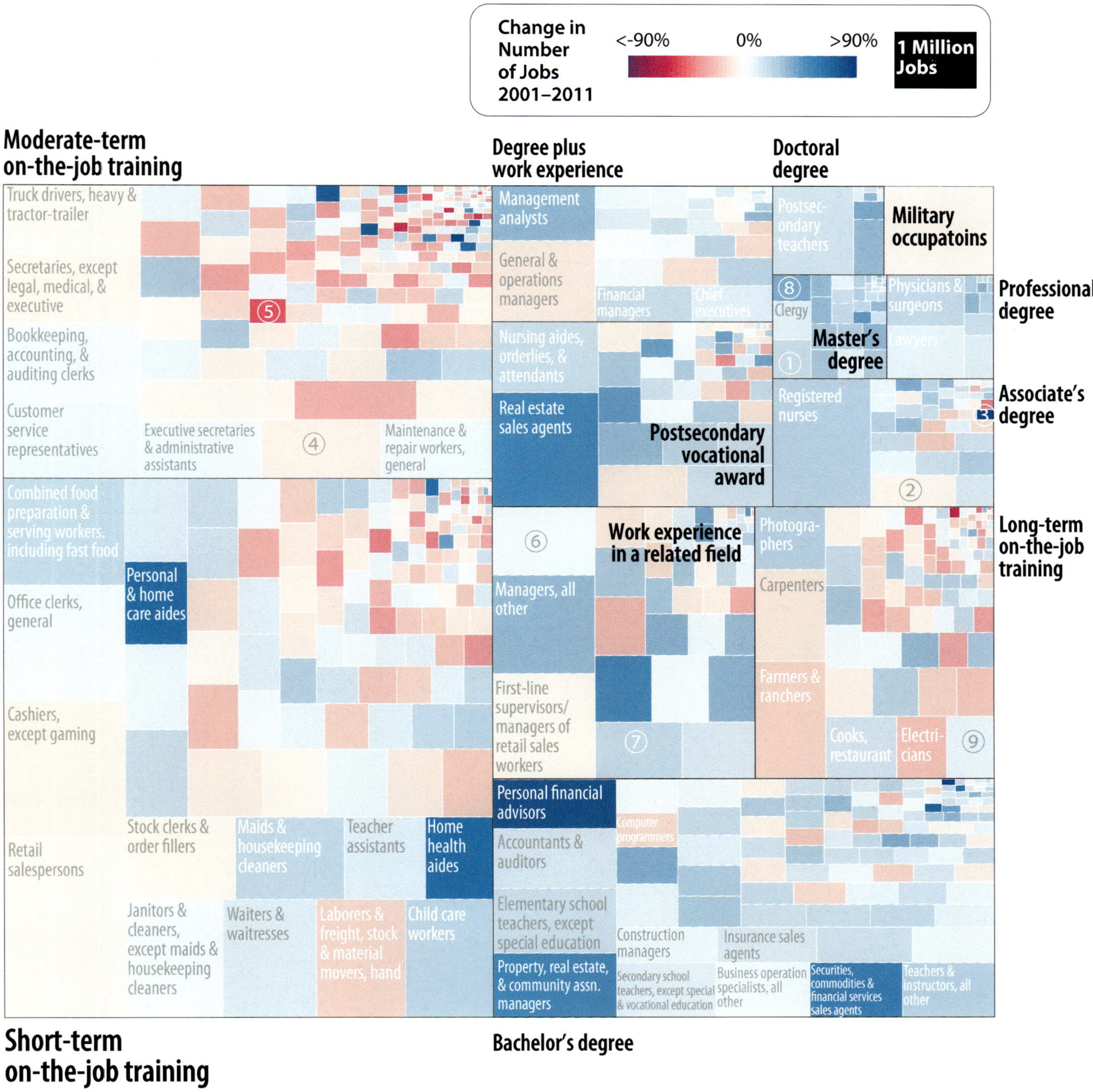

(1) School counselors
(2) Computer support specialists
(3) Geological & petroleum technicians
(4) Sales representatives, wholesale & manufacturing, except technical & scientific products
(5) Sewing machine operators
(6) First-line supervisors/managers of office & administrative support workers
(7) First-line supervisors/managers of production & operating workers
(8) Physical therapists
(9) Police & sheriff's patrol officers

Source: EMSI EconomicModeling.com (Compiled from data collected by BLS, BEA and US Census Bureau)

2011

Health & Social Assistance Occupations: Income

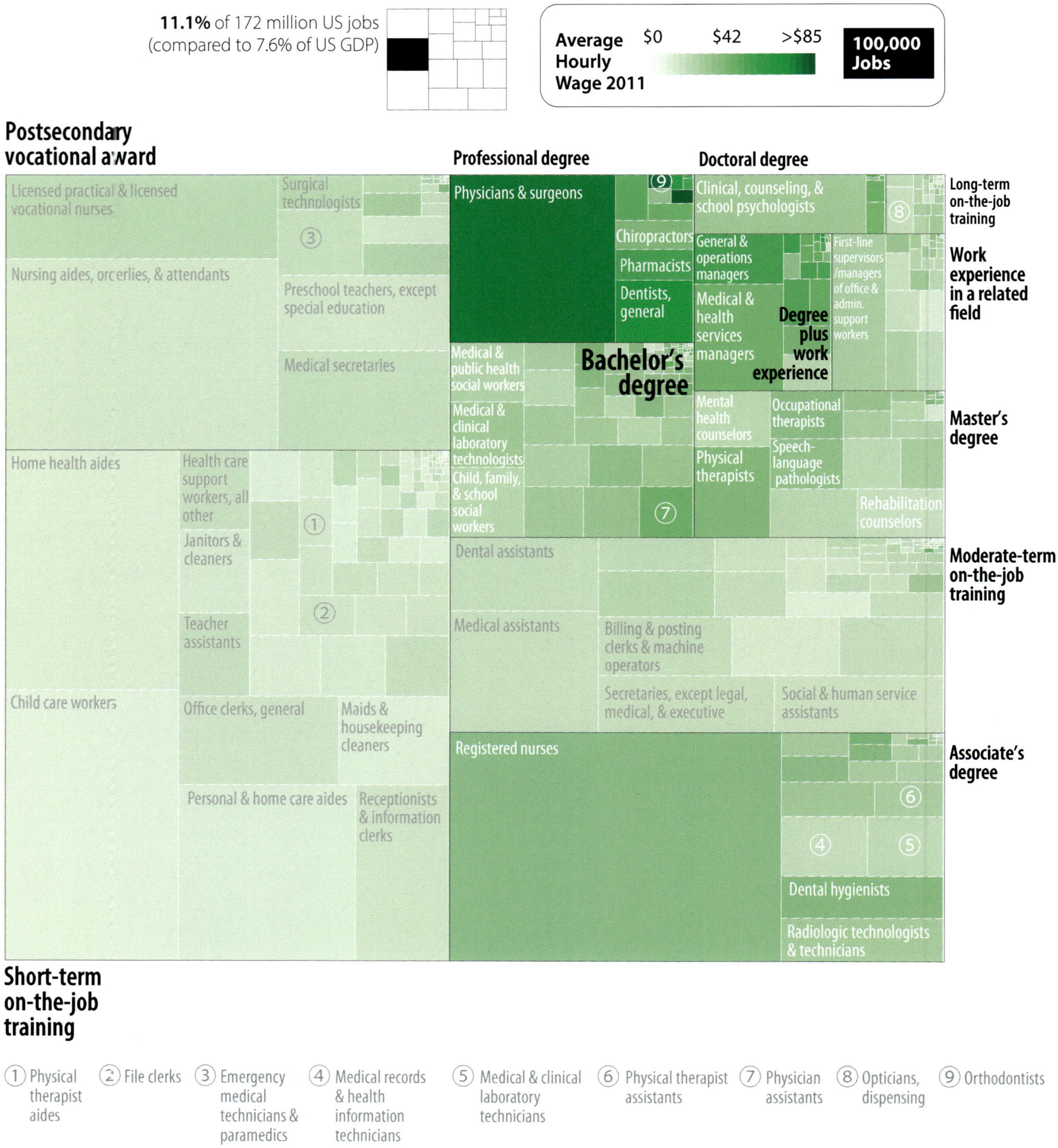

 Source: EMSI EconomicModeling.com (Compiled from data collected by BLS, BEA and US Census Bureau)

Health & Social Assistance Occupations: Job Growth

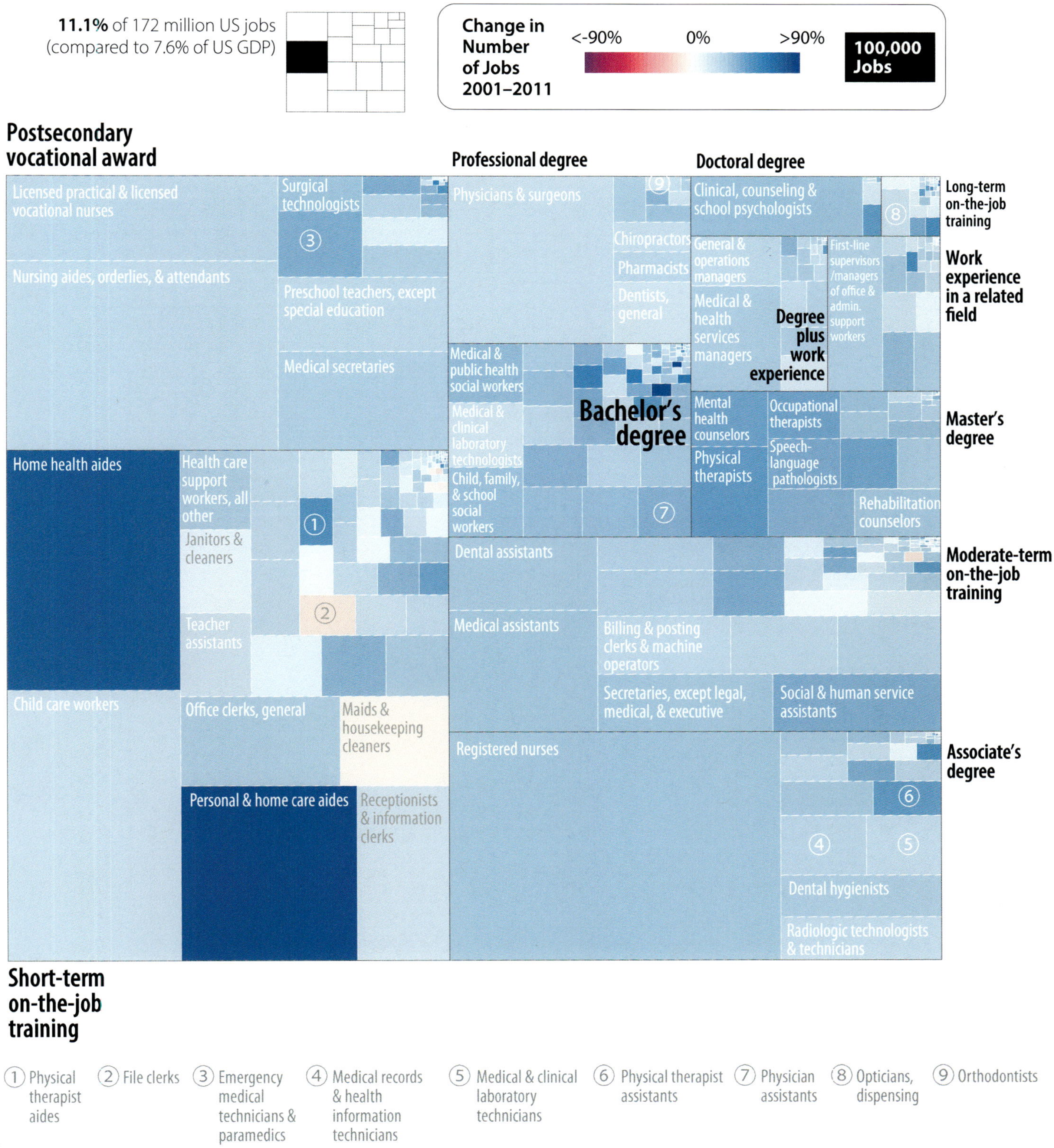

Source: EMSI EconomicModeling.com (Compiled from data collected by BLS, BEA and US Census Bureau)

2011

Information Occupations: Income

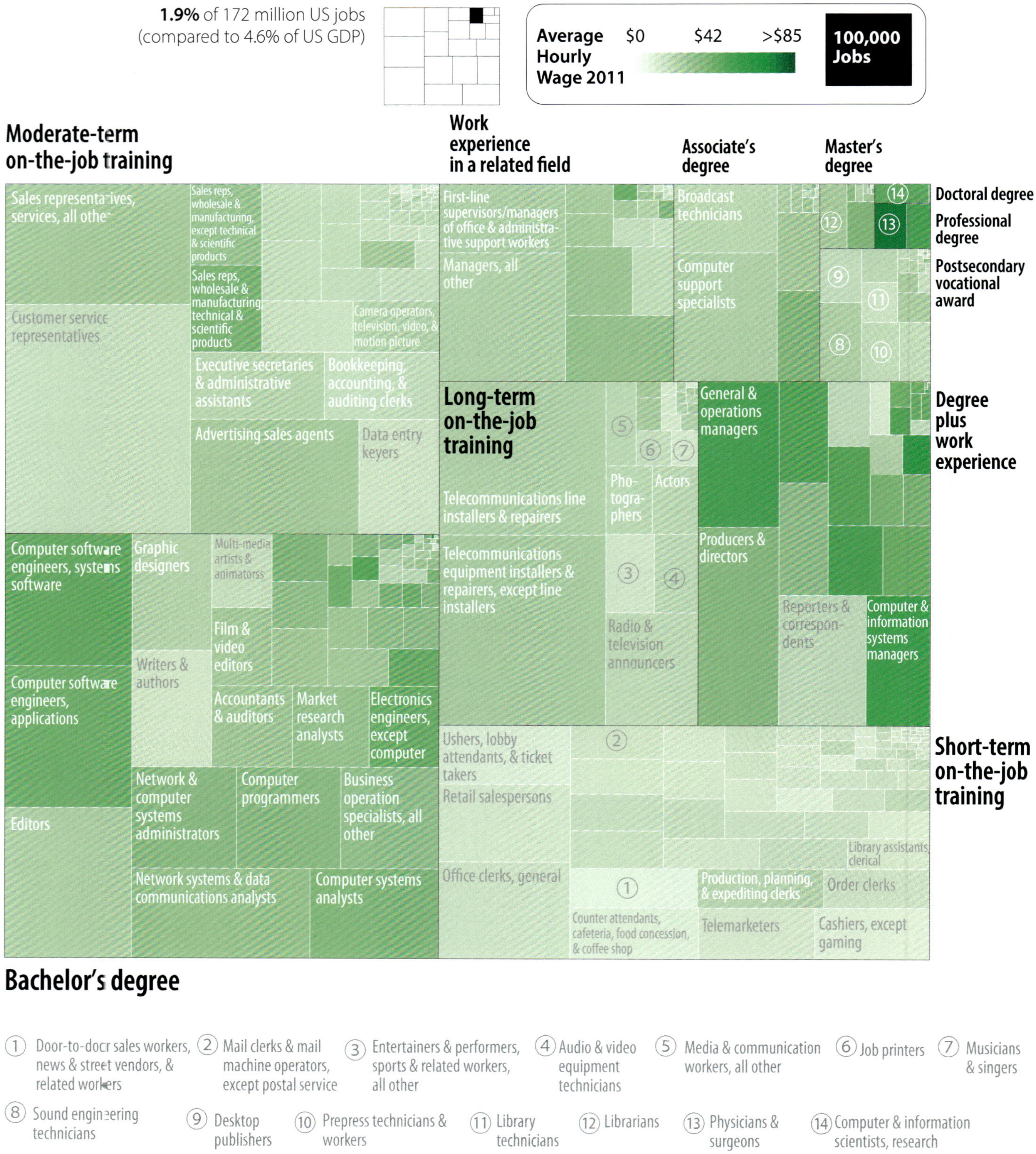

 Source: EMSI EconomicModeling.com (Compiled from data collected by BLS, BEA and US Census Bureau)

2001–2011

Information Occupations: Job Growth

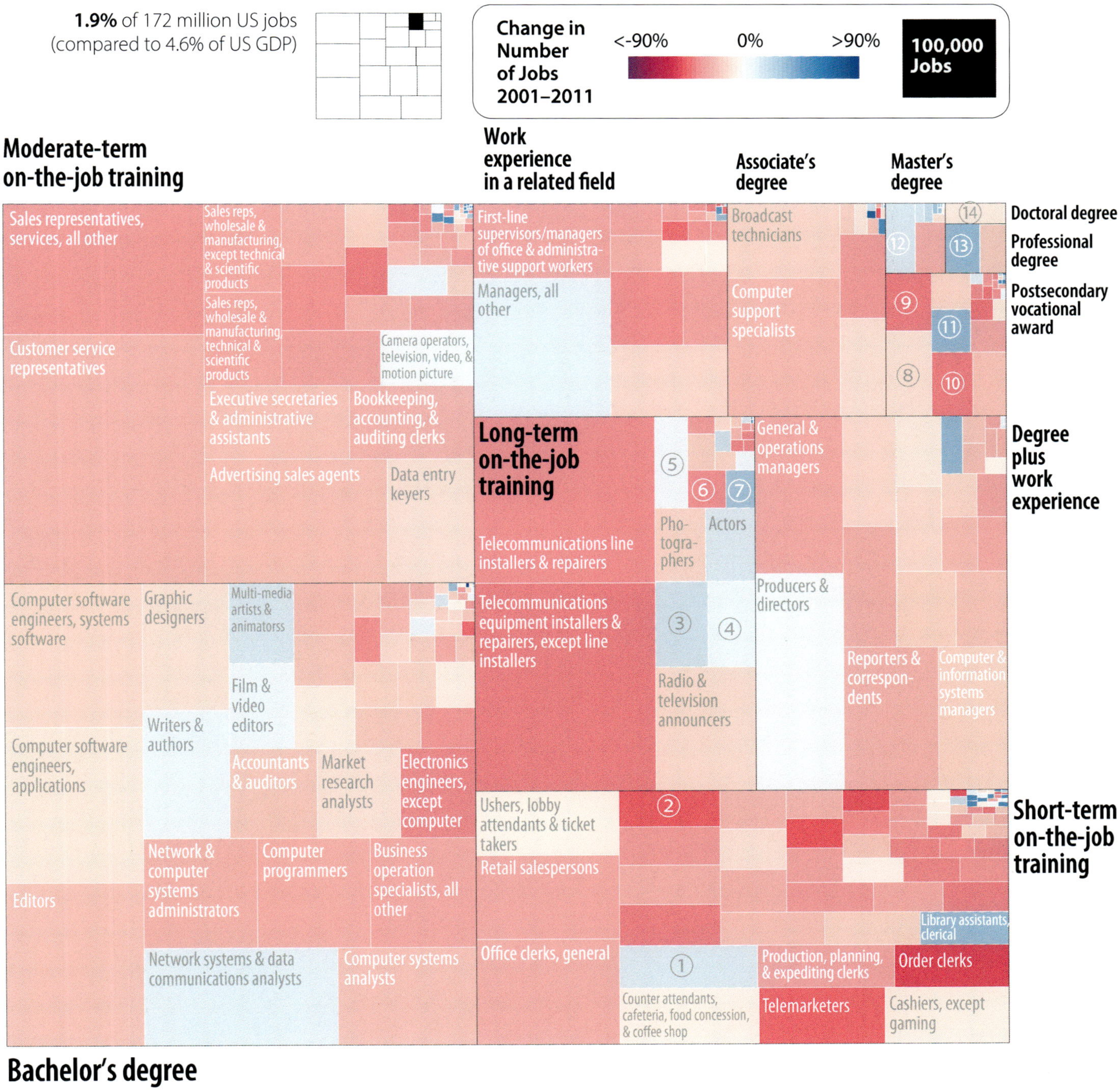

(1) Door-to-door sales workers, news & street vendors, & related workers
(2) Mail clerks & mail machine operators, except postal service
(3) Entertainers & performers, sports & related workers, all other
(4) Audio & video equipment technicians
(5) Media & communication workers, all other
(6) Job printers
(7) Musicians & singers
(8) Sound engineering technicians
(9) Desktop publishers
(10) Prepress technicians & workers
(11) Library technicians
(12) Librarians
(13) Physicians & surgeons
(14) Computer & information scientists, research

Source: EMSI EconomicModeling.com (Compiled from data collected by BLS, BEA and US Census Bureau)

2011

Government Occupations: Income

13.7% of 172 million US jobs (compared to 13.4% of US GDP)

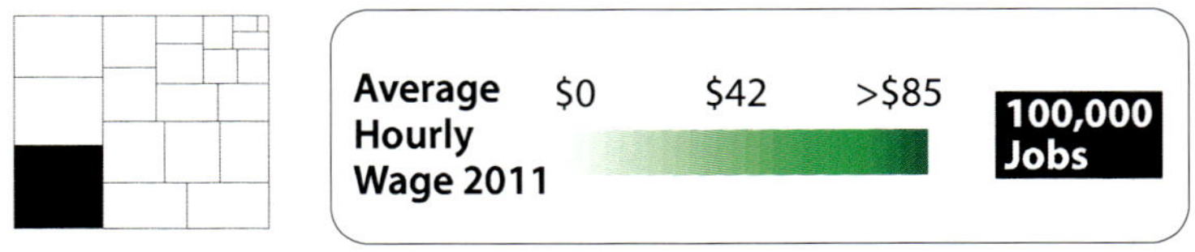

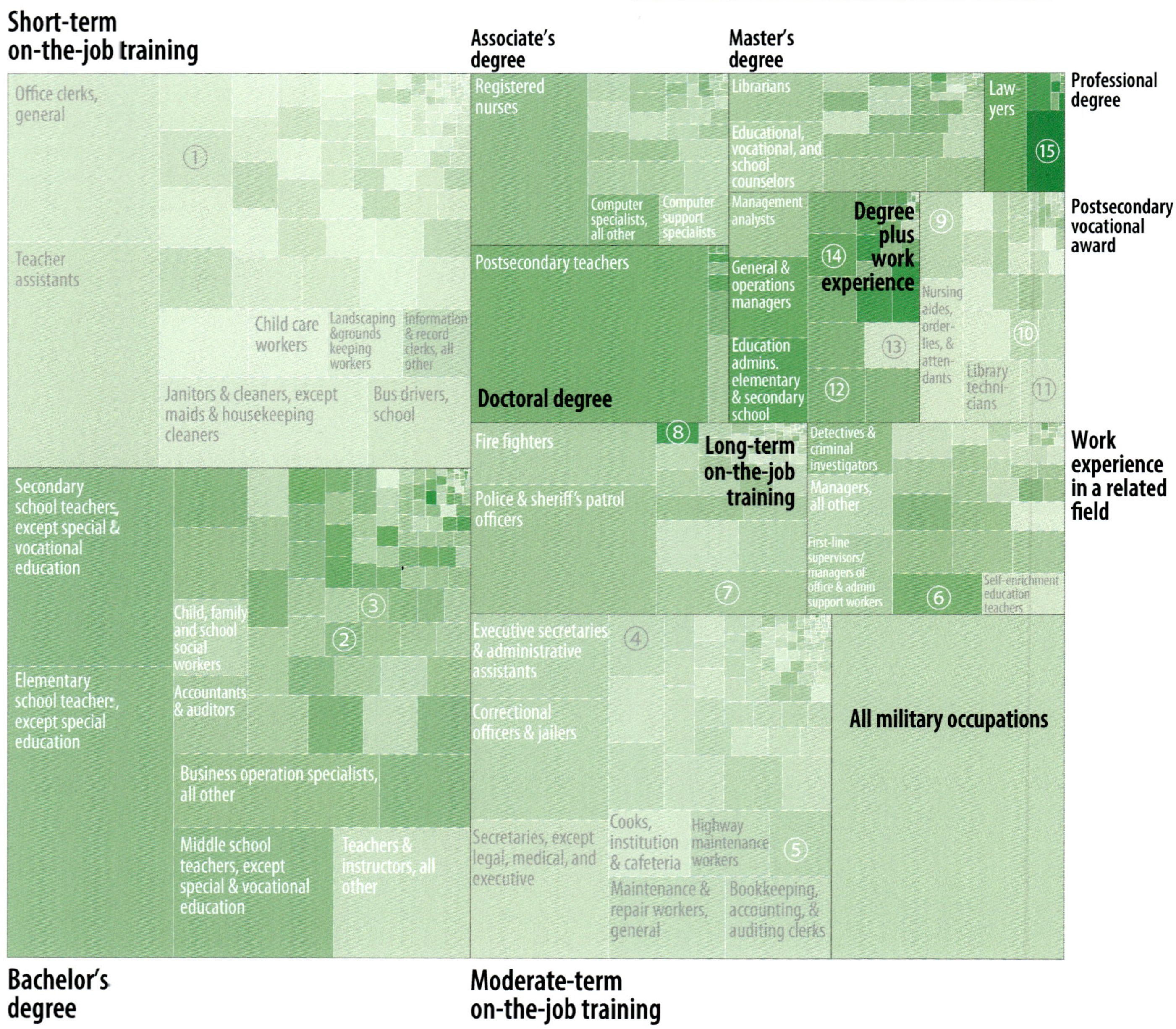

(1) Office & administrative support workers, all other (2) Computer programmers (3) Network systems & data communications analysts (4) Police, fire, and ambulance dispatchers (5) Eligibility interviewers, government programs (6) First-line supervisors/managers of police & detectives (7) Compliance officers, except agriculture, construction, health & safety, & transportation

(8) Air traffic controllers (9) Licensed practical & licensed vocational nurses (10) Bus & truck mechanics & diesel engine specialists (11) Emergency medical technicians & paramedics (12) Education administrators, postsecondary (13) Legislators (14) Judges, magistrate judges, & magistrates (15) Physicians & surgeons

 Source: EMSI EconomicModeling.com (Compiled from data collected by BLS, BEA and US Census Bureau)

2001–2011

Government Occupations: Job Growth

13.7% of 172 million US jobs (compared to 13.4% of US GDP)

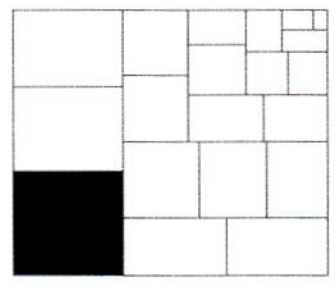

Change in Number of Jobs 2001–2011 <-90% 0% >90% **100,000 Jobs**

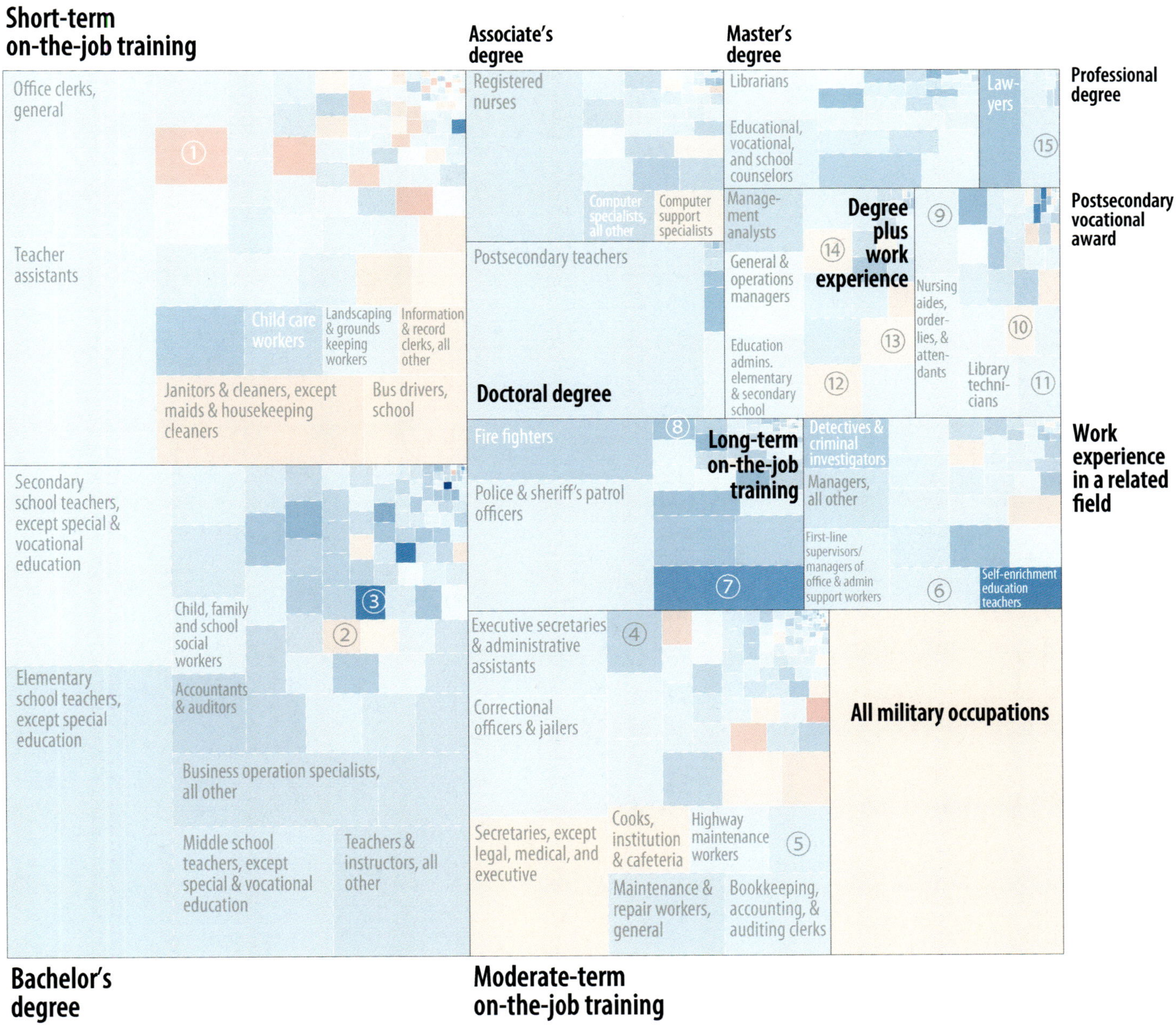

① Office & administrative support workers, all other ② Computer programmers ③ Network systems & data communications analysts ④ Police, fire, and ambulance dispatchers ⑤ Eligibility interviewers, government programs ⑥ First-line supervisors/managers of police & detectives ⑦ Compliance officers, except agriculture, construction, health & safety, & transportation ⑧ Air traffic controllers ⑨ Licensed practical & licensed vocational nurses ⑩ Bus & truck mechanics & diesel engine specialists ⑪ Emergency medical technicians & paramedics ⑫ Education administrators, postsecondary ⑬ Legislators ⑭ Judges, magistrate judges, & magistrates ⑮ Physicians & surgeons

Source: EMSI EconomicModeling.com (Compiled from data collected by BLS, BEA and US Census Bureau)

2011

Finance & Insurance Occupations: Income

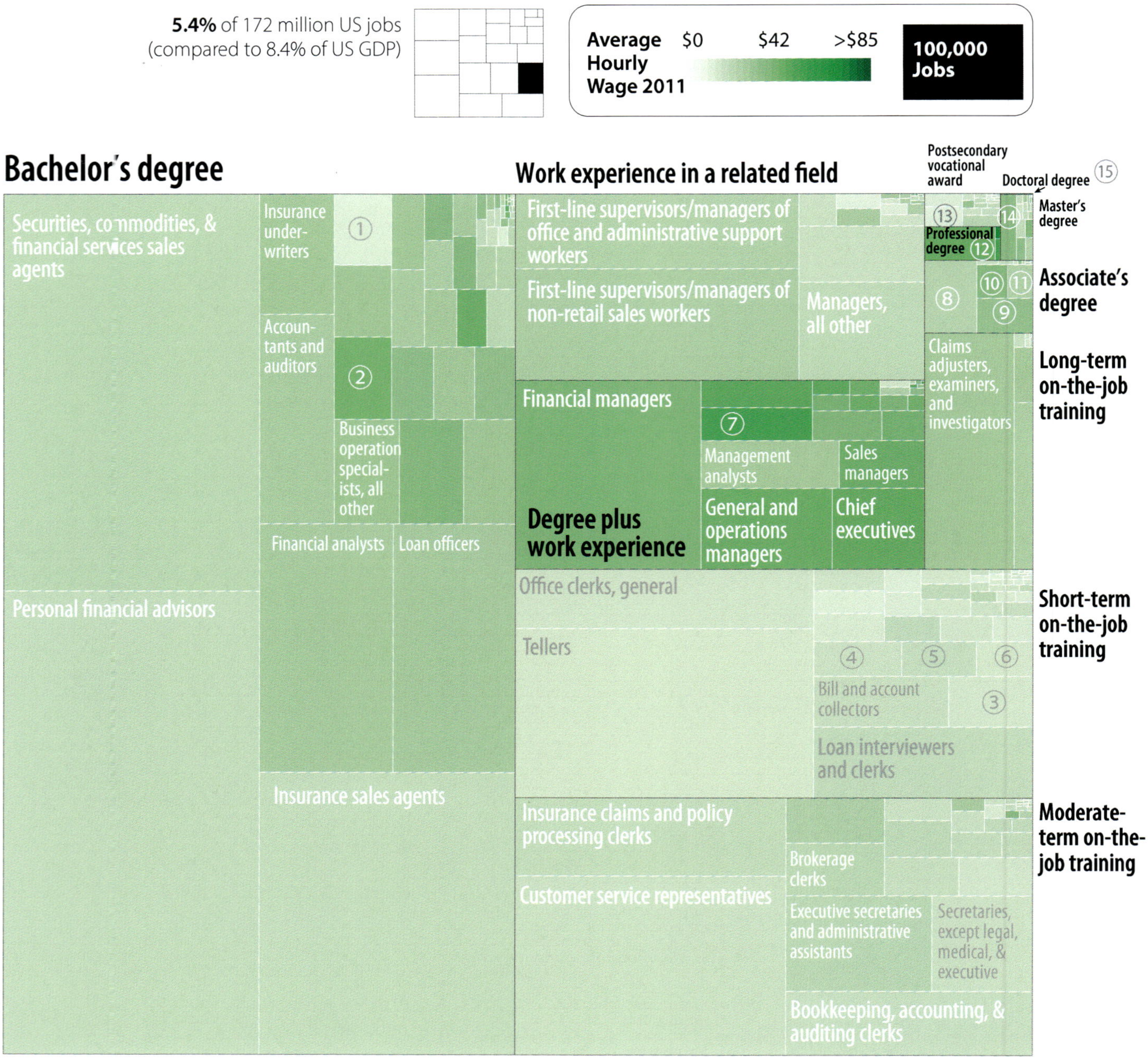

(1) Property, real estate, & community association managers
(2) Computer software engineers, applications
(3) Receptionists & information clerks
(4) Office & administrative support workers, all other
(5) Credit authorizers, checkers, & clerks
(6) File clerks
(7) Marketing managers
(8) Computer support specialists
(9) Registered nurses
(10) Computer specialists, all other
(11) Paralegals & legal assistants
(12) 3 Professional degree occupations: Lawyers, Pharmacists, Physicians and surgeons
(13) Real estate sales agents
(14) Operations research analysts
(15) 2 Doctoral degree occupations: Postsecondary teachers, Mathematicians

 Source: EMSI EconomicModeling.com (Compiled from data collected by BLS, BEA and US Census Bureau)

2001–2011

Finance & Insurance Occupations: Job Growth

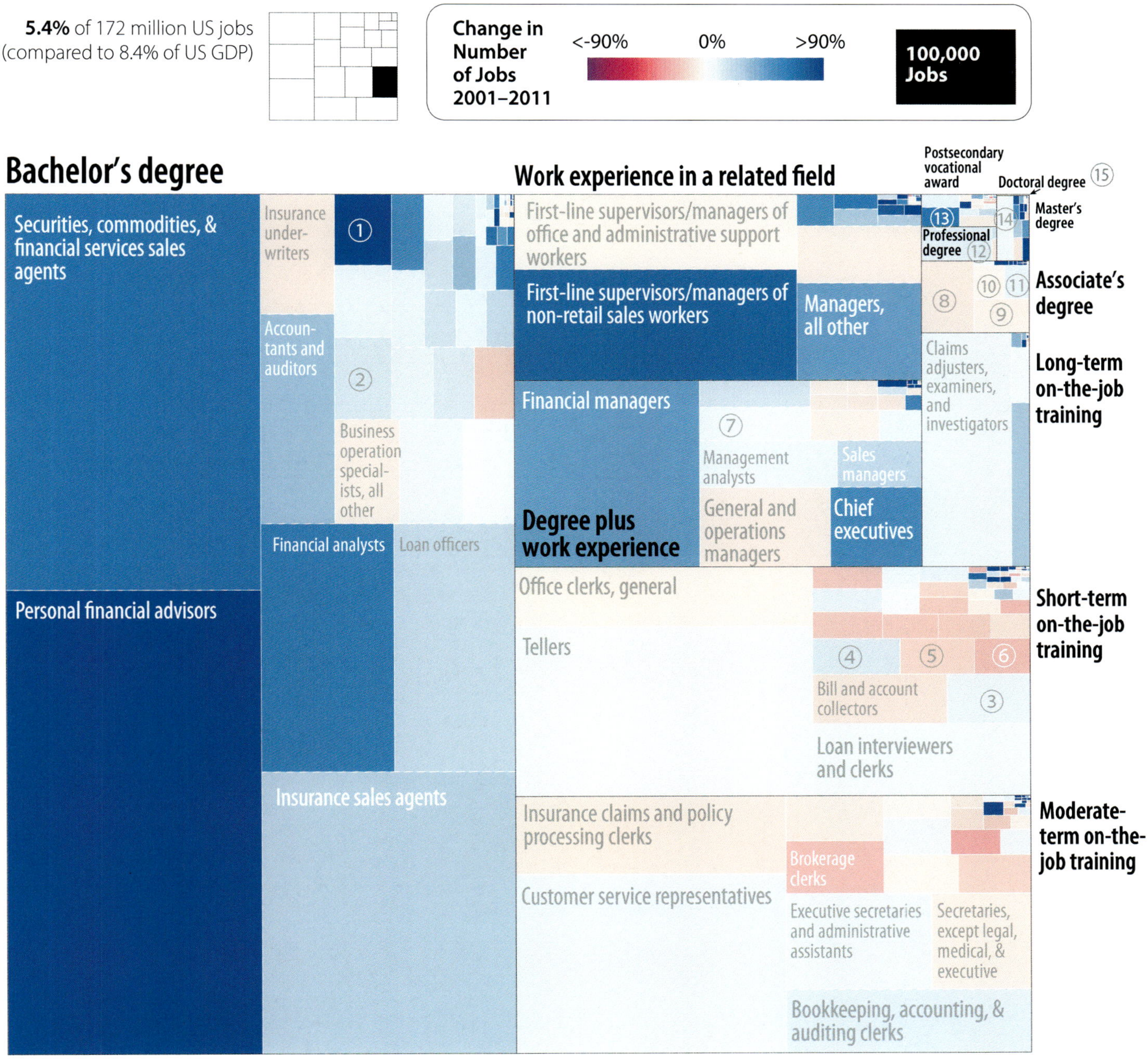

(1) Property, real estate, & community association managers (2) Computer software engineers, applications (3) Receptionists & information clerks (4) Office & administrative support workers, all other (5) Credit authorizers, checkers, & clerks (6) File clerks (7) Marketing managers (8) Computer support specialists

(9) Registered nurses (10) Computer specialists, all other (11) Paralegals & legal assistants (12) 3 Professional degree occupations Lawyers Pharmacists Physicians and surgeons (13) Real estate sales agents (14) Operations research analysts (15) 2 Doctoral degree occupations Postsecondary teachers Mathematicians

Source: EMSI EconomicModeling.com (Compiled from data collected by BLS, BEA and US Census Bureau)

2011 Accommodation & Food Occupations: Income

7.0% of 172 million US jobs (compared to 2.7% of US GDP)

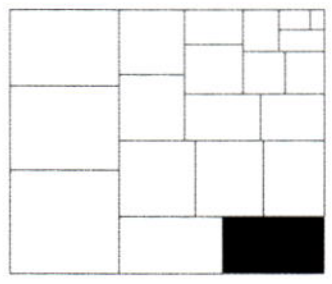

Average Hourly Wage 2011 $0 $42 >$85

100,000 Jobs

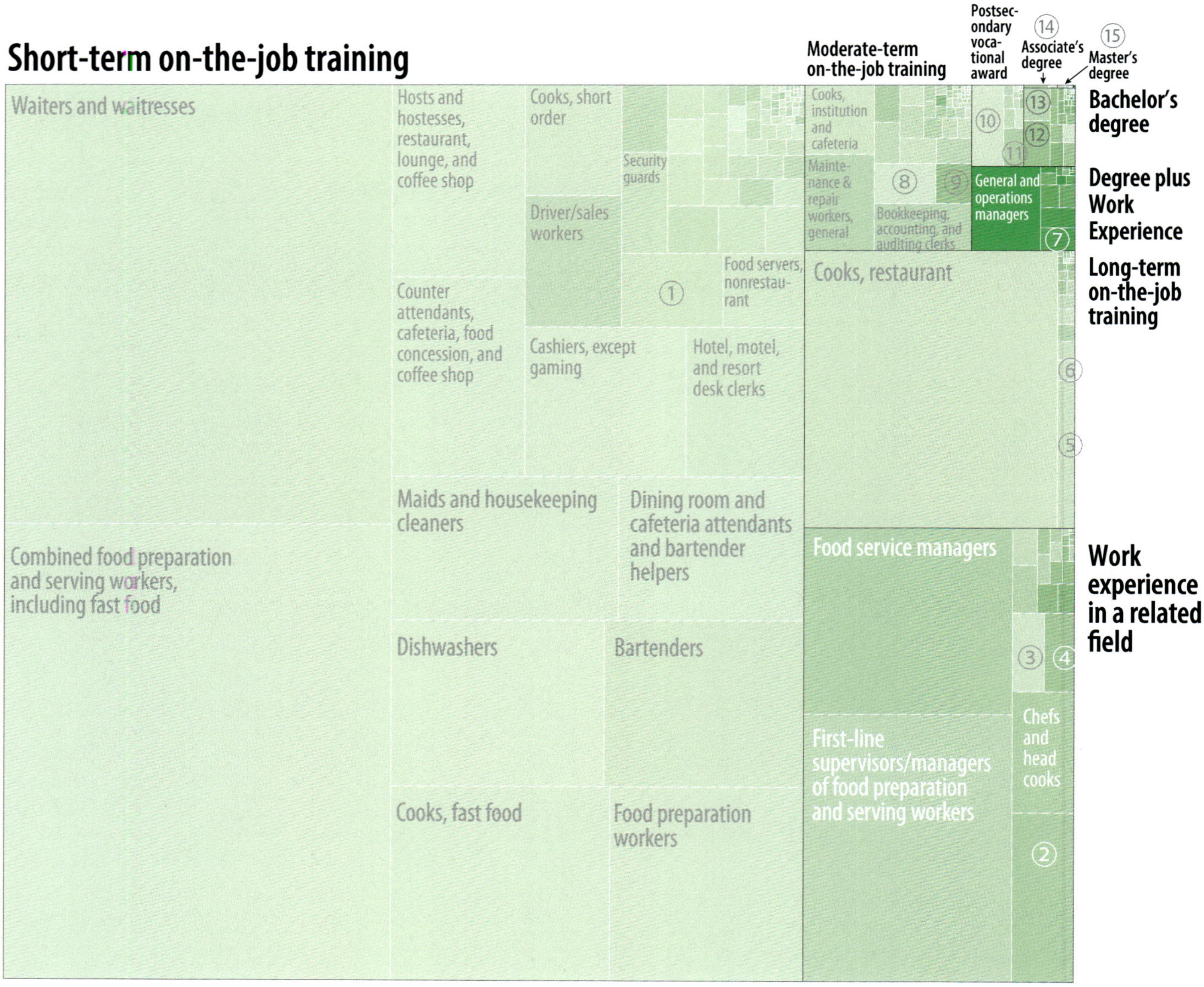

(1) Janitors and cleaners, except maids and housekeeping cleaners (2) Lodging managers (3) First-line supervisors/managers of housekeeping and janitorial workers (4) First-line supervisors/managers of office and administrative support workers (5) Bakers (6) Musicians and singers (7) Chief executives (8) Laundry and dry-cleaning workers

(9) Sales representatives, services, all other (10) Gaming dealers (11) Massage therapists (12) Accountants and auditors (13) Meeting and convention planners (14) Two largest Associate's degree Computer support specialists; Interior designers (15) Two largest Master's degree Educational, vocational, & school counselors; Rehabilitation counselors

 Source: EMSI EconomicModeling.com (Compiled from data collected by BLS, BEA and US Census Bureau)

2001–2011

Accommodation & Food Occupations: Job Growth

7.0% of 172 million U.S. jobs.
(compared to 2.7% of U.S. GDP)

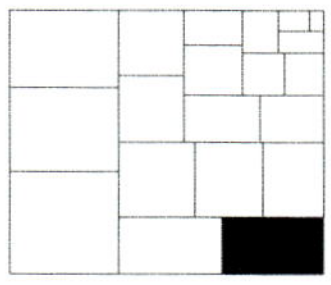

Change in Number of Jobs 2001–2011 <-90% 0% >90%

100,000 Jobs

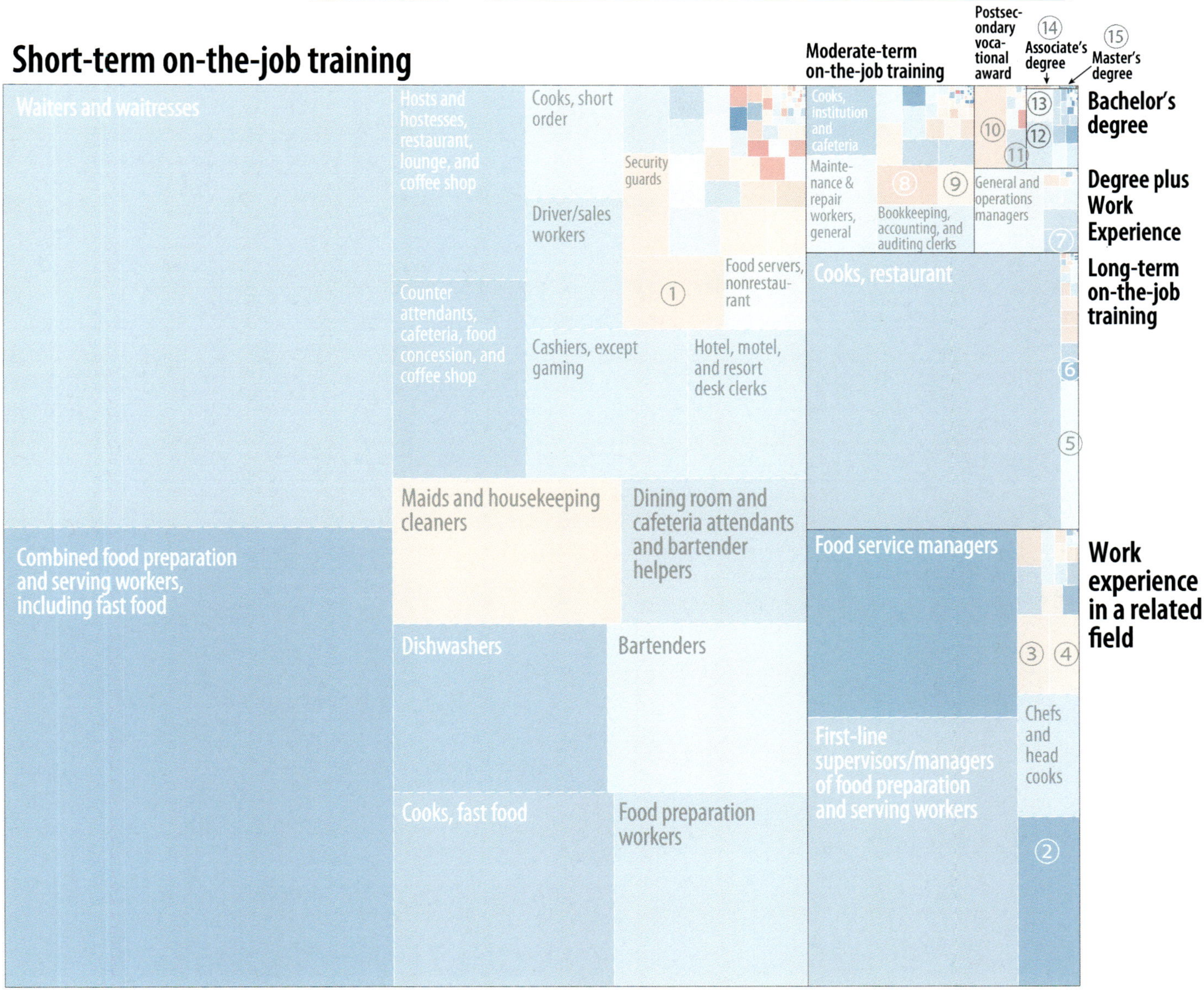

(1) Janitors and cleaners, except maids and housekeeping cleaners (2) Lodging managers (3) First-line supervisors/managers of housekeeping and janitorial workers (4) First-line supervisors/managers of office and administrative support workers (5) Bakers (6) Musicians and singers (7) Chief executives (8) Laundry and dry-cleaning workers

(9) Sales representatives, services, all other (10) Gaming dealers (11) Massage therapists (12) Accountants and auditors (13) Meeting and convention planners (14) Two largest Associate's degree Computer support specialists; Interior designers (15) Two largest Master's degree Educational, vocational, & school counselors; Rehabilitation counselors

Source: EMSI EconomicModeling.com (Compiled from data collected by BLS, BEA and US Census Bureau)

2011

Manufacturing Occupations: Income

7.1% of 172 million US jobs
(compared to 11.7% of US GDP)

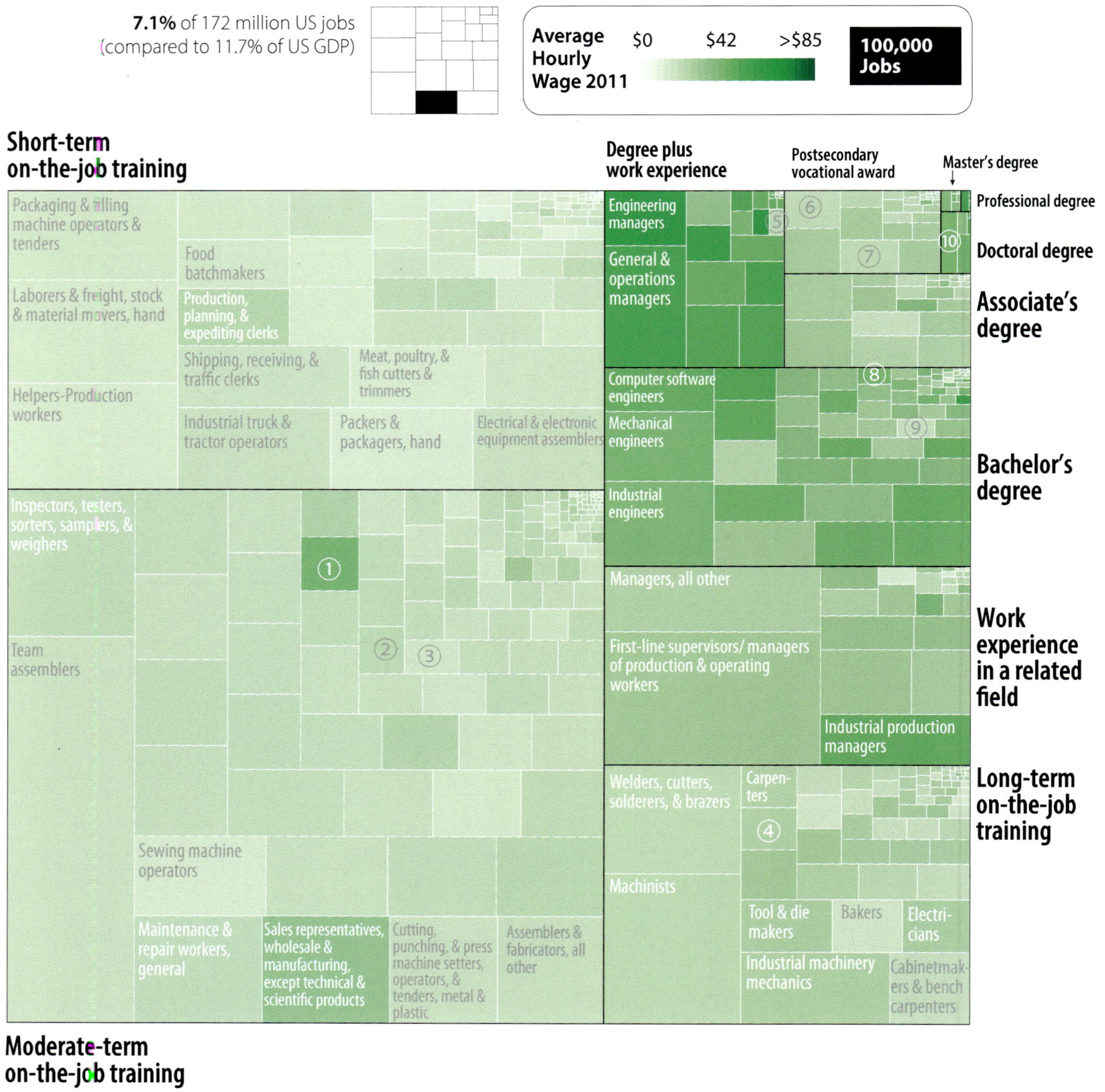

(1) Sales representatives, wholesale & manufacturing, technical & scientific products

(2) Separating, filtering, clarifying, precipitating, & still machine setters, operators & tenders

(3) Textile winding, twisting, & drawing out machine setters, operators, & tenders

(4) Aircraft structure, surfaces, rigging, & systems assemblers

(5) Art directors

(6) Prepress technicians & workers

(7) Jewelers & precious stone & metal workers

(8) Multi-media artists & animators

(9) Biomedical engineers

(10) Medical scientists, except epidemiologists

 Source: EMSI EconomicModeling.com (Compiled from data collected by BLS, BEA and US Census Bureau)

2001–2011

Manufacturing Occupations: Job Growth

7.1% of 172 million US jobs
(compared to 11.7% of US GDP)

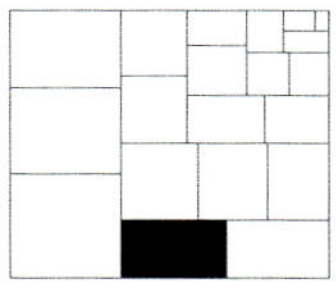

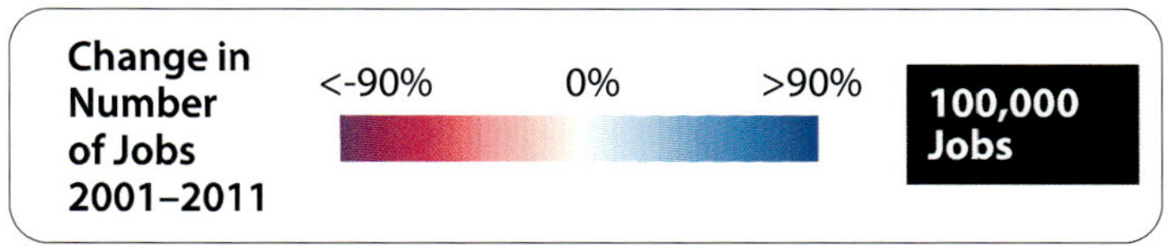

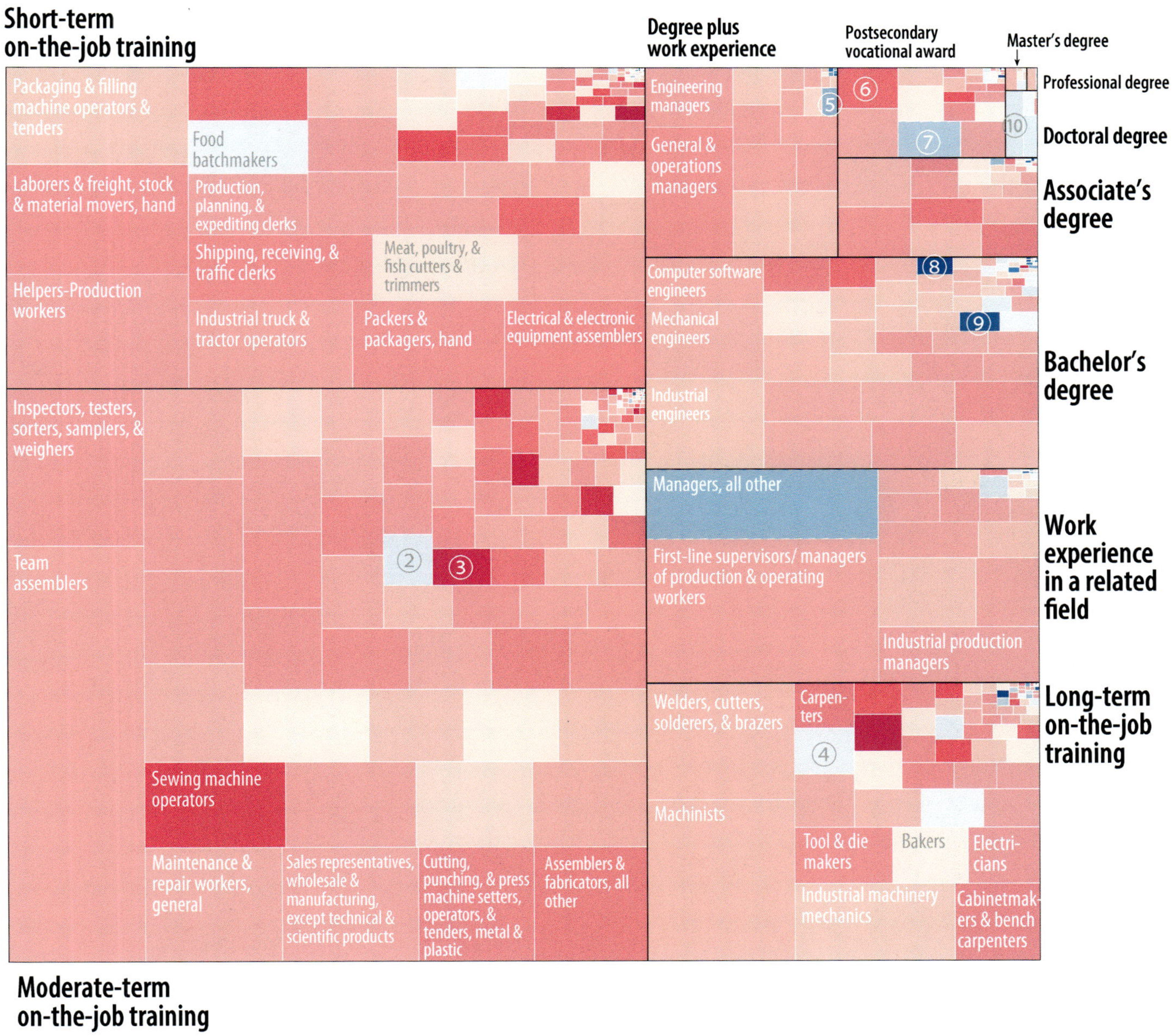

(1) Sales representatives, wholesale & manufacturing, technical & scientific products
(2) Separating, filtering, clarifying, precipitating, & still machine setters, operators & tenders
(3) Textile winding, twisting, & drawing out machine setters, operators, & tenders
(4) Aircraft structure, surfaces, rigging, & systems assemblers
(5) Art directors
(6) Prepress technicians & workers
(7) Jewelers & precious stone & metal workers
(8) Multi-media artists & animators
(9) Biomedical engineers
(10) Medical scientists, except epidemiologists

Source: EMSI EconomicModeling.com (Compiled from data collected by BLS, BEA and US Census Bureau)

2011

Professional, Scientific, & Technical Services: Income

6.9% of 172 million US jobs (compared to 7.5% of US GDP)

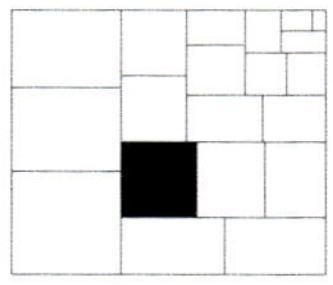

Average Hourly Wage 2011 $0 $42 >$85

100,000 Jobs

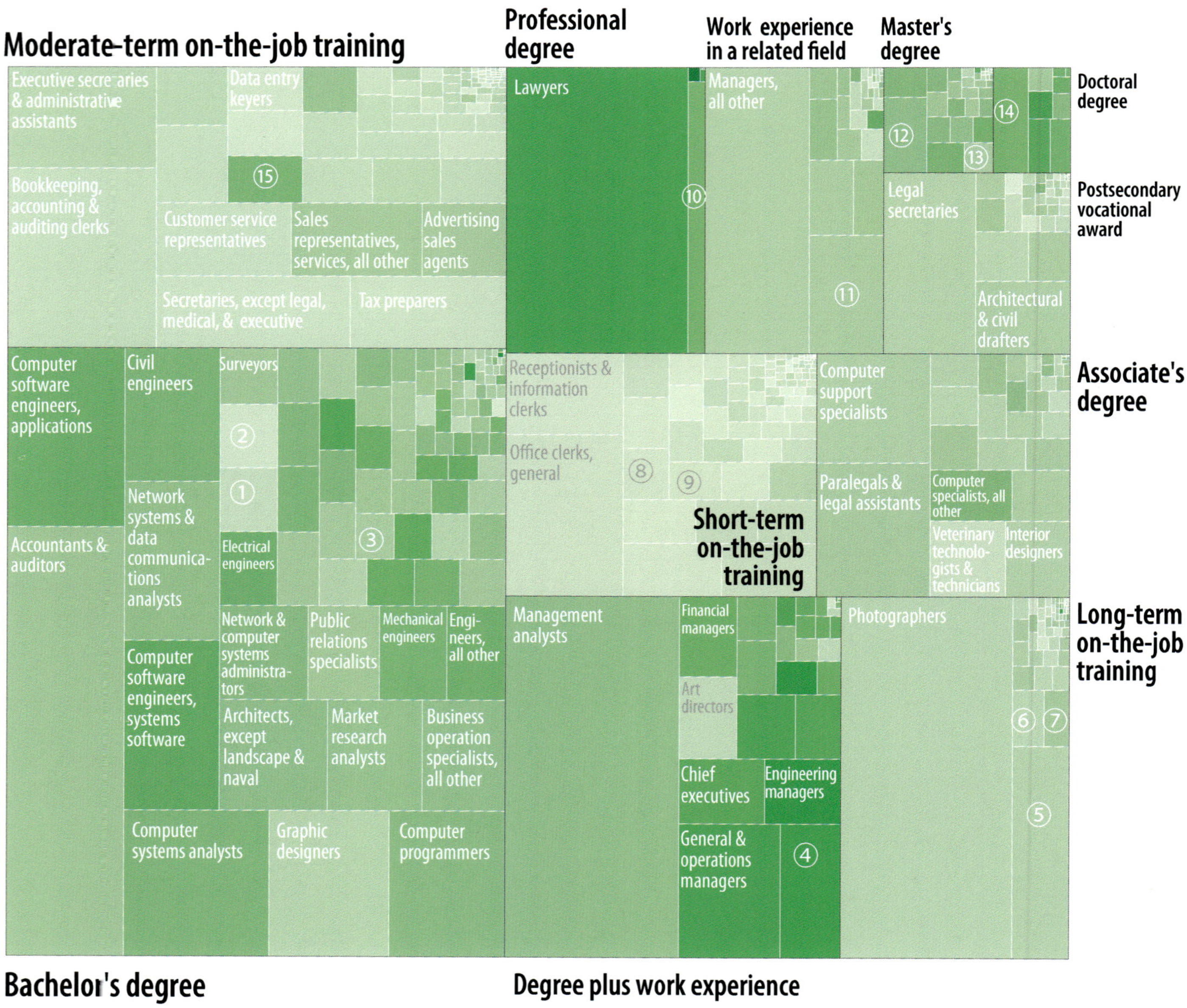

① Multi-media artists & animators
② Writers & authors
③ Personal financial advisors
④ Computer & information systems managers
⑤ Interpreters & translators
⑥ Media & communication workers, all other
⑦ Compliance officers, except agriculture, construction, health & safety, & transportation
⑧ File clerks
⑨ Mail clerks & mail machine operators, except postal service
⑩ Veterinarians
⑪ First-line supervisors/managers of office & administrative support workers
⑫ Environmental scientists & specialists, including health
⑬ Educational, vocational & school counselors
⑭ Medical scientists, except epidemiologists
⑮ Sales representatives, wholesale & manufacturing, technical & scientific products

 Source: EMSI EconomicModeling.com (Compiled from data collected by BLS, BEA and US Census Bureau)

2001–2011

Professional, Scientific, & Technical Services: Job Growth

6.9% of 172 million US jobs (compared to 7.5% of US GDP)

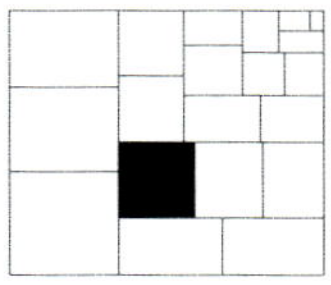

Change in Number of Jobs 2001–2011

<-90% 0% >90%

100,000 Jobs

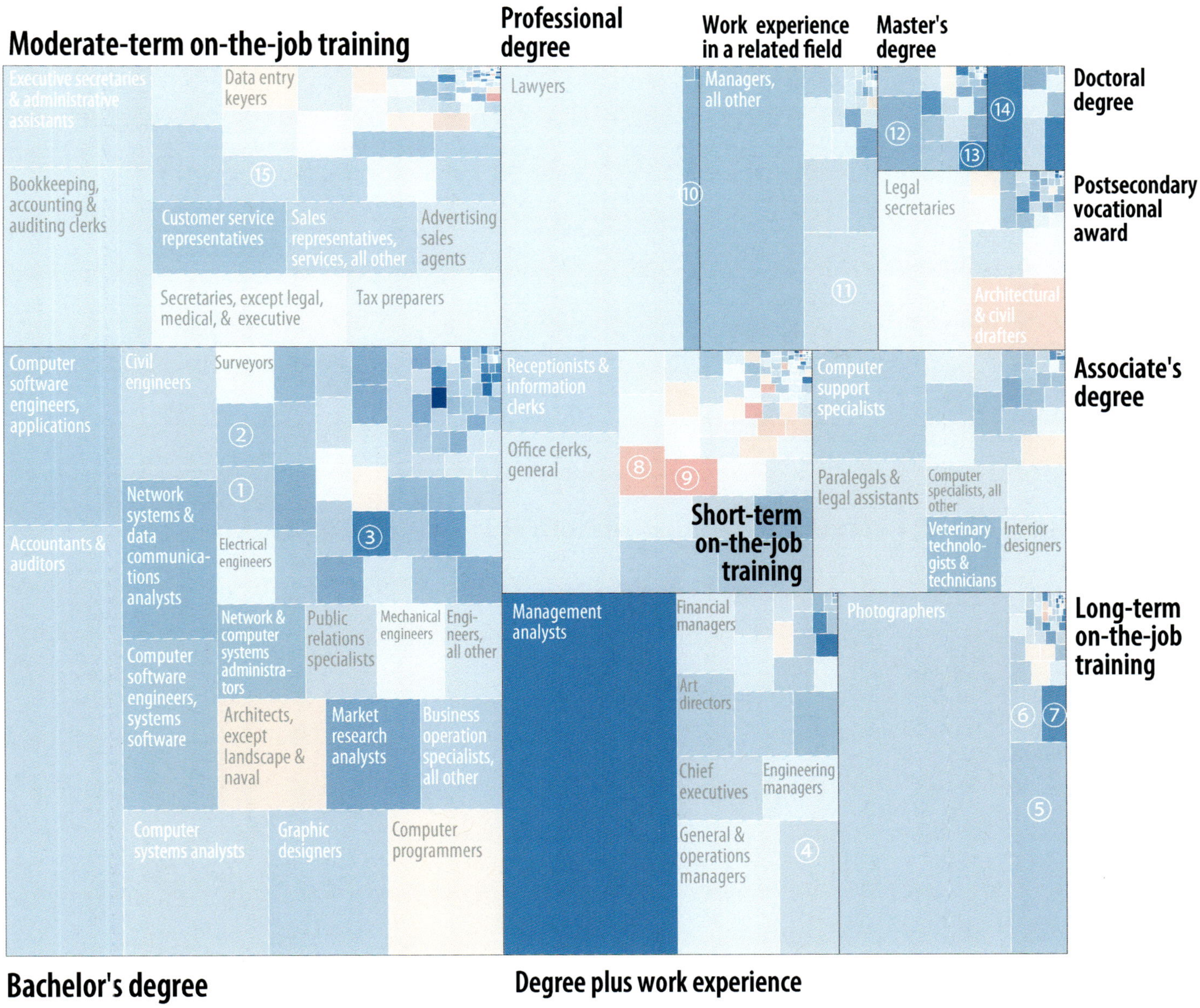

(1) Multi-media artists & animators (2) Writers & authors (3) Personal financial advisors (4) Computer & information systems managers (5) Interpreters & translators (6) Media & communication workers, all other (7) Compliance officers, except agriculture, construction, health & safety, & transportation (8) File clerks

(9) Mail clerks & mail machine operators, except postal service (10) Veterinarians (11) First-line supervisors/managers of office & administrative support workers (12) Environmental scientists & specialists, including health (13) Educational, vocational & school counselors (14) Medical scientists, except epidemiologists (15) Sales representatives, wholesale & manufacturing, technical & scientific products

Source: EMSI EconomicModeling.com (Compiled from data collected by BLS, BEA and US Census Bureau)

2001–2011

Admin Services, Waste Management, & Agriculture

Administrative, Support, Waste Management, and Remediation Services

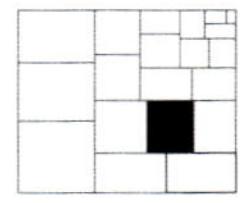

6.0% of 172 million US jobs (compared with 2.8% of US GDP)

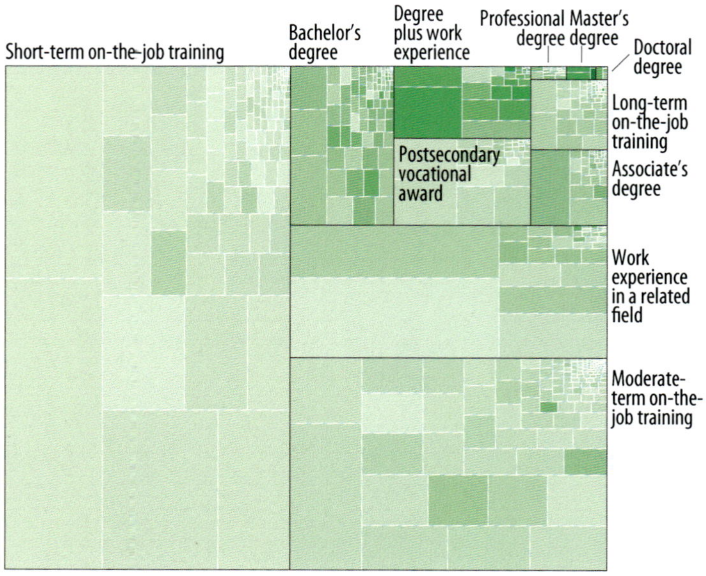

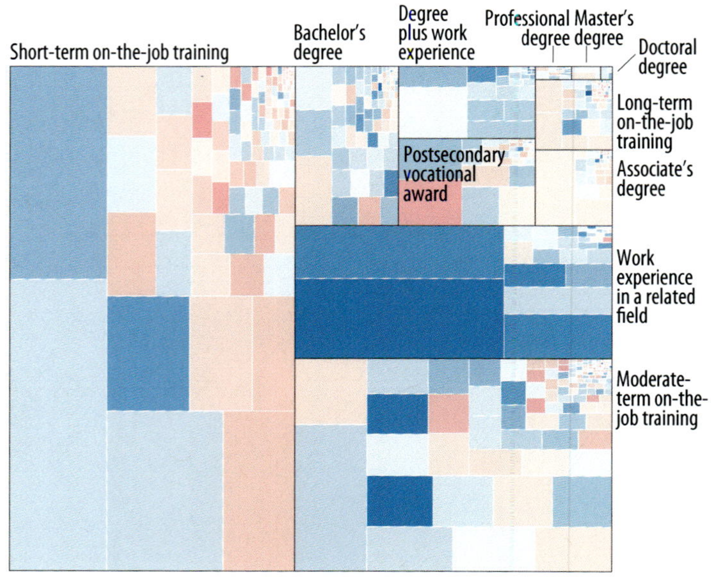

Agriculture, Forestry, Fishing, and Hunting

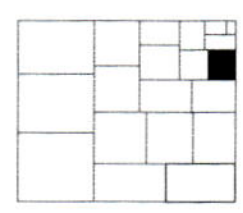

2.0% of 172 million US jobs (compared with 1.1% of US GDP)

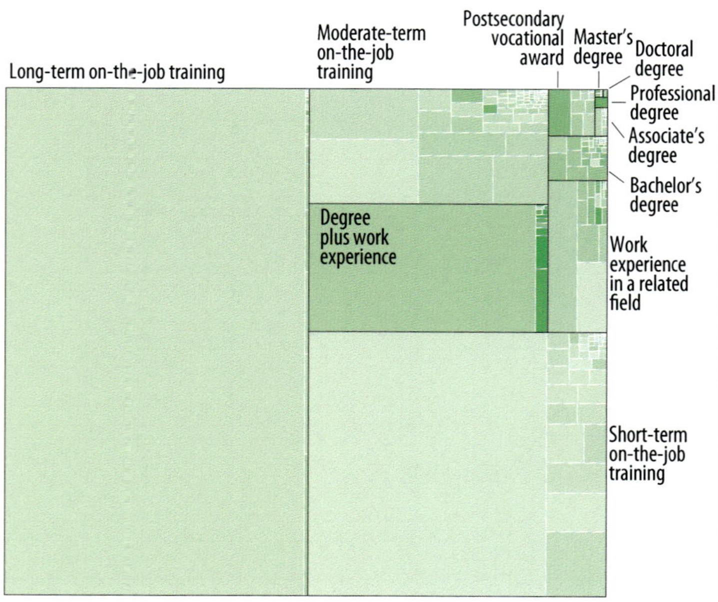

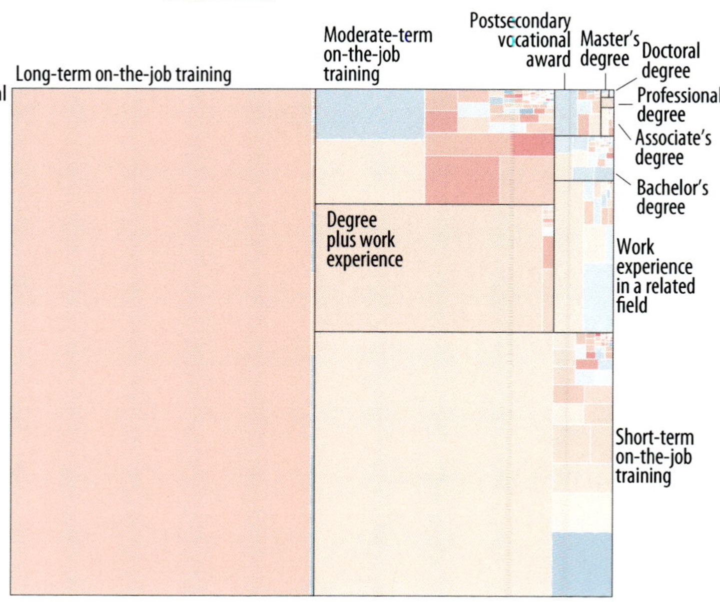

Average Hourly Wage 2011 $0 $42 >$85

Change in Number of Jobs 2001–2011 <-90% 0% >90%

 Source: EMSI EconomicModeling.com (Compiled from data collected by BLS, BEA and US Census Bureau)

2001–2011

Real Estate & Retail Trade

Real Estate and Rental and Leasing

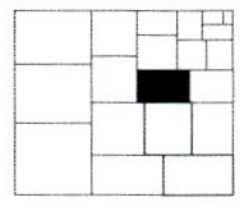

4.3% of 172 million US jobs
(compared with 12.7% of US GDP)

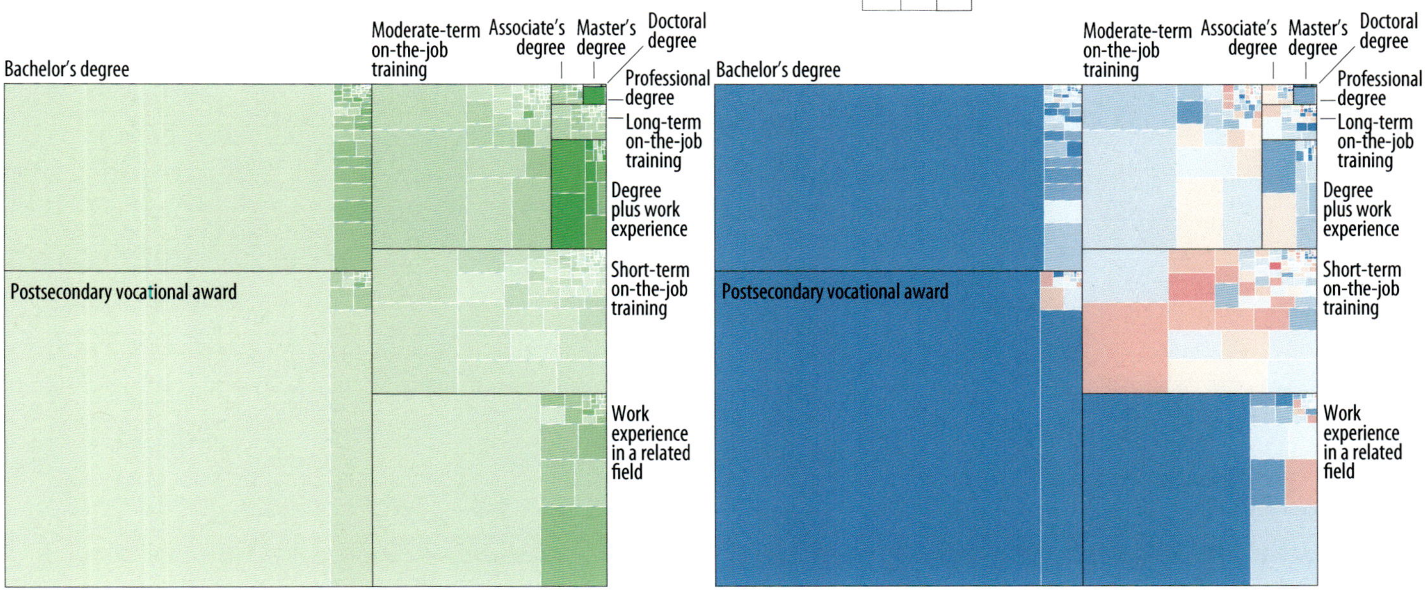

Retail Trade

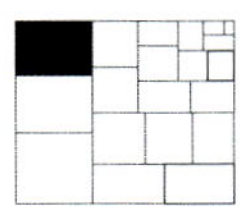

10.1% of 172 million US jobs
(compared with 5.9% of US GDP)

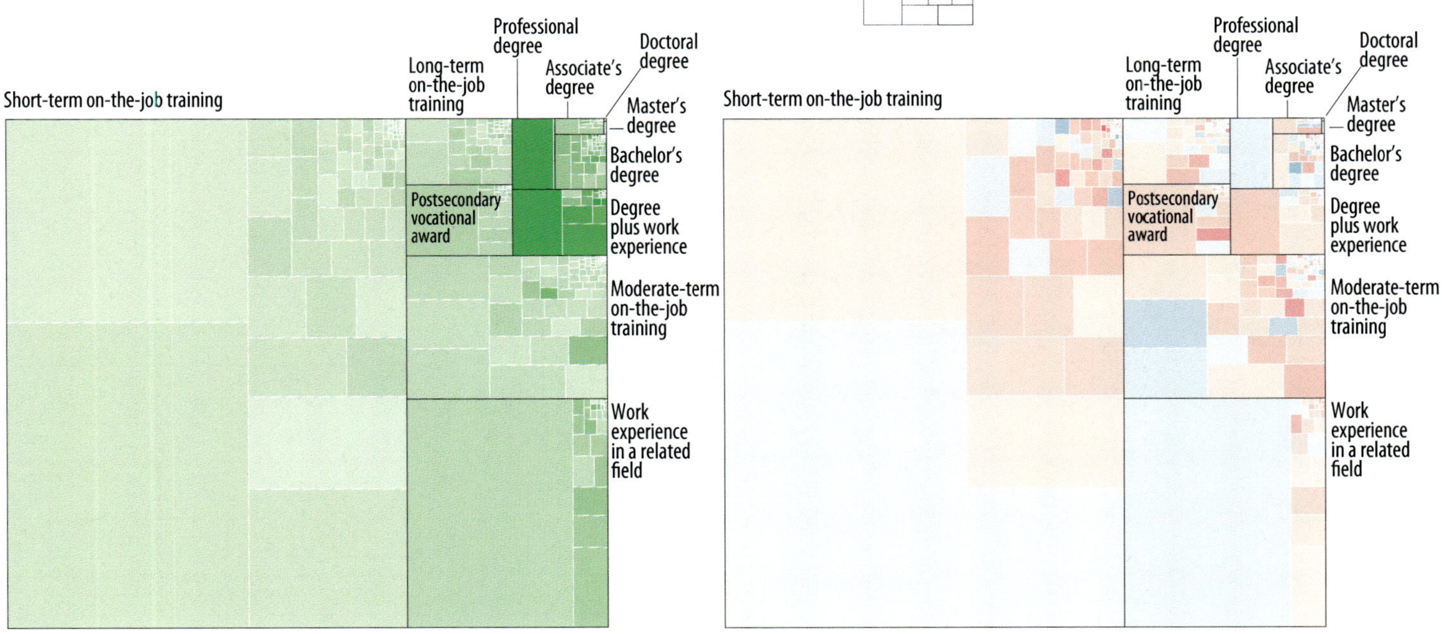

Average Hourly Wage 2011 $0 $42 >$85

Change in Number of Jobs 2001–2011 <-90% 0% >90%

2001–2011

Education & Construction

Educational Services

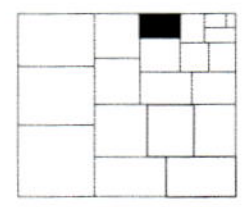

2.4% of 172 million US jobs (compared with 1.1% of US GDP)

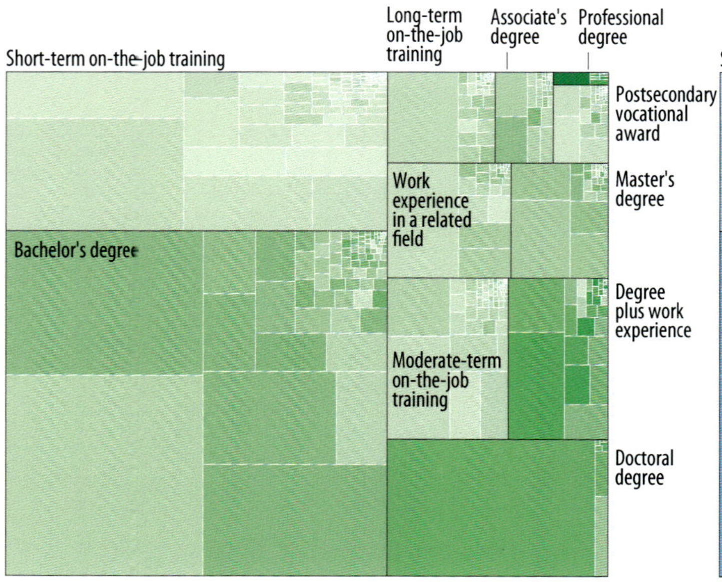

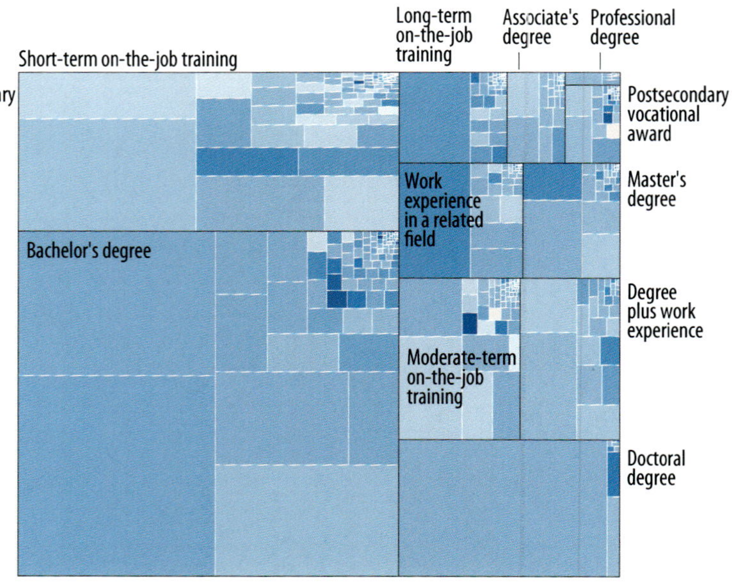

Construction

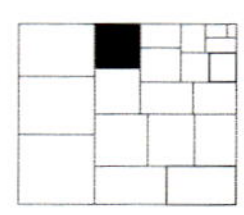

5.2% of 172 million US jobs (compared with 3.4% of US GDP)

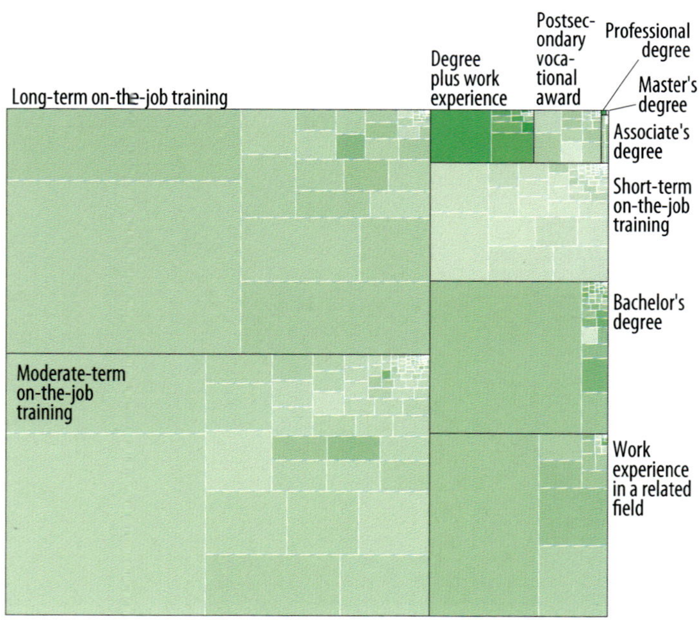

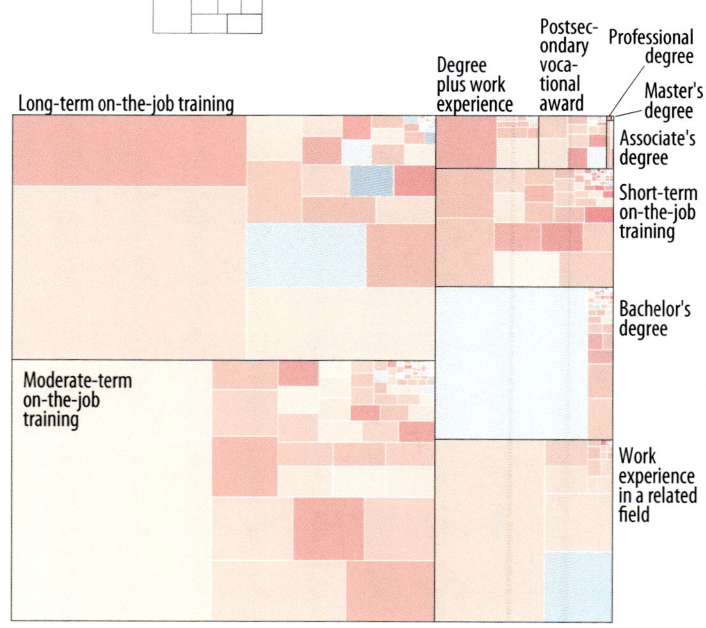

Average Hourly Wage 2011

Change in Number of Jobs 2001–2011

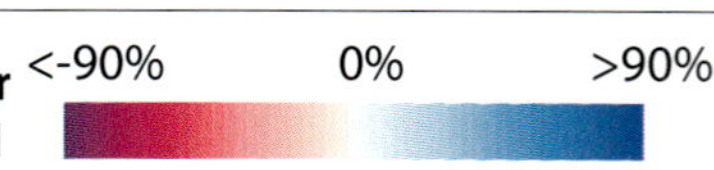

 Source: EMSI EconomicModeling.com (Compiled from data collected by BLS, BEA and US Census Bureau)

2001–2011

Mining & Utilities

Mining, Quarrying, and Oil & Gas Extraction

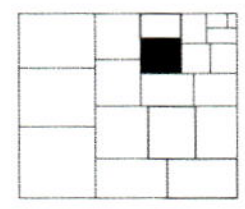

0.8% of 172 million US jobs
(compared with 1.9% of US GDP)

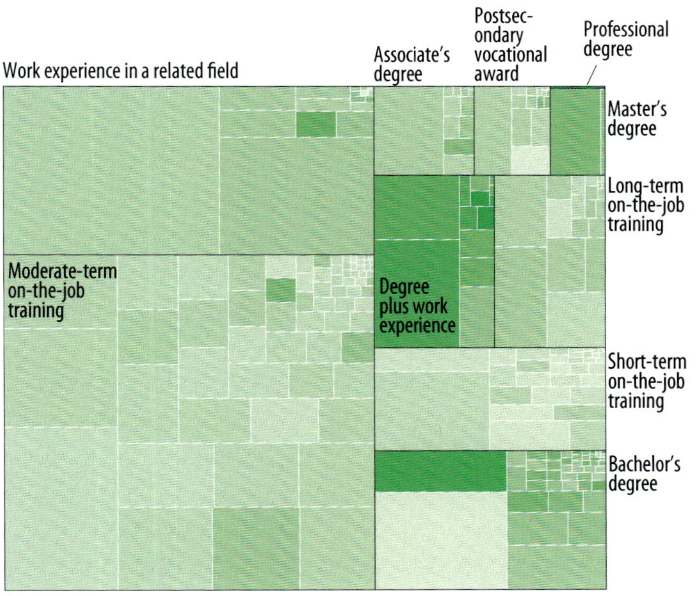

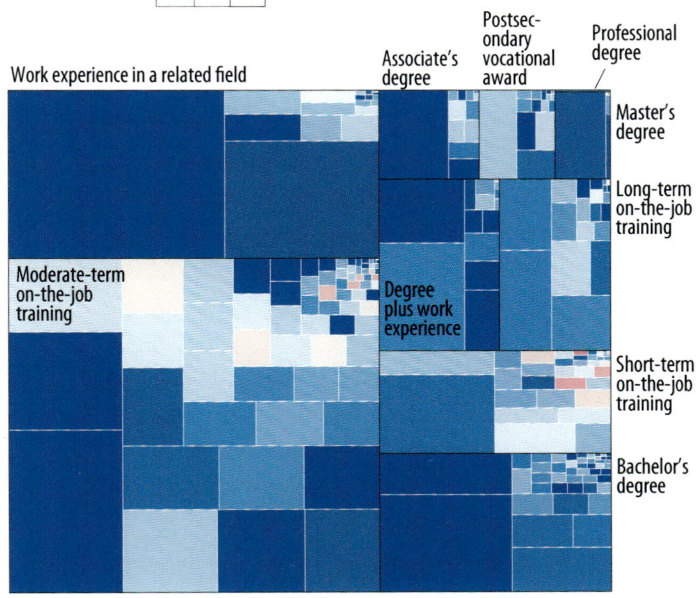

Utilities

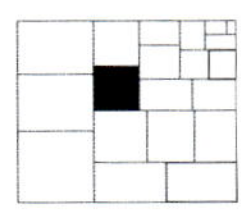

0.3% of 172 million US jobs
(compared with 1.9% of US GDP)

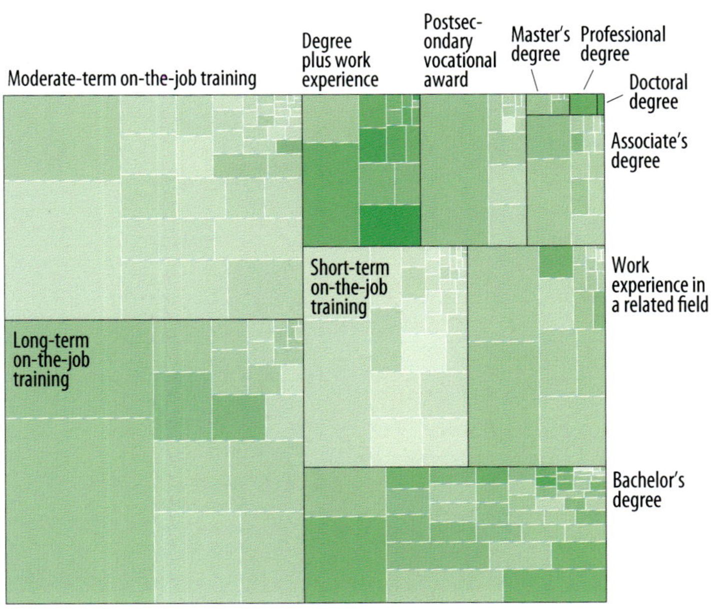

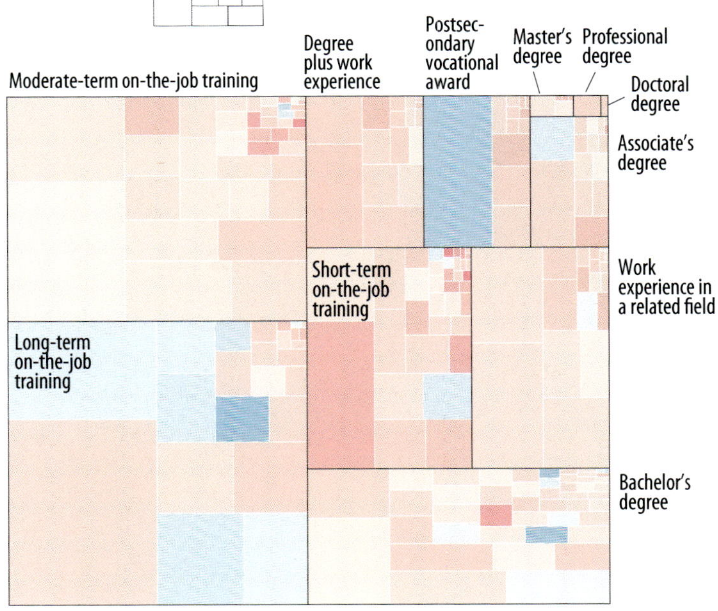

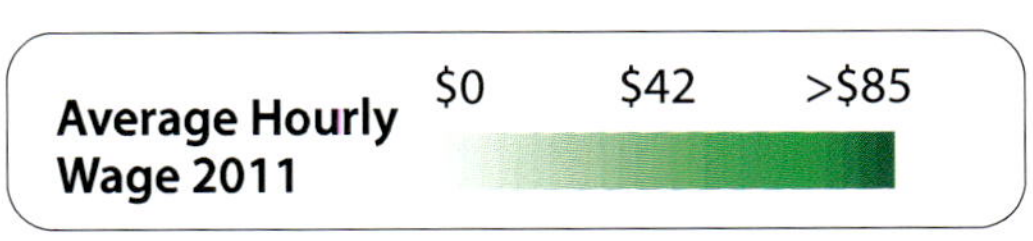

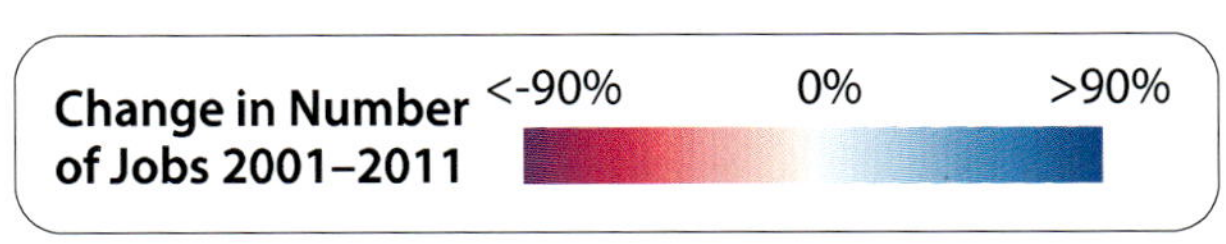

Source: EMSI EconomicModeling.com (Compiled from data collected by BLS, BEA and US Census Bureau)

2001–2011

Wholesale Trade & Transportation and Warehousing

Wholesale Trade

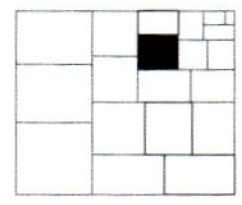

3.5% of 172 million US jobs (compared with 5.5% of US GDP)

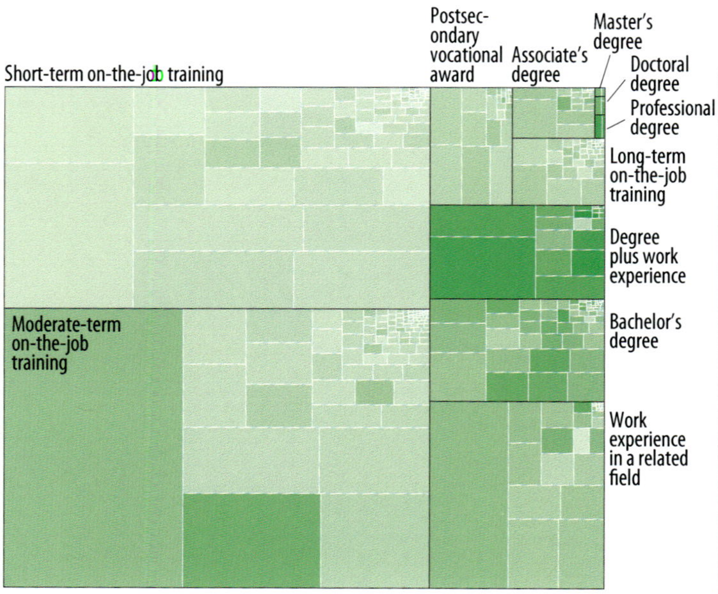

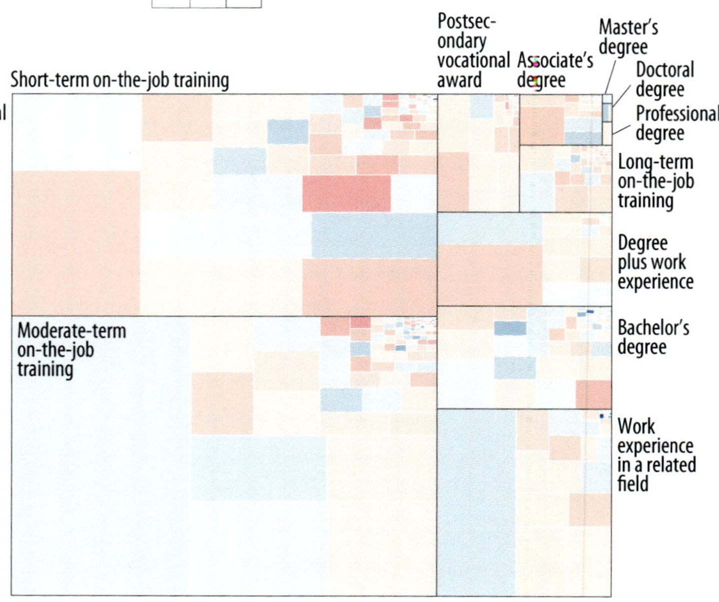

Transportation and Warehousing

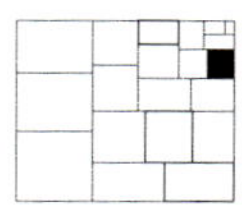

3.6% of 172 million US jobs (compared with 2.8% of US GDP)

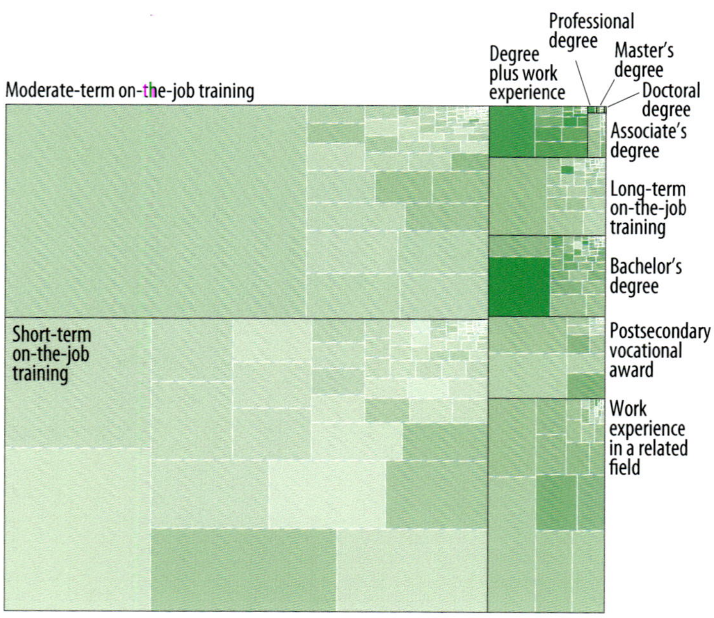

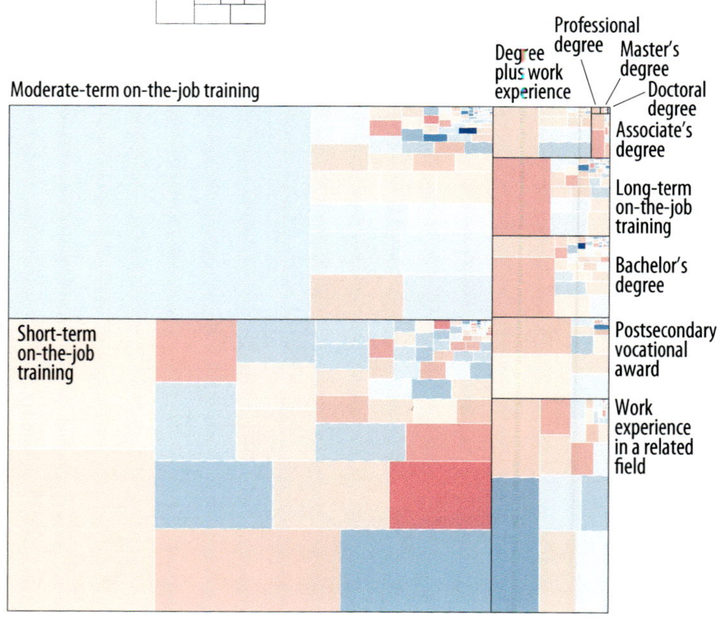

Average Hourly Wage 2011 $0 $42 >$85

Change in Number of Jobs 2001–2011 <-90% 0% >90%

 Source: EMSI EconomicModeling.com (Compiled from data collected by BLS, BEA and US Census Bureau)

2001–2011

Arts, Entertainment, and Recreation & Other Services

Arts, Entertainment, and Recreation

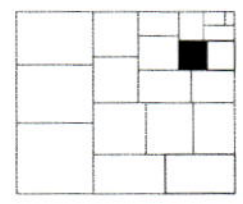

2.2% of 172 million US jobs (compared with 0.9% of US GDP)

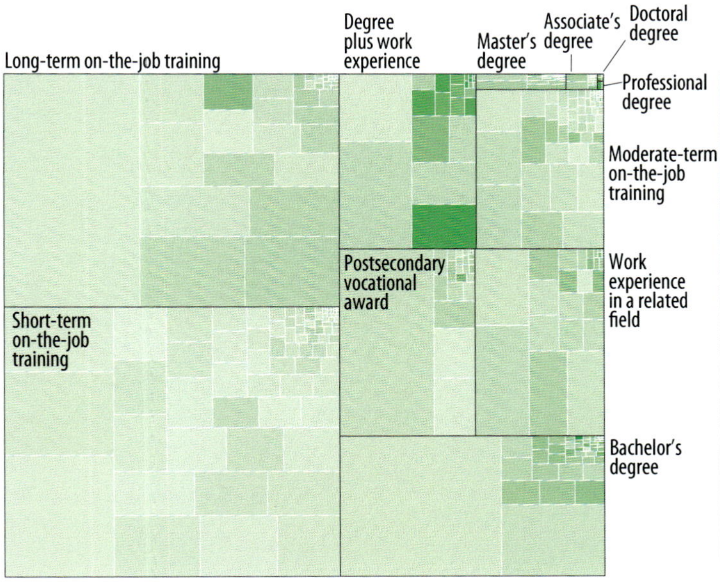

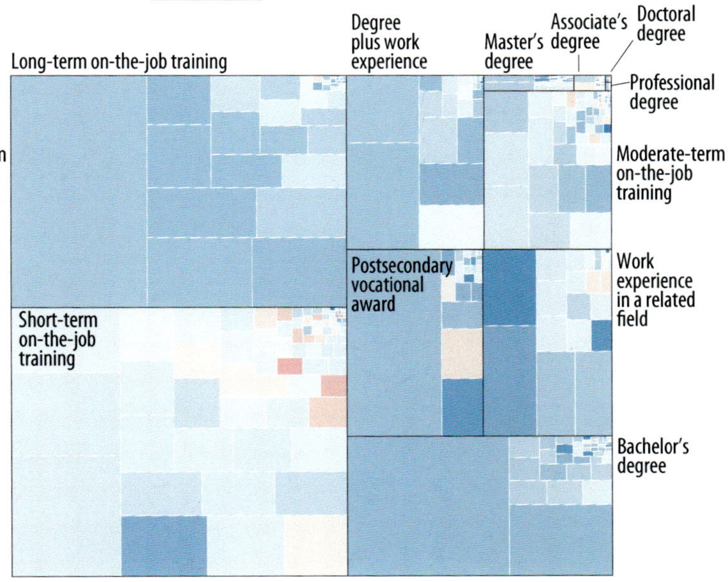

Other Services

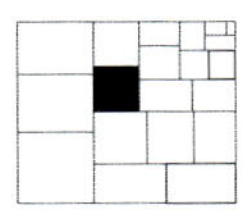

5.2% of 172 million US jobs (compared with 2.3% of US GDP)

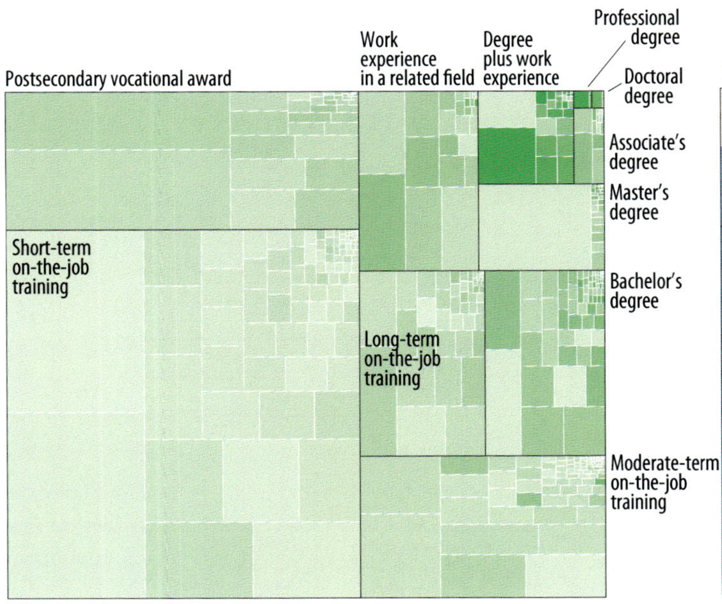

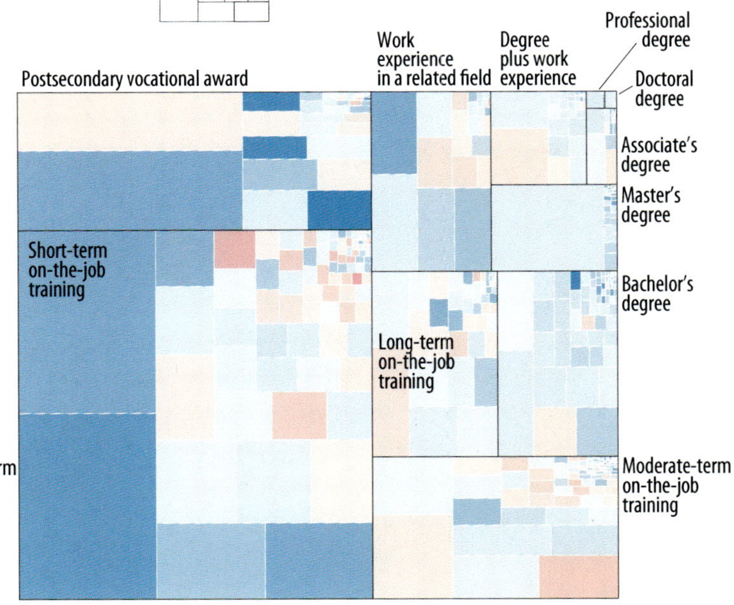

Average Hourly Wage 2011 $0 $42 >$85

Change in Number of Jobs 2001–2011 <-90% 0% >90%

Source: EMSI EconomicModeling.com (Compiled from data collected by BLS, BEA and US Census Bureau)

2001–2011

Management of Companies

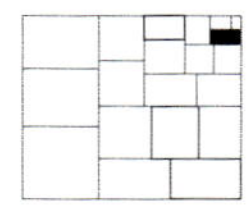

1.1% of 172 million US jobs
(compared with 1.7% of US GDP)

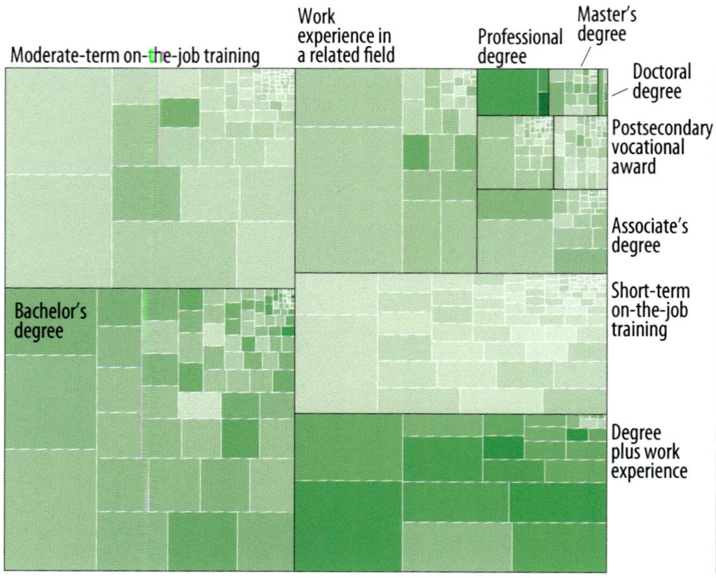

Average Hourly Wage 2011 $0 $42 >$85

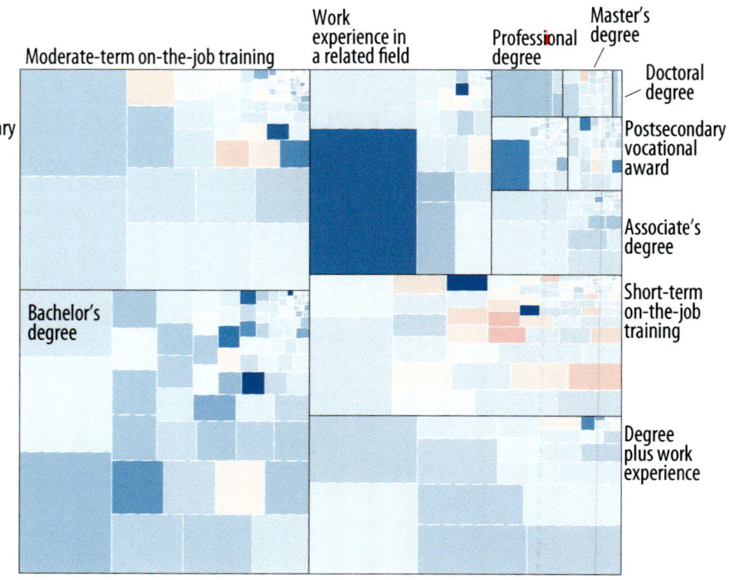

Change in Number of Jobs 2001–2011 <-90% 0% >90%

 Source: EMSI EconomicModeling.com (Compiled from data collected by BLS, BEA and US Census Bureau)

STANDARD OF LIVING

As incomes have grown dramatically over the last 100 years, patterns of family spending have changed. Food and clothing are relatively less expensive, while more money is spent on bigger and better housing. Although the poverty rate dropped to 12.6% by 1970, it has not changed significantly in the last 40 years.

1901–2002

Family Spending in the 20th Century

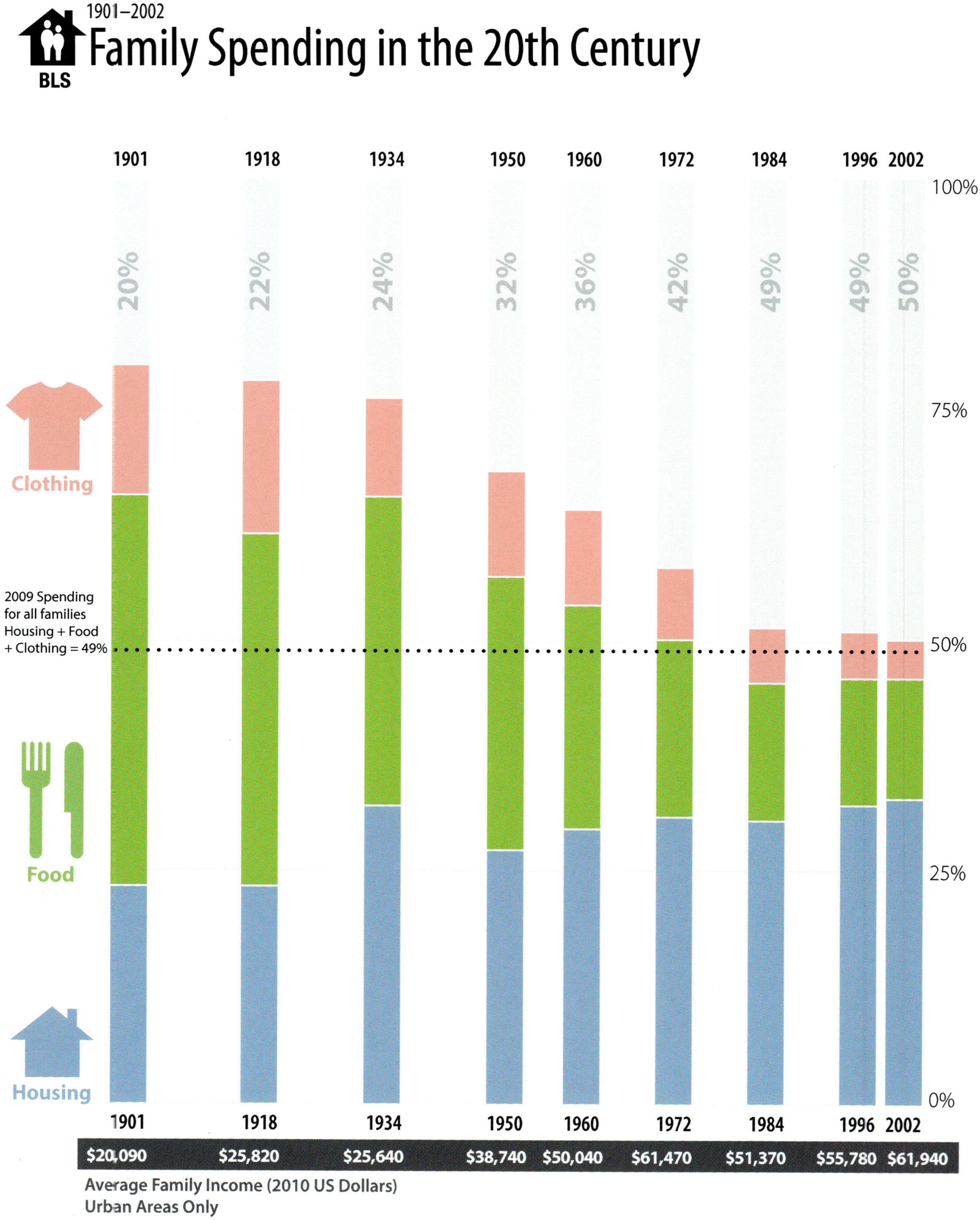

 Sources: US Bureau of Labor Statistics, "100 Years of US Consumer Spending: Data for the Nation, New York City, and Boston," Report no. 991

2009

Family Spending by Income Groups

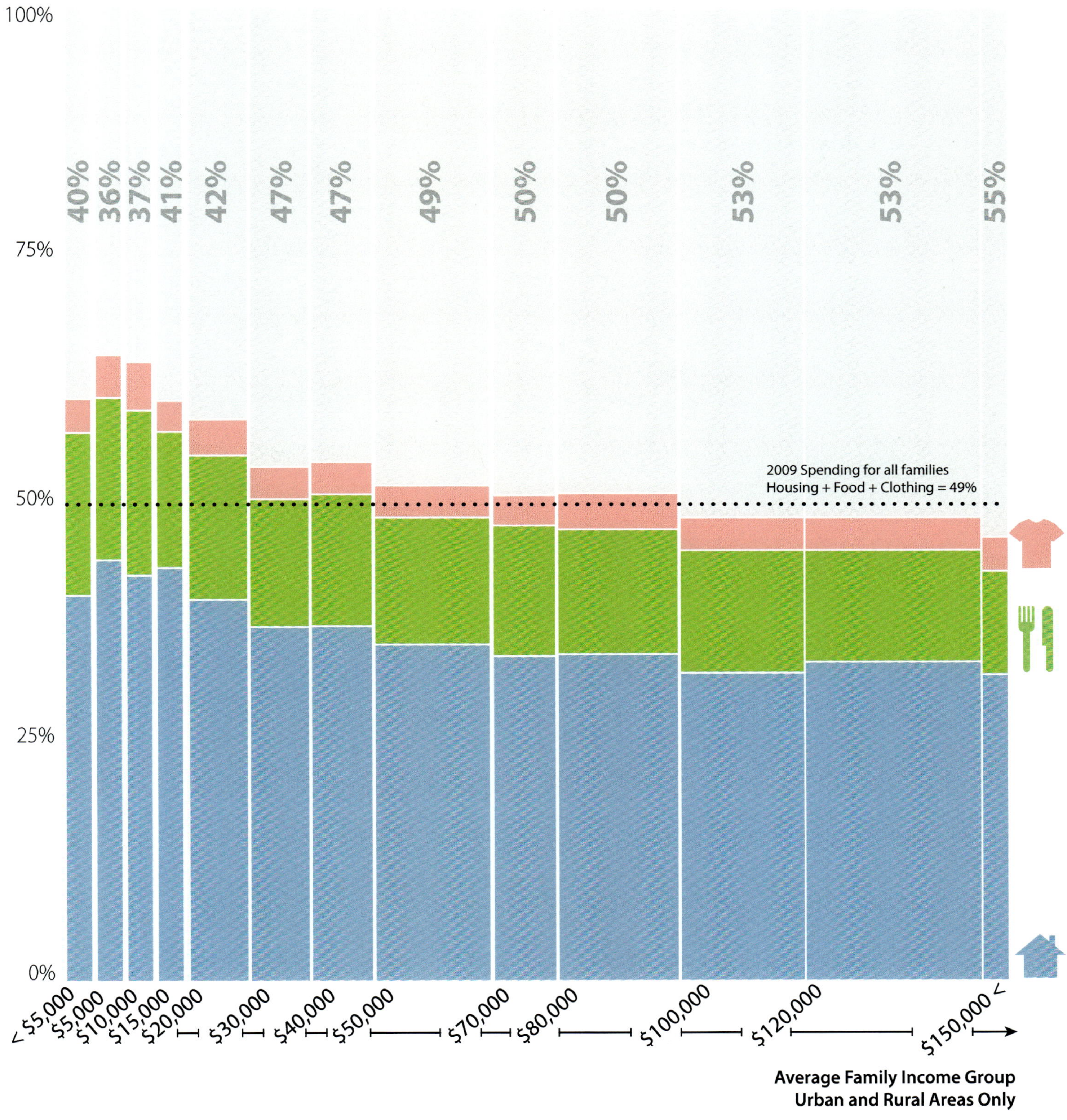

Source: US Bureau of Labor Statistics

1901–2002

Cost of Housing in the 20th Century

BLS

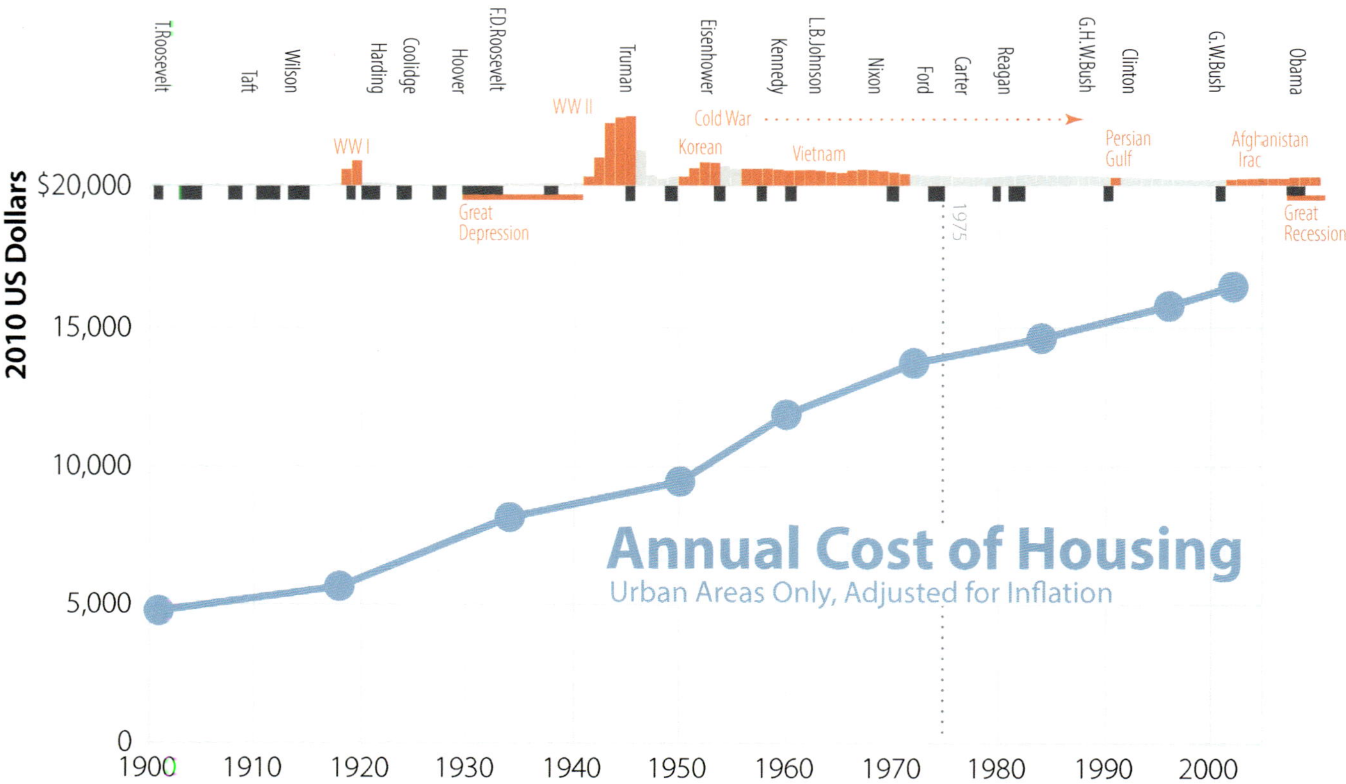

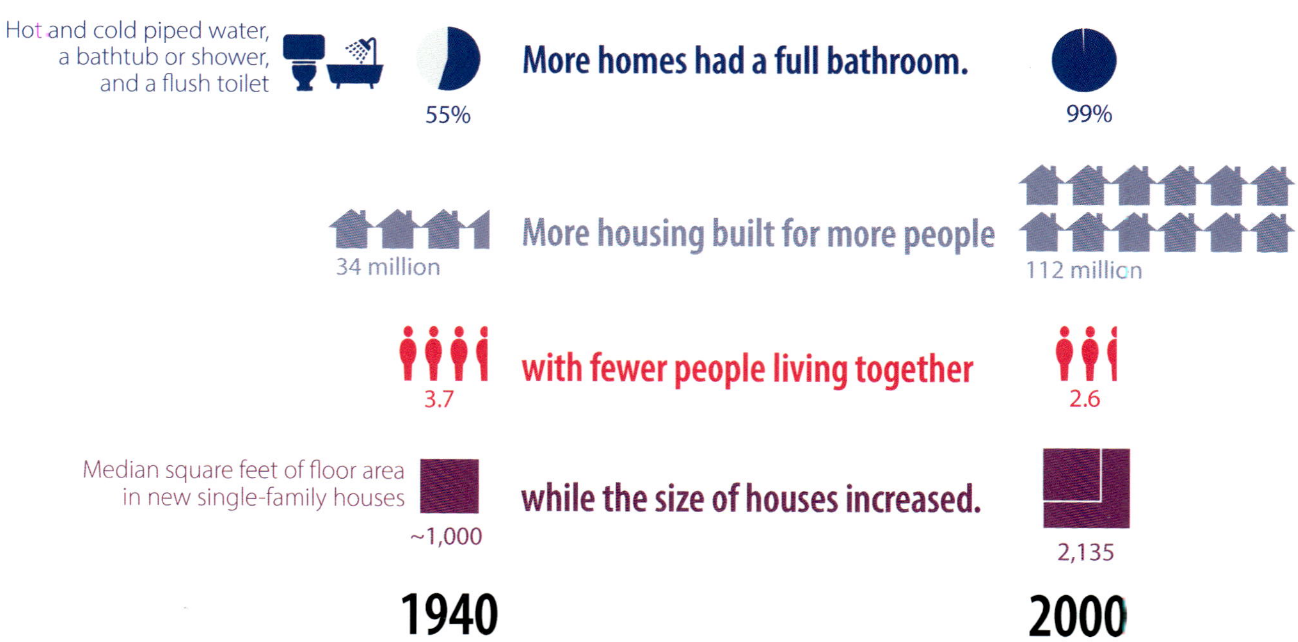

 Sources: US Bureau of Labor Statistics, "100 Years of US Consumer Spending: Data for the Nation, New York City, and Boston," Report no. 991 • US Census Bureau

Various

1900–2010

Income Growth in the 20th Century

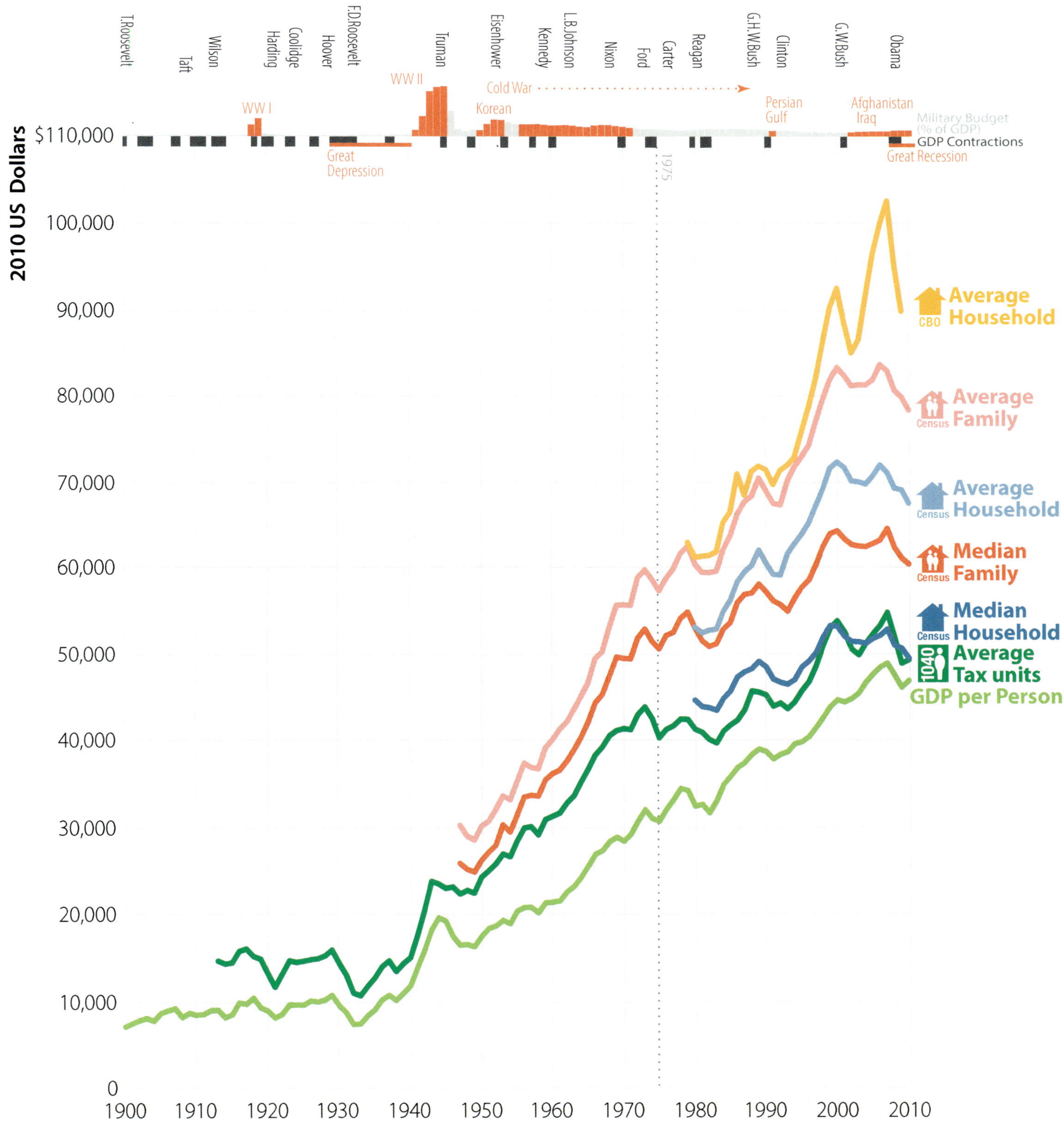

Sources: US Census Bureau • Congressional Budget Office, Average Federal Taxes by Income Group • US Bureau of Economics Analysis

1913–2010

Average Income

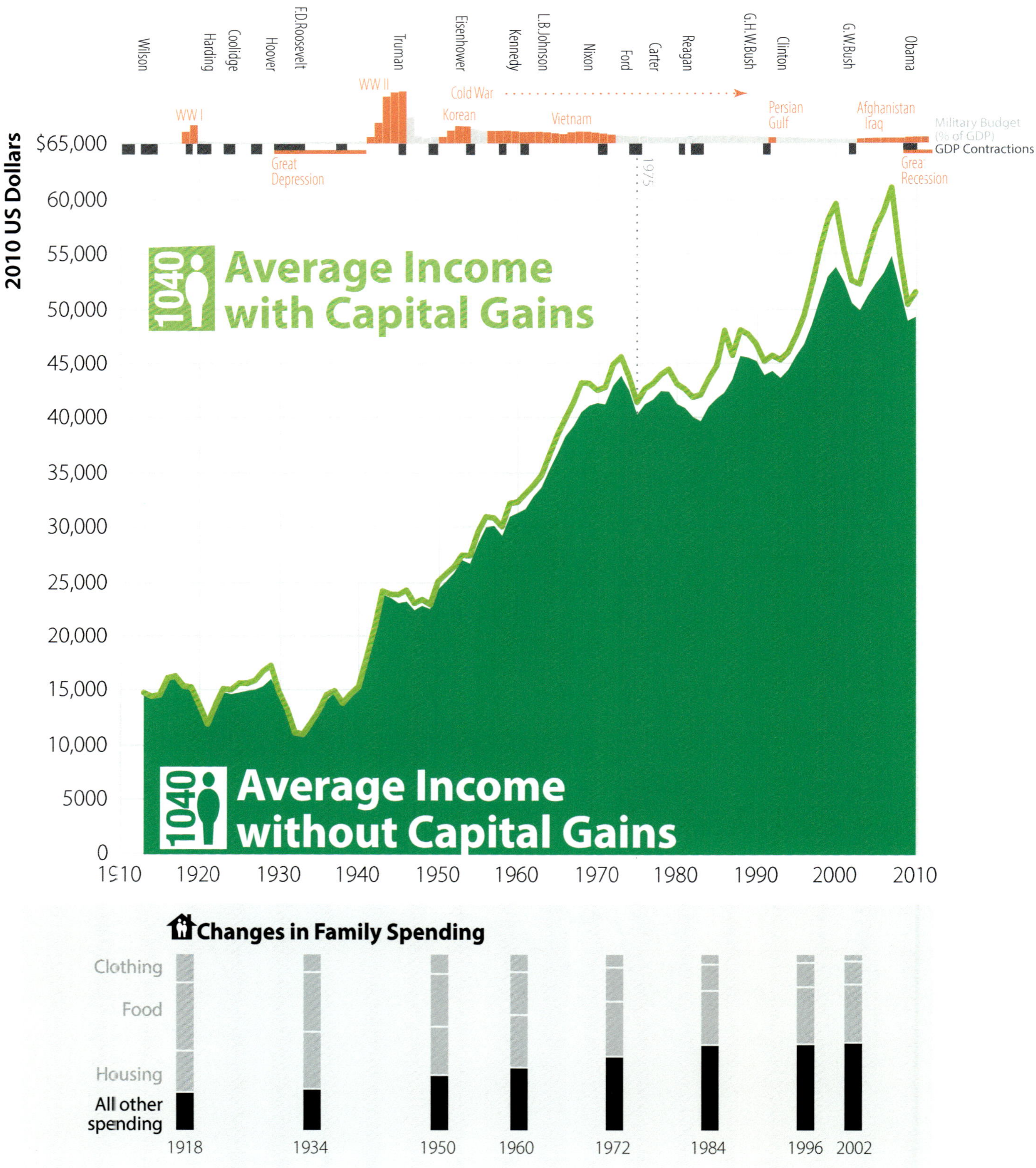

 Sources: World Top Incomes Database, March 2012 (Compiled from data collected by IRS) • US Bureau of Labor Statistics, "100 Years of US Consumer Spending: Data for the Nation, New York City, and Boston," Report no. 991

1979–2010

Salaried and Hourly Wage Workers

BLS

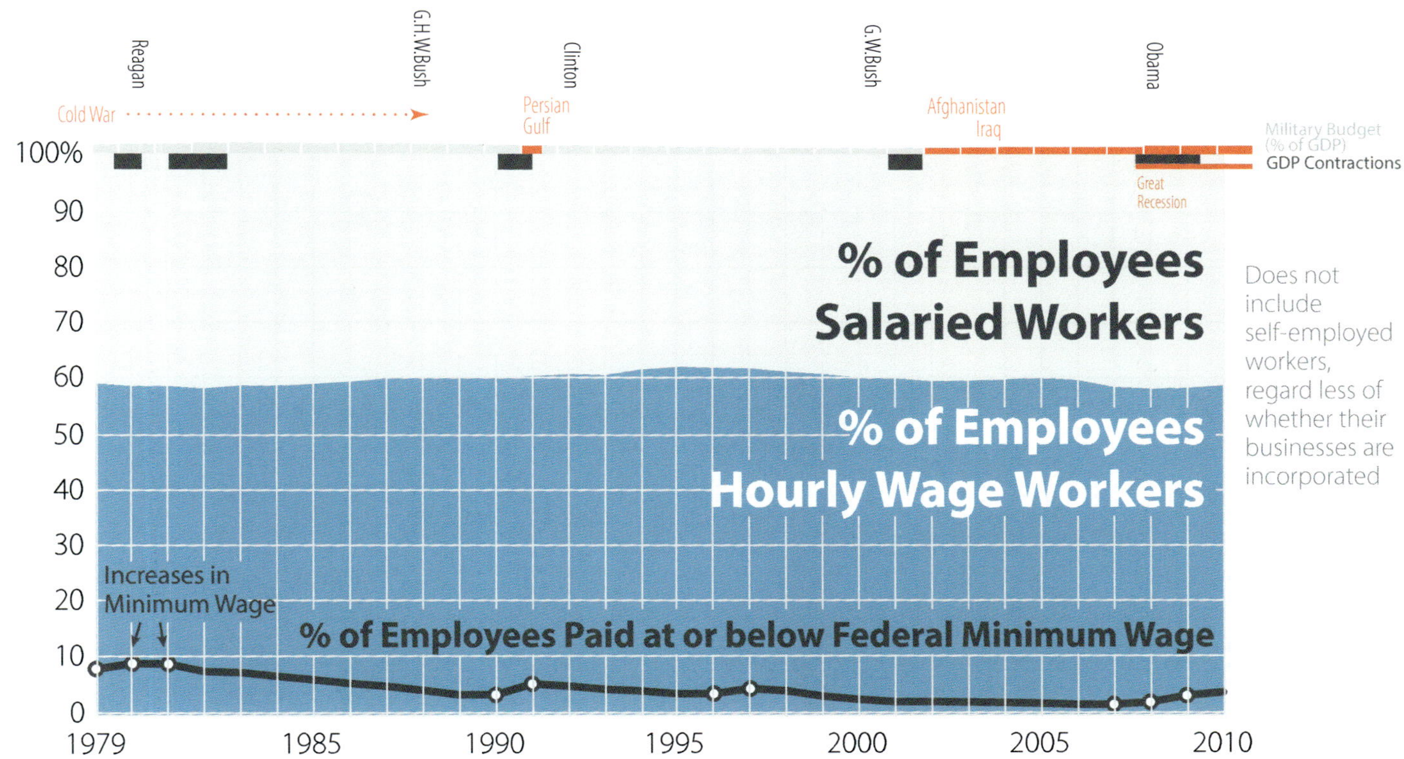

Number of Hourly Workers

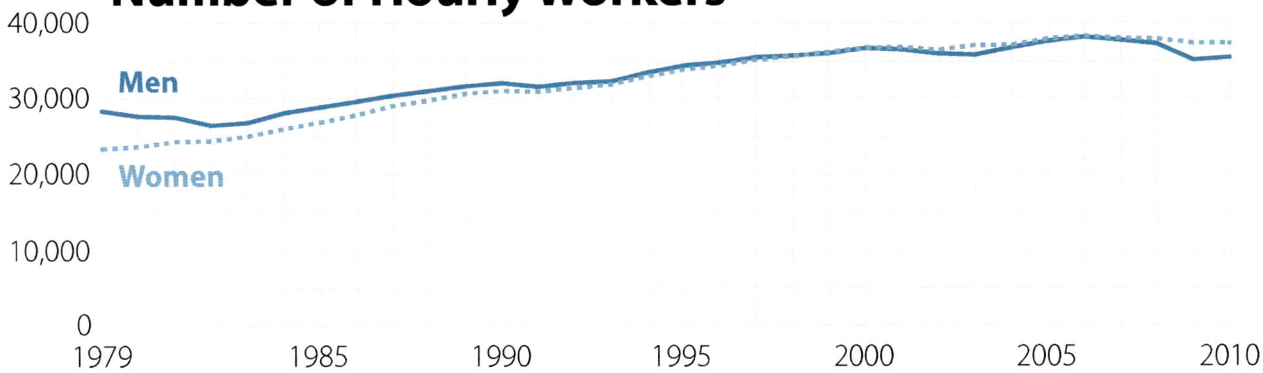

Minimun Hourly Wage

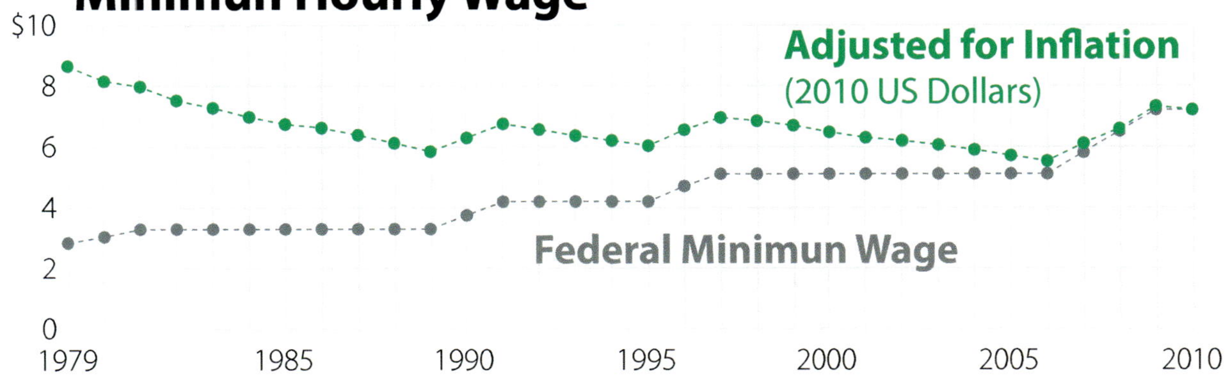

Source: US Bureau of Labor Statistics

1959–2010

Poverty Threshold

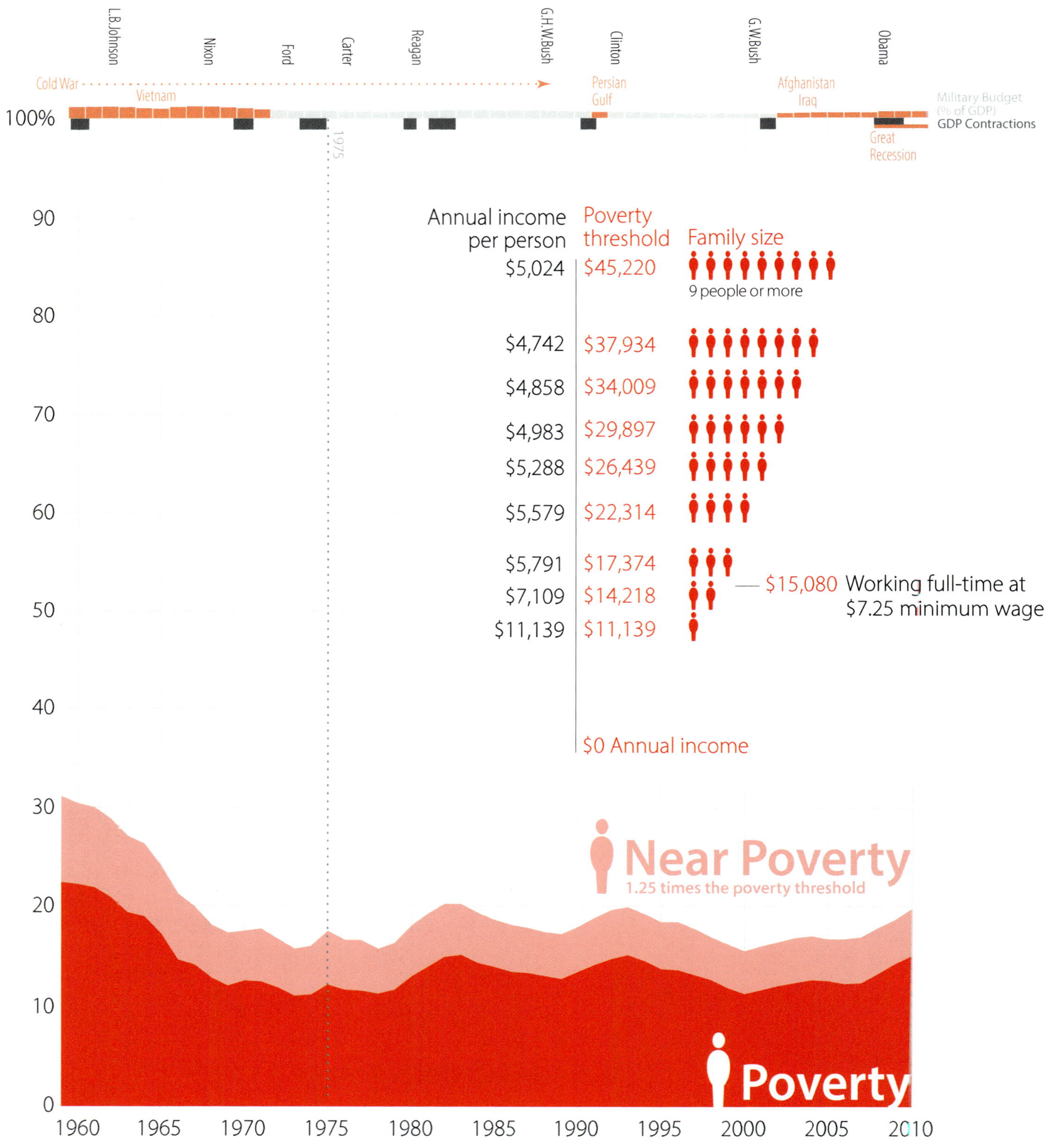

 Source: US Census Bureau, Historical Poverty Tables and Current Population Survey

Poverty thresholds are based on a family's "money income" (not including in-kind benefits or capital gains) and vary according to the size of the family and the ages of the family members but not by geographic location. Poverty thresholds are updated for inflation each year using the CPI-U. The poverty thresholds first were established in the 1960s to calculate how much it cost to feed a family using a nutritionally adequate food plan designed by the US Department of Agriculture. Then, the total cost of living was estimated, assuming that a family of three or more people spent about one-third of their after-tax income on food (determined using survey data). Over the years, this calculation has been modified—for example, using the CPI rather than price changes of items in the food plan—but the basic approach has remained unchanged.

Source: US Census Bureau, "How the Census Bureau Measures Poverty"

About the Guide

Published January 2013

The data graphics were created using a combination of OmniGraphSketcher, R statistical package, and Adobe Illustrator. Data formatting and calculations were performed in Microsoft Excel, while AnyBizSoft PDF Converter for Mac helped extract data tables from PDF files. The font used is Adobe Myriad Pro.

All data graphics and diagrams are original to this book. However, additional icons needed were taken from NounProject.com and are believed to be in the public domain or purchased from DutchIcon.com and Handbook of Pictorial Symbols by Rudolf Modley.

Copyright

ISBN
978-1-937504-45-8 Paperback
978-1-937504-46-5 Hardcover
978-1-937504-47-2 eBook

Additional information can be found at VisualizingEconomics.com.

A Custom Worthy Edition
Published by
Worthy Shorts, Inc.
39 Crosby Street
New York, NY 10013
www.worthyshorts.com

Mu brandon, Catherine
An Illustrated Guide to Income in the United States
CW108

Acknowledgments

I was able to create *An Illustrated Guide to Income in the United States* with the help of my backers on Kickstarter.com (some of whom are listed below) and a New Media Women Entrepreneurs grant from the J-Lab at American University funded by the McCormick Foundation.

Aaron Anzalone • Aaron Tan • Alex Whalen • Andrew Bullock • Andy Singh • Arjay Ramey • Ashvin B. Chhabra • Barclay A. Dunn • Barney Maccabe • Baton Lane • Bill Caemmerer • Bob Wyman • Brian Earl • Brian Kelsey • Britt J. James • Brooks Hall • Bruce Ostly • Bry Willis • Cain Hoy • Carolyn Hidy • Cate Long • Charles Teague • Chaseman1973 • Chris Pears • Christine Cooper • Christopher G Smith • D.J. Trindle • Dan Heath • Daniel Aronen • Daniele Bartoccioni • Danny Bates • Dave Gilson • Dave Haas • Dave Savage • David Chan • David Conway • David H Munson • David Joerg • David W. Stewart • Deepinder Singh • Dick Zander • Donald stevens • Doug Elliott • Douglas C. Bennett • Dr. Mirko Junge • Dr. Todd Beer • Drew Suder • DrTaxSacto • Ed Cowden • Edward Choi • Eric Appesland • Eric Carter • Fleur Levitz • Furball the Tiger • geewhiz • Gene Gualtieri • George Ciobanu • Glenn R NIcol • Gokay Saher • Gong Szeto • Gregory Swingholm • Gwendolyn Patrick • H D Goodman • H. Jude Boudreaux, CFP® • Hal Varian • Harold and Melissa Taylor • Harvey Summers • Indy Chakrabarti • J Hudson • Jack Hart • James B. Schreiber, Ph.D. • James E. Kneser • James Jarrett • James N. Simone • James Norris • Jane Williams • Jascha Franklin-Hodge • Jason T. Heinhorst • Jason W. Carney • Jeff Bernstein • Jeff D. Hamann • Jeff Gibson • Jeff Hammerbacher • Jeffrey Horn • Jen Lowe • Jenni Hyyppä • Jeoffry B. Gordon, MD, MPH • Jeremy Commandeur • Jessica and Trevor Esch • Joe Mako • Joel Noble • Johannes B • John Constantine • John Kelley • John Markos O'Neill • John R. Dougan • John W. Rodat • John Whitaker • Johnathan Stein • Jonathan Alfonso • Jonathan, MyMoneyBlog.com • Joseph Brown • Joseph Ratto • Josh Kawaii-Bogue • Joy Deborah Robison & Ian Hargraves • JustinChung.com • Kaleem Khan • Karl Makepeace • Kathryn Trabert • Kelly A. Olsen • KendallTodd, Inc. • Kevin McBride • Komnieve Singh • Lamar Showalter • Larry D Stoddard • Lawrence Lipkin • Leslie Densmore • Lori McNabb • Lorna Brodtkorb • Lotus M Jones • Lynne Brown • Marcie Davis • Mark E. Madsen • Mary R Valls • Mary Stromquist • Matt Henderson • Matt Johnson • Matt Thompson • Matthew A Carroll • Matthew Trumbull • Mauricio Vasquez • Michael Abrahams • Michael Pusateri • Michael R.A. Corsaro • Mike Liveright • Mike Schwab • Mirko Lorenz • Mitchell Abdullah • Moira Saucedo • Murray gm • Myra Boime • Norris Krueger • Paul Haahr • Pete Magsig • Peter minuk • Ralph Dratman • Randall Lockridge • Randy Nyce • Reed Cataldo • Rick Huntington • Robert Minichino • Robert Snyder • Ryan Dobbe • Sam Pizzigati • Sara Swenson • Scott W • Sean Rutledge • Stephen Bruckert • Steve Kleine • Steve McClary • Steve Vance • Steve W • Steve Wehba • Susan Hughes • Susan White • SVT Group • Ted Kerr • Tim Ruszel, Ruszel Design Co. • Timothy Winn • Toby Schachman • Tony Bagwell • Tony Kim • Tony Turrin • Van Living • Vikram Kulkarni • VisualBudget.org • W. Lane McColl III • Walter Tyree • Wendy M. Anderson • Wendy Rahn • William Byars • William Neuhauser • Yoga Prakasa (PT Bumi Salihara) • Yury Gitman

In addition, my brother's mapping skills and knowledge of the US census data proved to be invaluable, along with the feedback I received from my mother, friends, and supporters.

Selected Bibliography

There are many surveys on salaries, top-earning celebrities, CEOs of public companies, and hedge fund managers, but when it comes to data covering all income in the United States, there are four main sources: the US Census Bureau, Bureau of Labor Statistics, Bureau of Economic Analysis, and Internal Revenue Service.

CEOs, Celebrities, and Hedge Fund Managers

Forbes. "CEO Compensation, 2011." January 2012. http://www.forbes.com/lists/2011/12/ceo-compensation-11_rank.html.

———. "Celebrity 100, 2011." Spring 2012. http://www.forbes.com/lists/2012/celebrities/celebrity-100_2011.html.

———. "Historical Chart: Two Decades of CEO Pay." December 2012. http://www.forbes.com/lists/2011/12/ceo-pay-20-year-historical-chart.html.

Taub, Stephen. "Really Big Bucks." *Institutional Investor's Alpha,* April 2006, 18–30.

———. "The New Tycoons." *Institutional Investor's Alpha,* April 2007, 40–57.

———. "The Kings of Cash." *Institutional Investor's Alpha,* April 2008, 34–49.

———. "Brother, Can You Spare a Billion." *Institutional Investor's Alpha,* April 2009, 37–47.

———. "The Rich List." *AR: Absolute Return + Alpha,* April 2010, 29-42.

———. "The Rich List." AR: *Absolute Return + Alpha,* April 2011, 33–48.

Countries

Central Intelligence Agency. *CIA World Factbook.* July 2011. https://www.cia.gov/library/publications/the-world-factbook/.

Maddison, Angus. "Statistics on World Population, GDP and Per Capita GDP, 1–2008 AD." July 2011. http://www.ggdc.net/MADDISON/oriindex.htm.

Education

Snyder, Thomas D., and Sally A. Dillow. "Digest of Education Statistics 2010." 2010 Digest Tables Directory, Table 8. 2011. http://nces.ed.gov/programs/digest/2010menu_tables.asp.

United States GDP, GINI, and Recessions

National Bureau of Economic Research. "US Business Cycle Expansions and Contractions." Summer 2011. http://www.nber.org/cycles.html.

US Census Bureau. American FactFinder. Fall 2011. http://factfinder2.census.gov/faces/nav/jsf/pages/searchresults.xhtml?refresh=t.

Historical Wages

Officer, Lawrence H., and Samuel H. Williamson. "The Annual Consumer Price Index for the United States, 1774–2011." MeasuringWorth.com, 2012. http://www.measuringworth.com/uscpi/.

———. "Annual Wages in the United States, 1774–Present." MeasuringWorth.com, 2011. http://www.measuringworth.com/uswage/.

US Bureau of Labor Statistics. "Employment, Hours, and Earnings from the Current Employment Statistics survey (National) SIC." June 2011. http://data.bls.gov/cgi-bin/surveymost?ee.

———. "National Compensation Survey." Fall 2012. http://www.bls.gov/ncs/data.htm.

———. "Table B-8. Average hourly and weekly earnings of production and nonsupervisory employees on private nonfarm payrolls by industry sector, seasonally adjusted." November 2012. http://www.bls.gov/webapps/legacy/cesbtab8.htm.

Households

US Census Bureau. "Families and Individual Money Income in the United States: 1945. Table 2." September 2011. http://www2.census.gov/prod2/popscan/p60-002.pdf.

———. "Income of Families and Persons in the United States: 1950. Table 1." September 2011. http://www2.census.gov/prod2/popscan/p60-009.pdf.

———. "Income of Families and Persons in the United States: 1960. Table 5." September 2011. http://www2.census.gov/prod2/popscan/p60-037.pdf.

———. "Income, Poverty, and Health Insurance Coverage in the United States: 2010. Table A-2." September 2011. http://www.census.gov/prod/2011pubs/p60-239.pdf.

———. "Historical Income Tables: Households." June 2011. http://www.census.gov/hhes/www/income/data/historical/household/index.html.

———. "Table HINC-06. Income Distribution to $250,000 or More for Households: 2010." June 2011. http://www.census.gov/hhes/www/cpstables/032011/hhinc/new06_000.htm.

Taxes

Citizens for Tax Justice. "Top Federal Income Tax Rates Since 1913." November 2011. http://www.ctj.org/pdf/regcg.pdf.

Congressional Budget Office. "The Distribution of Household Income and Federal Taxes, 2008 and 2009." August 2012. http://www.cbo.gov/publication/43373.

Hungerford, Thomas L. "Taxes and the Economy: An Economic Analysis of the Top Tax Rates Since 1945." Congressional Research Service, Report no. R42729. September 12, 2012. http://www.fas.org/sgp/crs/misc/R42729.pdf.

Tax Foundation. "Federal Individual Income Tax: Exemptions and Treatment of Dividends, 1913–2006." Spring 2012. http://taxfoundation.org/article/federal-individual-income-tax-exemptions-and-treatment-dividends-1913-2006.

Tax Policy Center. "Historical Corporate Top Tax Rate and Bracket." Spring 2012. http://www.taxpolicycenter.org/taxfacts/displayafact.cfm?Docid=65.

———. "Historical Individual Income Tax Parameters." Spring 2012. http://www.taxpolicycenter.org/taxfacts/displayafact.cfm?DocID=543&Topic2id=30&Topic3id=39.

Government

Correlates of War. "National Material Capabilities." Summer 2011. http://www.correlatesofwar.org/COW2%20Data/Capabilities/nmc3-02.htm.

Texas Tribune. "Government Employee Salaries." June 2011. http://www.texastribune.org/library/data/government-employee-salaries/.

US Department of Defense, Defense Finance and Accounting Service. "Military Members." Pay Tables. July 6, 2012. http://www.dfas.mil/dfas/militarymembers/payentitlements/militarypaytables.html.

Occupation and Industries

Bakija, Jon, Adam Cole, and Bradley Heim. 2008. "Jobs and Income Growth of Top Earners and the Causes of Changing Income Inequality: Evidence from U.S. Tax Return Data." Working Paper no. 2010-24, Williams College, Department of Economics, revised January 2012. http://web.williams.edu/Economics/wp/BakijaColeHeimJobsIncomeGrowthTopEarners.pdf.

EMSI (Economic Modeling Specialists International). Summer–Winter 2011. http://www.economicmodeling.com/.

US Bureau of Economic Analysis. "Gross Domestic Product (GDP) by Industry Data." June 2012. http://www.bea.gov/industry/gdpbyind_data.htm.

US Bureau of Labor Statistics. *Occupational Outlook Handbook*. 2012. http://www.bls.gov/ooh/.

US Census Bureau. "North American Industry Classification System." 2012. http://www.census.gov/cgi-bin/sssd/naics/naicsrch?chart=2012.

Poverty

US Census Bureau. Current Population Survey, Historical Poverty Tables. August 2011. http://www.census.gov/hhes/www/poverty/data/historical/.

———. "How the Census Bureau Measures Poverty." October 2012. http://www.census.gov/hhes/www/poverty/methods/measure.html.

Spending

Dolfman, Michael L., and Denis M. McSweeney. "100 Years of U.S. Consumer Spending: Data for the Nation, New York City, and Boston." Report no. 991, US Bureau of Labor Statistics. http://www.bls.gov/opub/uscs/.

US Bureau of Labor Statistics. "Table 2. Income Before Taxes: Average Annual Expenditures and Characteristics, Consumer Expenditure Survey, 2010." June 2011. http://www.bls.gov/cex/2010/Standard/income.pdf.

Sports

Freedman, Jonah. "The 50 Highest-Earning American Athletes: The Fortunate 50, 2010." *Sports Illustrated,* Summer 2011. http://sportsillustrated.cnn.com/specials/fortunate50-2010/index.html.

———. "The 50 Highest-Earning American Athletes: The Fortunate 50, 2011." *Sports Illustrated,* Summer 2011. http://sportsillustrated.cnn.com/specials/fortunate50-2011/index.html.

Haupert, Michael. "The Economic History of Major League Baseball." *EH.Net Encyclopedia,* edited by Robert Whaples. December 3, 2007. http://eh.net/encyclopedia/article/haupert.mlb.

"2010 Baseball Team Payrolls." About.com Baseball. July 6, 2012. http://baseball.about.com/od/newsrumors/a/2010baseballteampayrolls.htm.

USA Today. "USATODAY Salaries Databases." July 5, 2012. http://content.usatoday.com/sportsdata/baseball/mlb/salaries/player/top-25/2010.

Top Incomes

Internal Revenue Service. "The 400 Individual Income Tax Returns Reporting the Largest Adjusted Gross Incomes Each Year, 1992–2009." July 6, 2012. http://www.irs.gov/uac/SOI-Tax-Stats-Top-400-Individual-Income-Tax-Returns-with-the-Largest-Adjusted-Gross-Incomes.

Internal Revenue Service. "Statistics of Income Bulletin, Fall 2012." Washington, D.C. Decmeber 9, 2012. http://www.irs.gov/uac/SOI-Tax-Stats-Fall-Bulletin-2012.

Saez, Emmanuel, Thomas Piketty, Facundo Alvaredo, and Tony Atkinson. "The World Top Incomes Database." Summer 2012. http://g-mond.parisschoolofeconomics.eu/topincomes/.

Saez, Emmanuel, and Thomas Piketty. "Income Inequality in the United States." *Quarterly Journal of Economics,* vol. 118, no. 1 (2003): 1–39. http://elsa.berkeley.edu/~saez/pikettyqje.pdf.

Other

US Census Bureau "Definitions and Explanations of Terms." http://www.census.gov/main/www/glossary.html.